French

All you need to speak and understand French

Series editors: Pauline Swanton and Mike Zollo

Prentice Hall
is an imprint of

Harlow, England • London • New York • Boston • San Francisco • Toronto • Sydney • Singapore • Hong Kong
Tokyo • Seoul • Taipei • New Delhi • Cape Town • Madrid • Mexico City • Amsterdam • Munich • Paris • Milan

PEARSON EDUCATION LIMITED

Edinburgh Gate
Harlow CM20 2JE
Tel: +44 (0) 1279 623623
Fax: +44 (0) 1279 431059

Website: www.pearsoned.co.uk

ISBN 978-0-273-74436-8

Insides design: Claire Robertson, Sarah Peden
Layout: Sarah Peden, Nomazwe Madonko
Illustrations: Martin Sanders
Publisher: Debbie Marshall
Development editor: Sue Purcell
Project editor: Emma Brown
Marketing: Fiona Griffiths
Senior production controller: Franco Forgione

Audio producer: Colette Thomson, Footstep Productions Ltd.
Sound engineer: Andrew Garratt
Presenters: Juliet Dante, Marilo Sanchez, Felix Callens, Philippe Smolikowski

Printed and bound in the UK by Ashford Colour Press Ltd.

The Publisher's policy is to use paper manufactured from sustainable forests.

Pearson Education is not responsible for the content of third-party websites.

Acknowledgements: p116 extract from *Temps Libre* by Denis C. Meyer www.hku.hk/ french/dcmScreen/lang2043/tempslibre.htm; p138 article from *France Soir* http:// www.francesoir.fr/divers/nouveaux-parfums-les-fragrances-ensoleillees-arrivent; pp168–169 'Déjeuner du matin' by Jacques Prévert from *Paroles* published by © Éditions Gallimard in 1946; p178 extract from blog *One Thing in a French Day* by Laetitia Perraut http://onethinginafrenchday.podbean.com/

Introduction

This course is for beginners who want to go beyond just getting by in French. It introduces you to the basic language you'll need whether you're learning for travel, for work, for personal fulfilment or for the sheer joy of it.

The course has been developed to show you how the language actually works, giving you a firm foundation for saying what you want to rather than just reproducing set phrases.

There's enough here for you to be able to make real inroads into a variety of daily exchanges. Making sure you have something to say is a vital step. Being willing and able to engage in a conversation, however rudimentary, is the very best way to improve your understanding and proficiency in the longer term.

To make another language your own, you need to get to grips with its grammar, the system of rules and regulations that makes it work. Grammar is pretty straightforward. Recognising and using language rules are activities that your brain is naturally geared up for. It is, after all, how you learned your own language. Other languages will throw up concepts that are unfamiliar but you don't have to be a grammar expert to recognise these and begin to use them for yourself. Like many fields of knowledge, grammar has engendered its own technical terms; you'll find these explained as you go through the book.

French and English have a great deal in common and making use of their similarities is a feature here. Exploiting close relationships can furnish useful shortcuts to making progress. It may also lead you to some surprising discoveries about English!

How does the book work?

Language learning is a matter of building skills and understanding little by little until you have the full picture. You'll find that the content of each of the chapters evolves from what has been learned before and leads you on to the next step.

Undertake the journey chapter by chapter to ensure that you progress logically and that the French you learn fits together in ways that will make it easier to memorise and to use. Even if you know some French already, follow the sequence, spending more time on areas with which you are less familiar.

The activities have been designed to develop your ability to speak French, understand when people answer you, and give you some experience of reading and writing. They make use of tried and tested techniques to help you become a more effective language learner, such as predicting, educated guesswork, memory building, gist reading and selective use of a dictionary.

As you work through, you will acquire a basic French vocabulary. Many of the words you'll meet are among the most commonly used in the language and so will be of value to everyone. You'll also have your own particular interests and reasons for learning and will want to build a personal vocabulary alongside the one you acquire from the text. Tips for doing this and for memorising new words are featured.

Learning how to learn a language is as important as learning the language itself. Understanding what needs to be learned, knowing how to go about learning and being aware of what works for you will contribute to your success. There is advice in the book on language-learning skills both within the chapters and in the additional sections: *The tools of the trade, Learning strategies* and *The four skills*.

A little creativity and risk are also necessary. There are moments when you will need to shed your inhibitions and take a chance on what you might say; there will be times when the text throws up unexpected challenges. Communication is never predictable, so relish the opportunity to test your nerve and your French.

One area in particular where you will need to let go of any preconceptions and inhibitions is pronunciation! Although many words may look familiar, they will never sound the same. This course takes you step by step through key sounds, showing how they equate to the written word. Spending time on pronunciation will improve your chances of understanding spoken French and being understood when you speak. It will also help you to go beyond what you find here, enabling you to pick up new French whenever and wherever you come across it.

Most of the activities have some form of audio accompaniment. These are flagged in the text with the following icon 🌐 and a track number for easy navigation. You'll be recommended to listen without looking at the text, listen with the text or use the audio to check answers to an activity. Activities that have no audio accompaniment are flagged with the following icon 🌐 . You'll find answers to all activities and transcripts of the audio in the back of the book.

You may need to work through units or parts of units several times before you feel confident that you've cracked the content. You may need to revisit units to refresh your memory. Repetition is a vital part of language learning. So study the text and play the audio any number of times to reinforce and practise what you've learned. The more, the better!

What's your role?

The book provides you with the 'knowledge' but asks to you to play an active role in your learning. As well as taking part in language exercises, think about the practicalities, such as when you're going to do your learning; be clear about your motivations and what you need to learn to do in French; be insightful about how you learn best and what you need to practise most.

You're in charge of the what, the when, the how and the how much. It's a really positive way to start because it means that you'll be able to tailor the learning to your own specific ends. New skills flourish when they are in constant use, so spend a few minutes each day thinking French. View this bilingual moment as a pleasure not a chore and it will soon become a natural part of your daily routine. You're on the brink of a really exciting journey, enjoy and **bonne chance!**

On y va!

- Look at links between French and English
- Learn words and phrases for meeting and greeting
- Pick up language-learning strategies

What have you let yourself in for? An exciting voyage of discovery that may change you forever.

You will learn to understand French, analyse it and use it for yourself; you will start to become a French speaker. This learning process can be applied to other languages; you will become a language learner. You will get close to a different culture, opening doors to new experiences and understanding.

The words

Modern French is derived from Latin, the same source as Italian, Spanish, Portuguese and Romanian. The collective name for these languages is 'Romance'. French and English have many words in common since much vocabulary in English also comes from Latin, through Norman French ('1066 and all that'), other Romance languages or directly from Latin itself in more recent times, particularly in the fields of science and culture.

As well as these influences, there has been considerable interchange between French and English of words and expressions in the fields of sport, pop music, business, science and computing (le football, le marketing, un e-mail). French has also acquired words from other languages that we have taken into English, such as Italian (spaghettis), Arabic (coton) and the indigenous languages of South America (tomate, chocolat).

A cognate is the term used to describe words descended from a common background. Take a look at this random sample of French words shared with English:

accent	accident	excellent	client	document
violent	intelligent	important	impossible	simple
imagination	interruption	million	religion	train
absence	justice	budget	culture	amateur
date	radio	final	village	famine

Even though they may look identical, French and English words will never sound the same. French has a different pronunciation system and in order to speak French you need to understand how this works and then practise sounds and utterances to get your mouth functioning in the French fashion. Correct pronunciation contributes a great deal to ensuring that you make your meaning clear.

 **activity 1**

A 1.02 Listen and repeat these words from the cognate list:

accent	violent	accident
client	imagination	interruption

B 1.03 Notice how -ent and -tion differ from their English pronunciation. What will **excellent, intelligent, action** and **nation** sound like in French? Listen to check.

Borrowed words

We've got used to food being described in French in restaurants and to buying French products in our shops. Any of these look familiar?

pâté	champagne	fondue	hors d'œuvres
petits pois	croissant	foie gras	nougat
mousse	fromage frais	mayonnaise	camembert
crème fraîche	gâteau	quiche	éclair

C 1.04 We tend to follow French rules when pronouncing these words in English; you can use this fact to glean invaluable insights into how French sounds. Try repeating the following out loud:

camembert	quiche	nougat	fromage frais
croissant	hors d'œuvres	petits pois	cuisine

In French the final letter is generally not pronounced: camember(t) not camembert, nouga(t) not nougat; h is generally silent ((h)ors d'œuvres); qu is a 'k' sound, rather than an English 'cw' (as in 'queen').

D 1.05 What sounds do these combinations of letters make: -eau, -ou, -oi? Say gâteau, bureau, mousse, bouffant, foie gras and je ne sais quoi out loud and then check with the audio.

Ch is a soft 'sh' sound in French, crème fraîche, champagne, not the English 'ch' (compare 'church'). The sound of the letter e is altered by the addition of an accent. É is a short sound (pâté, éclair), while è is a long sound (cafetière).

 **activity 2**

A 1.06 French pronunciation is very regular so you can transfer the rules that you learn from one word to another. How would you pronounce these? Check your answers with the audio.

roquefort	chocolat	moi	église
coulis	joie	eau	hôtel
chablis	croix	frère	

Stress

B 1.07 Listen to the following words on the audio. Can you spot them in the box? Cross them out as you listen.

chauffeur	village	justice	document
train	important	champion	budget
sport	impossible	simple	encouragement

Did you notice that in French the stress falls lightly on the last syllable? In English the stress falls on different parts of the word: document, village, imagination, encouragement. Listen again and repeat the words.

 **learning tip**

If you can, get into the habit of recording your voice as you listen to the audio and respond to the cues. Then compare yourself to the voices on the audio. This process puts a valuable distance between yourself and your voice and helps you see which particular sounds need more practice.

 **activity 3**

The crossover between French and English gives you a fighting chance of being able to understand what you read.

Can you hazard a guess at what the following text is all about? Highlight the words that are familiar and that look like English to help you make sense of the whole:

> Le chef du Restaurant Aragon adore les produits de la région. Il préfère offrir à ses clients des ingrédients saisonniers. Le restaurant est très populaire et les réservations sont nécessaires.

Meeting and greeting

Alongside all these words the two languages have in common, you may already be familiar with expressions such as bonjour *hello/good morning/ good afternoon*, bonsoir *good evening* and au revoir *goodbye*.

 **activity 4**

A **1.08** Practise saying these expressions with the audio. You'll spot the oi and ou sounds from the exercises above.

Now listen to some people exchanging pleasantries and names in a formal setting, maybe meeting each other for the first time. Listen out for bonjour, bonsoir and au revoir and fill in the gaps in the transcript below:

● .... madame, je m'appelle Louis Duval.
● .... monsieur, je m'appelle Madeleine Dugard.

● .... Madeleine. À bientôt!
● .... Louis.

● .... monsieur, je m'appelle Paul Bousquet. Je vous présente Jérôme Martin.
● Enchanté, messieurs. Je m'appelle Charles Fournier.

● .... messieurs, dames. Je m'appelle Henri Lacroix.
● Enchantée, monsieur. Je m'appelle Sylvie Gauthier. Je vous présente Jean-Claude Arnaud, Victor Bellenger et Catherine Hugo.
● Enchanté, messieurs, madame.

- .... Henri. À bientôt!
- .... Sylvie.

B Listen again; this time concentrate on the words that come directly after bonjour and bonsoir. You should hear: monsieur, madame, messieurs and mesdames. Monsieur and madame are the French equivalents of 'Mr' or 'sir' and 'Mrs' or 'madam'.

In English we might say 'Good morning, Mr Davies' but we're unlikely to say 'Good morning, sir'. In French when you greet someone you don't know very well it is normal to add their title but not their surname. When the speaker is addressing more than one man, they say Bonjour, messieurs, more than one woman Bonjour, mesdames and a mixed group Au revoir, messieurs, (mes) dames.

 **activity 5**

1.09 Try these greetings and farewells for yourself:

| **1** greeting | **2** greeting | **3** farewell |

| **4** greeting | **5** farewell |

 **activity 6**

A bientôt

A 1.10 Now look back at the exchanges in Activity 4. Can you find the words for 'Pleased to meet you' (just one word in French), 'See you soon' (two words) and 'Can I introduce ...' (three words)? Underline them and listen to the audio to remind yourself what they sound like.

enchanté

je vous présente

You will have noticed that the expression for 'Pleased to meet you' has two different forms: enchanté and enchantée. You use enchanté if you are a man and enchantée if you are a woman.

B 1.11 What would you say in response to the following? Listen to check your answers.

1 Je vous présente Béatrice Cartier.   *enchantée*
2 Au revoir. À bientôt.   *au revoir*
3 Je vous présente Antoine Lafarge et Didier Fallon.   *enchanté*
4 Bonjour monsieur/madame. Je m'appelle Fabienne Durand.
   enchantée

 **activity 7**

1.12 Back to the previous exchanges. This time look for the way in which you would say 'I am called'. To ask someone their name, you'd say Vous vous appelez comment? Listen and repeat with the audio and then play your part in the conversation:

- Say good morning (to a woman).   *Bonjour madame*
- Bonjour. Vous vous appelez comment?
- Reply.   *Je m'appelle R.G*

- Bonsoir. Je vous présente Madeleine Dugard.
- Say that you're pleased to meet her.   *Enchantée madame*

- Say good evening and ask what the man is called.   *Bonsoir, vous vous appeler comment?*
- Je m'appelle Henri Lacroix.
- Say that you are pleased to meet him.
   Enchanté monsieur
- Au revoir.
- Say goodbye and see you soon.   *Au revoir, a bientôt*

Putting words together

Being able to use another language, any language, involves tackling a number of different elements such as words, rules, pronunciation and culture.

You've already made a start. You know that the last letters of French words are not usually pronounced; you know that in formal situations greetings are accompanied by titles; you know that if you're talking to more than one person the title changes; you will have worked out that **vous** is the French word for 'you' and je means 'I'. In other words you are in the process of collecting rules.

You really need to understand the rules of the language to be able to create appropriate and relevant things to say for yourself. Language rules are referred to as 'grammar' and grammar has acquired an unfortunate and undeserved reputation for being difficult and tedious.

Quite a few of us have had no formal training in the grammar of our own language. Nevertheless, we are born with the ability to deduce these patterns and structures without having them explained. Most of us communicate well and we can recognise when others are not using our language properly. As adult learners we have the advantage of being able to reactivate our innate grammar skills and apply these to the new language to help us learn faster. And don't forget that making grammatical mistakes is also a vital part of the learning process.

How are you today?

In most languages meet and greet situations are composed of a number of conventions, one of which is making enquiries about people's well-being. In French the phrase you use is Comment allez-vous? *How are you?*

 **activity 8**

A **1.13** Now listen to the exchanges on the audio and identify which of the following mean 'well', 'very well' and 'not bad'.

Comment allez-vous?   Très bien.   Bien.

Pas mal.   Et vous?

B **1.14** Have a go for yourself – take part in the following conversations by following the prompts on the audio.

- Bonjour. Comment allez-vous?
- Say that you're well.   *Bien merci*
  Je vais

- Bonjour. Comment allez-vous?
- Say 'not bad' and ask how she is.   *pas mal et vous ?*
- Bien, merci.

- Offer an appropriate greeting (to a woman) and ask how she is.
- Je vais bien, merci. Et vous?   *Bonjour madame, comment allez vous ?*
- Say 'very well, thank you'.   *Très bien merci*

Learning another language is a cumulative activity. As you can see here, Comment allez-vous? links naturally to the greeting bonjour and gives you something more to say when you are introduced. Language also recycles itself. You'll find the words and phrases in this chapter recurring in different contexts throughout the book. You can use très bien ('very well' here) to pass comment on an idea, meal, film, hotel etc, since it also means 'very good'. Make a point of looking out for familiar words in unfamiliar contexts.

Talking of familiar words, what is the French for 'thank you'? Its companion is s'il vous plaît *please* (literally 'if it pleases you').

Translation

Learning another language often involves comparing it with your own language and spotting the similarities. This does not mean that you should translate everything word for word; in fact that is often entirely the wrong thing to do. You've met the two questions Vous vous appelez comment? and Comment allez-vous? If you were to translate these questions literally you would come up with 'You call yourself how?' and 'How do you go?', neither of which makes a lot of sense in English. Remember what the equivalent English expression is, rather than just what the individual words mean. Je vais bien in this context means 'I'm well' not 'I go well'.

Take a look at the two texts below. The French text has been entered into an online translation service. The English version generated by the service gives a graphic illustration of the shortcomings of direct translation!

Bonjour, monsieur. Comment allez-vous ? Je suis enchanté de faire votre connaissance.

Hello, Mister. How do you go? I am magic to make your knowledge.

Enchanté de faire votre connaissance *Pleased to make your acquaintance* is the full version of the phrase enchanté(e) that you met above.

Getting familiar

The meeting and greeting that you have done so far has taken place in formal contexts where people don't know each other. There are different ways of greeting people that you know well. Salut is the French equivalent of 'hi' and you'd expect to hear a first name used with it. Salut is used at any time, day or night, and it is also a familiar form of 'goodbye'.

 activity 9

A 1.15 Which people are saying 'hi' and which 'goodbye'? Listen without looking at the transcript and tick the appropriate box.

	Hi	Goodbye
Sophie		
Jérôme		
Nicolas		
Christine		
Paul		
Jean-Claude		

B Now look at these exchanges:

● Salut Sophie. Comment vas-tu?
● Salut. Je vais bien, merci.

● Salut Jean-Claude. Ça va?
● Salut Marie-Thérèse. Ça va très bien merci.

Underline the phrases used to ask how people are (there are two). Compare Comment vas-tu? with its formal equivalent Comment allez-vous? There are two words for 'you' in French, vous and tu. Vous is used when you're talking to people you

> A verb is a word that denotes any kind of action ('think', 'imagine', 'walk', 'sing', 'increase') or state of being ('live', 'exist').

don't know or don't know well, when you're addressing more than one person (Sophie et Paul, comment allez-vous?) or when you're talking to someone who is older. You'll have spotted that it's not just the word for 'you' that changes; formal and informal modes of address cause the verb to change too:

Comment <u>allez</u>-vous?, Comment <u>vas</u>-tu?

You'll be getting plenty of practice with verbs throughout the book so keep an eye out for the different forms. As a first-time visitor to a French-speaking country it is always wise to play safe and stick to **vous**. Once you get to the point of making friends you may be *formally* invited to *informally* address your contact! **On se tutoie?** means 'Shall we call each other **tu**?'.

<u>Ça va</u> has a number of equivalents ('you OK?', 'how are you?', 'alright?') and it is both question and answer:

Ça va, Paul? *You OK, Paul?*
Ça va, merci. *Fine, thanks.*

It's a recyclable phrase. It might crop up as a means of checking that you've understood instructions (Ça va? *Got it?*) or that you're comfortable with a choice (Ça va? *Are you OK with that?*). Watch out for it in future conversations.

 language tip

> French, like many other languages, has different ways of saying 'you', depending on how well you know someone and how many people you're talking to. In a similar way English used to have these variations with 'thou' or 'thee' and 'you' or 'ye'.

 pronunciation

1.15 Have you noticed how the voice rises at the end of a question and goes down slightly at the end of a statement? This is intonation, a word used to describe the cadence of language. Intonation is different in English and French so it's important to learn how it works. It's particularly important for a phrase like Ça va?, which can be both question and answer; the only way of telling which is from the intonation. Listen again to the exchanges above and repeat for practice.

Test case

 activity 10

1.16 Can you play your part in the following exchanges? You're going to adopt different roles as you go through the exercise for a bit more practice.

- Bonjour, Monsieur. Comment allez-vous? *Bonjour monsieur. Je vais bien merci, et vous?*
- Return the greeting and say that you are well. Ask how he is.
- Bien, merci. Je vous présente Christine Dufour. *Enchanté. Je m'appelle Paul*
- Say that you're pleased to meet her and tell her that your name is Paul.

- Say good evening to Madame Clément and ask how she is. *Bonsoir Madame, comment allez vous?*
- Bonsoir, Madame Grieux. Je vais bien, merci. Et vous?
- Say you are very well and introduce Henriette Margaux. *Je vais bien. Je vous présente Henriette.*

- Salut, Philippe. Ça va?
- Return the greeting and say that you're fine. Then say 'bye' and 'see you soon'. *Ça va, merci, Au revoir, A bientôt*

The written word

Reading and writing, as well as being things you might like to be able to do in French, provide ways to record what you have learned, to practise what you've learned and to learn new things for yourself. So mastering the rules of writing in French and, perhaps more importantly, remembering the pronunciation rules that help convert the written word into speech are very valuable activities for the language learner.

learning tip

It is worth investing time and effort getting to grips with the pronunciation of new vocabulary. If you get into the habit of relating the sound of a word with its written form you will soon find that French pronunciation rules become second nature. Research has shown that if you can look at a word and sound it correctly in your head, you are far more likely to be able to remember it.

French and English share the same alphabet and, for the most part, the same punctuation symbols (full stops, commas etc) for the same purposes. You'll have noticed one difference in words like crème, présente, bientôt, ça. French makes use of accents.

Four of the most common are:

- ` a **grave** accent, seen on a, e and u
- ´ an **acute** accent, seen on e
- ^ a **circumflex** accent, seen on a, e, i, o and u
- ̧ a **cedilla**, seen on c

Sometimes accents make a difference to the sound of a letter. The cedilla changes the c from a 'k' to an 's' sound, so ça is pronounced *sa*. As you've already heard, when e has a grave accent over it, it sounds like the 'e' in shed (crèche), and when it has an acute accent over it the sound changes to *ay* as in 'say', but without pronouncing the 'y' (café).

Some accents, like the ô in bientôt, are there for historical reasons and make no difference to the sound. Occasionally accents are used to denote the difference in meaning between two words that are spelt the same. Ou in French means 'or' but où means 'where'.

 word builder

A circumflex accent can denote a missing s in French, and an é at the beginning of a French word often equates to an 's' at the beginning of an English word. If you put the s back you may end up with something familiar: mât → *mast*, forêt → *forest*, épices → *spices*.

Activity 11

What might the following words mean?

hôpital	hôte	étudiant	épine	étrange
île	honnête	école	éponge	étrangler
hâte	arrêt	écarlate	étendard	

Endgame

Can you identify which word in this list has not come into English via French?

omelette	courgette	serviette	aubergine	bidet
duvet	sheet	parachute	abbatoir	savant

2 Vous avez un plan?

- Make enquiries
- Discover nouns and their gender
- Learn about singular and plural

The words

 activity 1

1.17 Certain locations may be of particular interest for the language learner: un hôtel, un café, un restaurant, un office de tourisme.

Using your experience of cognates and some educated guessing match the items to the place in this table:

un hôtel	un plan de la ville *tourisme*
	des omelettes
un restaurant *des spécialités*	un parking *hôtel*
	des sandwichs
	un menu à prix fixe
un café *des omelettes*	une chambre pour deux personnes
	une liste des spectacles
un office de tourisme *un plan de la ville*	des spécialités de la région *rest*

Now listen to the audio and repeat each of the words and phrases, paying particular attention to the way they sound.

 **learning tip**

Listening followed by repetition is a good way of fixing new vocabulary in your mind. Listening first enables you to get a grip on pronunciation before you have a go. It's quite hard to 'unlearn' bad pronunciation so try each word several times before moving on and go back to listen again to any words that you are still unsure of at the end of an exercise.

Getting what you want

 **activity 2**

1.18 The most straightforward way of getting what you want is to simply say its name, and add 'please' (**s'il vous plaît**). Listen to these people asking for things and tick them off in the list on the previous page.

Making enquiries

It's useful to be able to check availability by asking 'Do you have/have you got ...?'. **Vous avez ...?** is the phrase you need.

 **activity 3**

A **1.19** Listen to seven people asking for different items. Following the example given, make a note of where each person is in the grid below.

e.g. **1** Vous avez un plan de la ville?

Dans un office de tourisme	Dans un restaurant	Dans un hôtel
1		

B **1.20** Now over to you:

In a café (**dans un café**), how would you ask if they have any:

1 omelettes

des om

2 sandwiches

des sandwich

Or in a department store (un grand magasin), how would you ask if they have:

3 a car park   **4** a café

un parking   un

 pronunciation

1.21 Did you notice that when you say vous avez you hear the final consonant of vous? It has a 'z' sound: vou - z - avez. The rule is that, although you don't usually sound the final letter of French words, if the next word begins with a vowel (a, e, i, o, u) or a silent h, you do. You can hear the rule again in des_omelettes and des_hôtels. This is called 'liaison'. When it comes to making sense of what you hear it's important to remember that liaison happens. You might find it relatively easy to guess what une omelette is but de-zomelettes might not be so straightforward.

You met some liaison in the last chapter. See if you can mark it up on these sentences:

Comment allez-vous?
Vous vous appelez comment?

Now listen to how all these phrases sound.

Making sense of what you hear

There is a tendency among language learners to want to get to the bottom of everything that is said, but in the early stages, picking out key words may be enough to get the gist of what's going on. Vous avez questions, for example, will often generate an answer that begins with either oui *yes* or non *no*, so you should be able to determine early on whether you are likely to get what you've asked for.

 **activity 4**

1.22 Listen to the three conversations and make a note of what they ask for and whether they get it or not. You'll hear the question Vous désirez? *Can I help you?*, a common opening gambit in shops, receptions, restaurants and cafés.

1. *guide de la region   No tc*
2. *table for two —*
3.

In transactional conversations such as these it's useful to recognise some common expressions: Voilà *there you are/there is* can be used to hand things over or point things out: Un guide? Voilà; Voilà un restaurant. Voilà has a companion word, voici, which means 'here you are/here is': Voici une liste des campings; Un café? Voici. Alors is a much-used word meaning 'well' or 'so'.

 brilliant activity 5

In exchanges like those you've just listened to you can often get by with a very limited number of set phrases together with the appropriate vocabulary in order to get what you want. Use the examples that you've worked with to play your part in the next conversations. You might want to spend a few moments thinking about how you will say what you need to before you begin.

A 1.23
- Greet the man at reception. *Bonjour monsieur*
- Bonjour monsieur. Vous désirez?
- Ask if they have a restaurant. *Vous avez un restaurant*
- Oui monsieur. Juste là.

B 1.24
- Greet the woman. *Bonjour madame*
- Bonjour madame. Vous désirez?
- Ask if they have a table. *Vous avez une table*
- Oui, bien sûr, suivez-moi.
- Ask if they have a fixed-price menu. *Vous avez un menu à prix fixe*
- Non madame, à la carte seulement.
- Ask if they have regional specialities. *Vous avez des specialités de la region*
- Oui madame, voici une liste.
- Order a coq au vin. *Un coq au vin s'il vous plaît*

brilliant learning tip

You would need a long time to learn all the words and rules necessary for you to operate in French as you do in your own language. The trick is to apply what you do know to a number of different situations and see what works and what does not. If you keep pushing out the boundaries in this way you will get a feel for what is right and wrong.

Gender wars

How are your powers of observation? Have you noticed that there are two different ways of saying 'a' – un and une. Why? In French all nouns are either masculine or feminine. We don't make this gender distinction in English (one of the very few languages that doesn't) but French does, so 'plan' is masculine and 'list' is feminine and the word for 'a' changes accordingly: un plan and une liste. You can probably see that there is no logical reason behind which items are masculine and which are feminine. Of course, when gender is implied in the meaning of the word like 'a girl' or 'a boy' it's easy to get it right (une fille, un garçon). The rest of the time you will need to learn the gender with the word.

The fact that French divides its nouns up into masculine and feminine is one of the things that most perplexes learners who are English speakers. Does it matter if you get gender wrong? Not usually. People will still understand. However, gender does have a profound effect on the language as a whole so, as a learner, you do need to be aware of it and factor it into your learning.

> Noun is the term given to living beings (i.e. people or animals), things, places and concepts (such as beauty or freedom).

 **learning tip**

When you learn new nouns always learn the appropriate words for 'a' too. So learn un café not just café and une bière not just bière. You will be very surprised, if you do this, how quickly you will get to grips with this rule.

More than one

 **activity 6**

Look at this description of the amenities in a town and underline the words that are in the plural. You'll notice the phrase il y a in the text; it means 'there is' or 'there are'.

À Lille, il y a un musée d'histoire naturelle, des monuments historiques, une cathédrale et des églises, des parcs, des jardins, un centre commercial, un marché, des boutiques, des restaurants, des bars, des hôtels. En fait, tout pour le touriste.

Look again at the text:

1 What is the French word for 'some'? *des*

2 What is the gender of cathédrale, musée, marché and centre? *m m m*

3 What might églises be? *churches*

4 Find the French word meaning 'for'. *pour*

You will see that to make a noun plural you normally add s. There are exceptions to this rule, e.g. un gâteau → des gâteaux. The plurals of words that end in -eau are made by adding x instead of s. Words ending in -al go a little further by changing the end of the word to aux in the plural: un journal *a newspaper* → des journaux *some newspapers*. In English we sometimes omit the words 'some' or 'any' with plurals: 'There are (some) cafés, bars and restaurants'. In French, however, you must always include des, which can mean both 'some' and 'any': Il y a des cafés, des bars et des restaurants.

Making sense of what you hear

ont de – 2 pers

Il n'y a pas de café

In order to understand French you need to get used to listening out for clues that are different from English. In English the word 'some' often warns you that a plural word is on the way and, in addition, you hear a change of sound at the end of the word: 'a document' → 'some documents'. In French, you only have des to help, since singular and plural usually sound the same: un document → des documents. Des works for both masculine and feminine nouns: une omelette → des omelettes; un plan → des plans.

 **activity 7**

A Create plurals for the following:

singular	plural
Example: un café	des cafés
un animal	*des animaux*
une région	*des régions*

2'00 Tues

un château	des châteaux
un accident	des accidents
un marché	des marchés
une ville	des villes
un cheval *horse*	des chevaux

B **1.25** Now listen to the audio, repeat the words and highlight the plural endings that you can actually hear.

 **activity 8**

A **1.26** Imagine that you're eavesdropping in the tourist office in Lille. Listen and answer the questions. See if you can also pick out the French for 'a lot' (beaucoup).

1 What was not available?
2 What sport featured in the requests?
3 What are there a lot of?
4 What shopping destination is mentioned?
5 Is there anywhere to go gambling?

The phrase il y a can be used to ask a question and also to make a statement: Il y a un marché à Lille? *Is there a market in Lille?*; Il y a un marché à Lille *There's a market in Lille.* It can be used to talk about singular and plural: Il y a un cinéma *There's a cinema*; Il y a des cinémas *There are some cinemas*; Il y a des cinémas? *Are there any cinemas?*

Il y en a ... means 'There are ... of them': Il y des hôtels? *Are there any hotels?*; Il y en a beaucoup *There are lots of them*.

B What would you say to find out if:
1 there is a bar?   Il y a un bar?
2 there are any campsites?   Il y des or Il y en a beaucoup des Campsite?
3 there is a castle?   Il y a un monument historique?
4 there is a cathedral?   Il y a cathédrale
5 there are any parks?   Il y en parcs.

⚜️ brilliant learning tip

Here are some useful phrases to help you collect and record new words direct from French speakers.

Ça s'appelle comment en français? *What's that (called) in French?*
Ça s'écrit comment? *How is it written/spelt?*

If you want to hear how these phrases sound go to the reference section at the back of the book.

By the way, did you recognise a word you met in Chapter 1? Je m'appelle ... *I'm called*; Ça s'appelle ... *That's called* ....

A word about cafés

French cafés are unique. They are part of the landscape of each town, where they make a strong statement about the fact that food, drink and interaction with other people lie at the heart of French life. You'll find a number of familiar things to eat and drink (un chocolat, une omelette, un hamburger) and some beverages that are close enough to English to guess (une bière, un café, un thé). You'll also find some exclusively French experiences:

Un croque-monsieur is sometimes described as a 'toasted cheese sandwich with ham' but the image conjured by the English translation won't match the reality of this snack.

Un kir is an apéritif, a mixture of white wine and blackcurrant liqueur. If you are really celebrating, you could choose un kir royal, which substitutes champagne for white wine.

Test case

⚜️ brilliant activity 9

A 1.27 Listen to the audio and work out where each of these two conversations is taking place.

1 .... *Store*

2 .... *Café*

B 1.28 Play your part in the audio conversation where you're meeting a friend to go to Café de la Gare:

- Salut, ça va?
- Return the greeting and say that you're fine. *Salut ça va*
- Voici le café de la Gare
- Ask the waiter if they have a table for two people. *Vous avez une table pour deux personnes?*
- Oui, voilà une table là-bas.

- Bonjour madame, monsieur. Vous désirez?
- Order a milky coffee and ask if they have any omelettes. *Un café crème s'il vous plaît. Vous avez des omelettes?*
- Ah non, je regrette, mais j'ai des sandwichs, un croque-monsieur ...
- Order a croque-monsieur. *Un croque-monsieur, s'il vous plaît*

C 1.29 You're in the tourist office. Play your part in the following conversation:

- Bonjour monsieur.
- Return the greeting and ask if he has a map of the town. *Bonjour monsieur, vous avez un plan de la ville*
- Oui, voilà monsieur.
- Say thank you and ask if there are any museums. *Merci, il y a des musées*
- Oui monsieur, il y en a beaucoup, le musée des vins, le musée des Beaux Arts.
- Say 'very good' and ask if there is a market. *Très bien. Il y a un marché*
- Oui monsieur, sur la Place Charles de Gaulle.
- Ask if he has a list of hotels. *Vous avez un liste d'hôtels s'il vous plaît*
- Oui, bien sûr, voici.
- Say thank you very much and take your leave. *Merci beaucoup, monsieur, Au revoir*

D Using the section about facilities in the city of Lille above, and with the help of the example below, create a similar description of what might be found in your home town. For example:

- À Newtown, il y a une église et un parc. Il y a des restaurants et des bars.
- À Grandtown il y a un centre commercial, des hôtels et un camping.

A Harston, il y a une église et un bois de poste
A Grantham il y a une église et un parc. Il y a des restaurants et des bars. Il y a un centre commercial, des hôtels mais er je regrette mais un camping

☀ brilliant word builder

Some sources say as much as 30% of English vocabulary is of French origin. As you have seen in Chapter 1, many words are identical. Others are very close and you can easily convert them from one language to the other by familiarising yourself with some key spelling patterns. In this chapter, you have come across la specialité *speciality*. You can transfer many other English words ending in '-ty' into French in the same way:

la beauté, la liberté, la fraternité, la sincérité, la légalité, l'irrégularité (f)

The endings of many other abstract nouns change in a similar fashion:

y → ie	l'économie (f), la biologie, la pharmacie, l'astrologie (f), l'astronomie (f), la géographie
ism → isme	le racisme, le tourisme, le réalisme, le pessimisme, le modernisme, le fascisme

Activity 10

Have a go at converting these words into French:

university, quality, philosophy, sociology, optimism, communism

Endgame

Your challenge is to collect ten new French words for food and drink from English sources, excluding a dictionary. You might use recipes, product packaging, menus or other people. Once you have your ten words, check them out with the dictionary, noting any gender details; create word maps for la nourriture *food* and les boissons *drinks* from your research.

tomate   crabe
salade   banane
orange   congette
carotte   crème
lentille   datte
olive .   figue
                  radis

3 On est où?

Where + when

- Ask where places are
- Talk about what you and other people do for a living
- Develop your understanding of nouns and gender
- Meet a key verb être *to be*

In the last chapter you found yourself asking for a whole list of items in different places using the phrases Vous avez...? and Il y a...? Now is your chance to find out where these places are.

Instant history

brilliant activity 1

Look at these signs. As with English street names, French street names provide a real cultural briefing. The following places are named after a battle; a writer and poet; a chemist; a president of France; and a World War One supreme commander. Which is which?

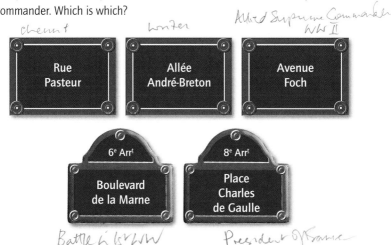

chemist   *writer*   *Allied Supreme Commander WW II*

| Rue Pasteur | Allée André-Breton | Avenue Foch |

| 6ᵉ Arrᵗ | 8ᵉ Arrᵗ |
| Boulevard de la Marne | Place Charles de Gaulle |

Battle in WWI   *President of France*

The words

 activity 2

1.30 Now see if you can sort these words into the appropriate column. Look up any you can't guess using your dictionary or the glossary. Beware, one word is to do with books, but may not be quite what it seems.

l'hôpital   le poste de police   l'arrêt de bus   la librairie
l'aéroport   la gare routière   le tabac   la station de taxis
le pressing   l'hôtel de ville   le supermarché   la poste   la gare

les magasins *shops*	les bâtiments municipaux *municipal buildings*	le voyage *travel*
le supermarché	Hospital	l'arret de bus
le pressing	la poste	l'aeroport
la librarie	l'Hotel de ville	la station de taxis
le tabac	le poste de police	la gare
		la gare routiere

Have a go at saying the words out loud, then listen and repeat to make sure that your pronunciation is working well.

Words for 'the'

In the last chapter you met the French words for 'a' and 'some'; here you will have already spotted words for 'the'. There are four of them: **le** is for nouns that are masculine (**le** supermarché); **la** is for nouns that are feminine (**la** gare); **l'** is used for masculine and feminine nouns that begin with a vowel (a, e, i, o, u) or a silent h (**l'**aéroport; **l'**hôtel) and **les** is for plural nouns whatever their gender (**les** stations de taxi; **les** arrêts). Did you notice that poste changes gender? <u>La</u> poste is 'the post office' and <u>le</u> poste de police is 'the police station'.

 activity 3

Complete the grid with **le, la, l', les**. Check on the rules for making nouns plural if you need to (see page 24).

	le/l'/la	les
un supermarché	*le*	*les*
un café	*le*	*les*
un bureau	*le*	*les*
un magasin	*le*	*les*
un canal	*le*	*les caneaux*
une avenue	*l'*	*les avenues*
un hôpital	*l'*	*les hopitaux*

Putting words together

 activity 4

A **1.31** Listen to these people in a hotel reception asking where places are. See how much you can understand without looking at the text first. Can you identify how to say 'where is' and 'excuse me'?

- Pardon, monsieur. Où est l'hôtel de ville, s'il vous plaît?
- Il est dans la rue Pasteur.
- Merci beaucoup.
- Je vous en prie.

Pardon means 'excuse me' when you are trying to attract someone's attention and also 'sorry' should you inadvertently bump into someone. You can also use it to ask for repetition as you do in English, or, in this context, you can say **Comment?**

B **1.32** Now listen to the next set of people asking where various places are. Work out where each location is and write it in the corresponding box. Along the way listen out for 'thank you very much' and the response 'it's nothing; it's a pleasure':

Market café	*Il est dans l'alley André Breton*
Post office	*Elle est place Charles de Gaulle*
Station	*Elle est dans la Rue Pasteur*

Merci Je vous en prie

Merci beaucoup is 'Thank you very much' and **Je vous en prie** means 'It's nothing' or 'It's a pleasure'.

 activity 5

1.33 Take a look at this map of a town.

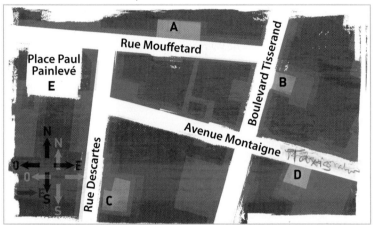

Ask where the following places are, listen to the answers and identify which letter they are on your map:

taxi rank   police station   dry cleaner's
bus station   flea market (le marché aux puces)

When you ask for directions, you'll get a variety of answers. Did you spot Il y en a un *There's one (of them)* as you listened?

Pardon, où est le pressing, s'il vous plaît? *Where's the dry cleaner's please?* **Alors il y en a un Boulevard de la Marne.** *Well, there's one on the Boulevard de la Marne.*

In English you don't need to say 'of them' but en is a fixture in French. Note too that you don't always need to say 'in the' in French, you can just say the name of the street: Boulevard de la Marne.

brilliant language tip

> Some words are hybrids. Le marché is the French for 'market' and, just as in English, you can add 'super' and 'hyper': un supermarché *supermarket*, un hypermarché *hypermarket*. Some other useful terms translate directly: le marché noir *the black market*, le marché monétaire *the money market*. Others are not so obvious: la bourse is the word for 'the stock market', literally 'the purse'.

Making sense of what you hear

It's all very well being able to ask where something is, but if you are lost, it's even more important to understand enough to get you where you want to be. If possible it is a good idea to predict some of the words and phrases you might hear so that you're ready for them. Words such as la rue *street*, la place *square*, dans *in* will help you orientate yourself in a conversation and literally too.

Although prediction can help, don't forget that the unexpected is common in communication. You've already met someone who didn't know where the bus station was: Je regrette, je ne sais pas *I'm sorry I don't know*. You may ask someone who will undermine your best intentions by ending the conversation with an abrupt Je n'ai aucune idée! *I've no idea* or Je ne suis pas d'ici *I'm not from here*.

Collect phrases that will be useful to slow down what is said or to be able to check what you have heard.

 activity 6

1.34 Here are two phrases to begin with.

Désolé(e), je n'ai pas compris. Voulez-vous répéter, s'il vous plaît? *Sorry, I didn't understand. Will you say it again, please.*

Vous avez dit (la Rue Pasteur)? *Did you say …?*

Play your part in the following conversation on the audio:
- Stop a man and ask where the hospital is.   *Pardon monsieur, ou est l'hôpital s'il vous plaît*
- Vous avez dit l'hôpital? Il est Boulevard de la Marne.   *Désolé je n'ais pas compris*
- Say sorry you didn't quite understand, ask him to repeat the instruction.   *Voulez vous répéter, s'il vous plaît*
- L'hôpital est Boulevard de la Marne.
- Check that he said Boulevard de la Marne.   *Vous avez dit Boulevarde de la Marne*
- Oui, c'est bien ça.

In the exchanges so far you may have spotted another example of the gender rule in action. Did you notice how the word for 'it' changes according to whether the building is masculine or feminine?

Où est le poste de police? Il est dans la Rue Pasteur.
Où est la poste? Elle est Place Charles de Gaulle.

Il est and elle est literally mean 'he is' and 'she is'. Given everything has a gender in French, there is no need for an extra word 'it' for inanimate objects as in English. Il is masculine 'it' and elle is feminine 'it'.

Introductions

 activity 7

A **1.35** Listen to these people saying what they do for a living.

Can you find the word for lawyer with a bit of lateral thinking? What do the other people do for a living?

B **1.36** Next you will hear some of these people being introduced to each other; fill in their professions on their business cards.

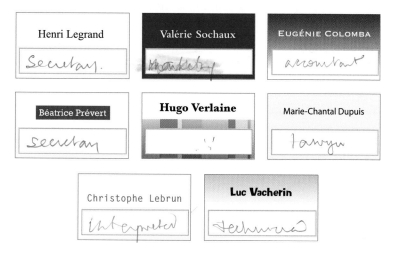

Have you noticed that, unlike English, French does not include the words for 'a' or 'the' when talking about jobs and professions?

She's the marketing director. Elle est directrice marketing.
He's a consultant. Il est consultant.

 activity 8

1.37 How would you introduce the following people and say what they do? Remember that Je vous présente is how you say 'can I introduce'.

Guillaume Souchet - avocat *Je vous présenter G S: Il est avocat*

Roselyne Flon - directrice générale *" . " . - R F. Elle est directrice générale*

Marguerite Dormoi - comptable *" r " r elle est comp-*

Pascal David - directeur qualité *~ . - . il est directn*

Alfred Laroche - interprète *, - - : il est interprète*

You've just introduced two directors, one male <u>directeur</u> qualité and one female <u>directrice</u> générale. The word for the work you do may change according to whether you are male or female. On the whole, female versions of jobs end in e but a number of other spelling changes can happen too.

 activity 9

A Use the examples to fill in the gaps in the table below:

masculine	feminine
un conduc<u>teur</u> *driver*	une conduc<u>trice</u> *un conducteur*
un acteur *une actrice*	*une*
un technic<u>ien</u> *un pharmacienne*	une technic<u>ienne</u>
	une pharmacienne
un avoca<u>t</u>	une avoca<u>te</u>
un étudiant	*une étudiante*
un secrétaire *un dentiste*	une secrétaire
	une dentiste
un infirm<u>ier</u> *nurse*	une infirm<u>ière</u>
un boulanger *baker*	*une boulangère*
un coiffeur *hairdresser* *un serveur*	une coiff<u>euse</u>
	une serveuse *waitress*

For historical reasons, and as a legacy from less emancipated times, some jobs only have a male form (un **professeur** *a teacher*, un **médécin** *a doctor*, un ingénieur *an engineer*) so Je suis professeur *I'm a teacher* works for both men and women. A dictionary will tell you whether there is a female version of the jobs you want to be able to talk about. Look for the French for your occupation. If you don't work you might say:

Je ne travaille pas. *I don't work./I'm not working.*
Je suis sans emploi/au chômage. *I'm unemployed.*
Je suis en retraite. *I'm retired.*
Je suis en recherche d'emploi. *I'm between jobs.*

B Change your identity

1.38 Imagine you are each of the following people and say who you are and what you do. Example: Je suis Michel Robert, je suis avocat. Listen to check your answers.

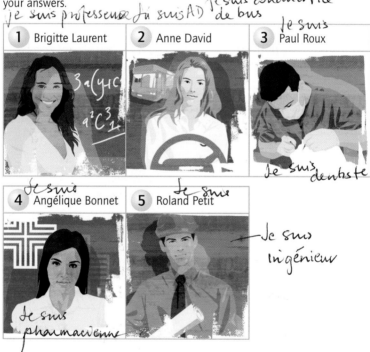

1 Brigitte Laurent   2 Anne David   3 Paul Roux

4 Angélique Bonnet   5 Roland Petit

Être ou ne pas être

In this chapter you have come across different parts of the verb 'to be': **je suis** *I am*; **il est** *he/it is*; **elle est** *she/it is* and **ils sont** *they are*. Go back and check where they occur. 'To be' in French is **être**, so what do you think the title of this section means?

When you search for verbs in a grammar reference you will find that they follow a format like this:

je suis	*I am*
tu es	*you are*
il/elle est	*he/she/it is*
nous sommes	*we are*
vous êtes	*you are*
ils/elles sont	*they are*

brilliant learning tip

If you learnt French at school you may remember chanting verbs out loud. There is something therapeutic about rote learning and you might set aside some time to commit verb patterns to memory. Think of them as the times tables of language learning. Linking learning of this sort to everyday actions such as walking to work or brushing your hair can sometimes help fix language in the mind.

Look again at être. Can you see the gender rule at work here? Focus on the 'they' part of the pattern. Ils sont means 'they are' when the people or things you are talking about are all masculine (a group of men or some sandwiches, for example) or a mixture of masculine and feminine (a group of men and women or sandwiches and omelettes). Elles sont is 'they are' when the people or things are all feminine (women or omelettes).

brilliant activity 10

A **1.39** Match these questions to the answers and check them on the audio:

1 Où sont Jérôme et Marianne? d	a Je suis dans l'hôpital.
2 Nous sommes où exactement? e	b Elle est dans la Rue Pasteur.
3 Où est la gare? b	c Elles sont dans la gare routière.
4 Où sont les toilettes? c	d Ils sont à la poste.
5 Tu es où? a	e Nous sommes dans l'Avenue Foch.

B **1.40** Now listen to these people. Can you answer these questions? You will hear ici meaning 'here' and aujourd'hui, which means 'today'.

1 Where is the person Marie-Claude is looking for? *Il est à Paris*
2 Which square is the office in? *Il est à place de liberté*
3 What job does the person who works for Dufour do? *Il est architect*

What a muddle! Look at the transcript of these exchanges. You should be able to spot various parts of être. Have you noticed that some of the things that are said are negative? Contrast je suis *I am* with je ne suis pas *I am not* (negative).

To make a verb negative in French you need to wrap ne and pas around it. Before a vowel the ne loses its e, just as le does: l'eau; il n'est pas.

 brilliant activity 11

Make the following sentences negative:

Example: Elles sont ici → Elles ne sont pas ici

1 Tu es professeur de mathématiques? *Tu n'es pas*
2 La poste est Place du Marché. *n'est pas*
3 Je suis dans le train. *ne suis pas*
4 Nous sommes à Paris. *ne somme pas*
5 Les portables *mobile phones* sont indispensables. *ne sonte pas*

Stock phrases

Since être is an extremely common verb you'll find it cropping up in a number of phrases and idioms that might be of use:

Je suis désolé(e). *I'm sorry.*
Je suis en retard. *I'm late.*
Je suis d'accord. *I agree.*
Vous êtes en bonne santé? *Are you in good health?*
Je suis aux anges. *I'm on cloud nine.* (literally 'I'm with the angels.')
Je suis dans les choux. *I'm bringing up the rear.* (literally 'I'm in the cabbages.')

Make sure that you look out for être and start a collection of useful phrases and idioms for yourself.

 **activity 12**

1.41 Listen to this phone call.

1 Where's Joseph and why is he apologising? *In the café at the station. He is late*
2 Where has Julie stopped off on her way? *— supermarket*

When you pick up a phone in France it's normal to begin the conversation with the word allô sometimes followed by oui. Allô is a version of 'hello' that's only used for phone conversations.

Where are you from?

 **activity 13**

A 1.42 Être crops up in the question Vous êtes d'où? *Where are you from?* (literally 'you are from where?'). In order to reply, you need the word de *from*, which loses an e when it's in front of a word beginning with a vowel. Look at the examples below and listen to them on the audio:

Vous êtes d'où?	Tu es de Londres?
Je suis de Paris.	Je suis de Birmingham.
Il est de Monte Carlo.	Ils sont de Dublin.
Nous sommes de Bruxelles.	Elles sont de Belfast.
Elle est d'Anjou.	Vous êtes de Cardiff?

Have you noticed that there is a French translation for London Londres? It won't take much effort to work out where Edimbourg might be. Both French and English have the habit of 'translating' names of cities (commonly capital cities), so what we call 'Brussels' is actually Bruxelles and choux de Bruxelles is a vegetable that you might want to avoid.

B 1.43 Listen to these people talking about where they're from and note down the places next to their names:

Monique Delahaye	*Marseille*
Thomas Espinasse	*Grenoble*
Michel and Thérèse Gallet	*Quebec*
Carole Rey	*Metz*
Habib Taieb	*Andorre*

Cast your mind over your family, friends and acquaintances. How will you say where they are from? And how will you answer the question: Vous êtes d'où?

~~Vous etes~~ Vons êtes du? Je suis de Yorki

Test case

 **activity 14**

Play your part in the conversations:

A 1.44 *Bonjour Madame, Je suis Mark T*
- Greet a new female colleague and tell her you're Mark Thompson.
- Enchantée, je suis Valérie de Lafayette. Je vous présente
  Jean-Pierre Renard. *Enchanté madam Vous êtes d'ici*
- Say that you're pleased to meet her. Ask if she's from round here. *Je suis*
- Non, je ne suis pas de Toulouse, je suis de Cahors. Et vous? *de Manchester*
- Say that you're from Manchester. Tell her that you are an interpreter. *Je suis*
- Ah bon, vous êtes ici pour la conférence, alors? *interprète*
- Say yes. Ask if he's an interpreter. *Oui. Vous êtes interprète*
- Non, je suis technicien. *On est*
- Ask where the conference room (la salle de conference) is.
- Elle est dans le hall d'exposition.
- Say thank you and take your leave. *Merci et au revoir*

B 1.45 Now you're out for the evening and you run into a friend of a friend.
- Greet the man and ask him how he is. *Bonjour mons. Comment allez vous?*
- Tres bien merci, et vous? *Très bien. Voici elle est professeur*
- Say very well and say this is (voici) Marthe Paoli, she's a teacher.
- Enchanté, vous êtes tous les deux professeurs, alors?
- Say no, you're not a teacher, you're an actor. *Non, je ne suis pas prof, Je suis actor*
- Tiens! Il y a un théâtre ici?
- Say yes, there's a theatre in rue Grenelle. *Oui, il y a un théâtre dan la rue Grenelle*

 **pronunciation**

1.46 If you put together the words for locations in la ville *the town* you would find quite a few with the letter r in them: la boulange<u>r</u>ie, la pha<u>r</u>macie, le <u>r</u>estau<u>r</u>ant, la <u>r</u>ue, le bouleva<u>r</u>d.

To make the r sound, your tongue stays flat behind your bottom teeth and the roof of your mouth vibrates as though you were gargling. There's a real pronunciation challenge for you in words that have r and u together, such as la <u>r</u>ue and la <u>r</u>uelle.

Practise saying the following words with the audio:

le restaurant   la rue   le boulevard   Henri   en retard
je regrette   la gare   bonjour   la directrice

If you have not already discovered the delights of YouTube (www.youtube.com) now is the time to do so. Search for Edith Piaf and listen to Je ne regrette rien, Milord and La vie en Rose for a wonderful exposé of the Parisian version of the r sound. For something a little subtler look for Charles Trenet singing La mer.

Reading

 activity 15

Comparing French and English texts provides an alternative to simply looking words up.

Victor Hugo is one name frequently found on road signs in France. To discover more about him look at this extract from his entry in Wikipedia.

> **Victor-Marie Hugo**, né le 26 février 1802 à Besançon et mort le 22 mai 1885 à Paris, est un écrivain, dramaturge, poète, homme politique, académicien et intellectuel engagé français, considéré comme le plus important des écrivains romantiques de langue française et un des plus importants écrivains de la littérature française.

political

Here's Wikipedia's English entry for Victor Hugo:

> **Victor-Marie Hugo** (26 February 1802 – 22 May 1885) was a French poet, playwright, novelist, essayist, visual artist, statesman, human rights activist and exponent of the Romantic movement in France.

The information varies between the texts. Without resorting to a dictionary can you work out what additional talents have been attributed to the man in the English text? Where was Hugo born and where did he die? You'll have noticed a number of cognates in the French text which will help you make sense of what is being said.

Endgame

In this chapter you have come across another group of words that, although not spelt identically, clearly have linguistic links. Take a look at the following:

victoire *victory*   directeur *director*
laboratoire *laboratory*   auteur *author*
territoire *territory*   acteur *actor*

Words that in English end with '-ory' frequently end in -oire in French. Words for jobs that end in -eur in French may have English equivalents ending in '-or', '-er'.

In the word search below look for the French words for:

history, pastor, memory, boxer, doctor (title), porter, employer, vendor, glory, ivory

If you don't like word searches, just try putting them into French!

E	E	V	C	G	X	E	R	V	U
R	R	E	U	N	R	M	U	E	O
I	P	I	E	I	V	P	E	N	M
O	X	O	O	W	T	L	T	D	W
V	N	M	R	L	Y	O	S	E	C
I	E	J	M	T	G	Y	A	U	Z
M	O	J	S	X	E	E	P	R	B
G	D	O	C	T	E	U	R	Z	I
R	U	E	X	O	B	R	R	I	G
W	I	E	R	I	O	T	S	I	H

4 Un tour des magasins

- Meet key words and phrases useful for shopping and eating
- Get to grips with numbers in French
- Pursue the gender issue

The words

As with most languages, certain endings on words provide clues as to what they might be. In English, shops often end in '-er': butcher's, grocer's, fishmonger's. The common ending for shops in French is -erie and all these words are feminine.

 activity 1

1.47 Have a go at matching the eight products below with the correct shop:

1 l'insectifuge _b_	a la boucherie	
2 le journal _e_	b la pharmacie	
3 le pain de campagne _c_	c la boulangerie	
4 les haricots verts _g_	d la pâtisserie	

5 le Brie de Meaux *h*	e la maison de la presse	
6 le bœuf *a*	f la poissonnerie	
7 l'éclair au chocolat *d*	g l'épicerie	
8 le saumon *f*	h la fromagerie	

Check that you have the correct answers and practise the pronunciation on the audio.

Shopping lists

Only you know what you are most likely to want to buy, so you might want to give that some thought and create a list of common items that you will need. When you do the activities in this chapter you could substitute the vocabulary that is most useful for you for the examples that are given.

Have a look below at these words for cheese, wine and bread:

le vin rouge *red* le vin blanc *white* le vin rosé le vin mousseux *sparkling*	le fromage au lait de vache *cow's milk* le fromage de chèvre *goat* le fromage frais	la fougasse la ficelle la couronne *crown* la flûte *small baguette*

Of course, much of the time, you'll be calling items by their type or brand name and when you do this they assume the same gender as the general term: un fromage, un camembert; un vin, un Bourgogne *Burgundy*; une voiture, une Peugeot etc.

 **cultural tip**

In la boulangerie you will find a range of different breads (des pains) that are variations of a baguette. Une flûte is a smaller version of une baguette and un grand pain larger. In addition you might ask for an alternative shape, une couronne (literally 'a crown'), a round loaf with a hole in the middle, or a different kind of bread, un pain de campagne *a country loaf*.

Shop talk

 activity 2

A 1.48 There are a number of key phrases that are useful for shopping. In the dialogue you will hear: Je voudrais ... *I would like*; C'est combien? *How much is that?* and C'est tout, merci *That's all, thank you.* Listen to the way these phrases are pronounced before you listen to the dialogue; practise saying them yourself.

Now answer these questions:

1 Which two shops are we in?   *bakery, chemist*

2 Which four items do they ask for?   *flûte, country loaf, antiseptic cream, insect repellent*

B How would you ask for the following items using Je voudrais ...?

1 a Bordeaux   *Je voudrais un*

2 six chocolate eclairs   *" " six*

3 a country loaf   *" " un pain de campagne*

4 a rosé wine   *" " un vin rosé*

 **learning tip**

Don't forget too that pointing and shopping go together perfectly. Even the most competent linguist is unlikely to know all the words for local specialities, so a judicious finger accompanied by Un comme ça, s'il vous plaît *One of those, please* can always get you what you want.

Number crunching

C'est combien? is one way of asking how much something is. Combien is the word for 'how much' or 'how many'. In English if you want to discover the cost of something you might say: 'How much is it?' or 'How much do I owe you?' (Je vous dois combien?), 'How much does it cost?' (Ça coûte combien?), and so on. A similar menu of options is available in French but start with C'est combien and remember to be on the lookout for other ways of asking the price.

You'll find a numbers section on page 185. Before you tackle the following exercises, learn the numbers one to 20 and the words for 30, 40, 50, 60, 70, 80, 90. Number learning is particularly good for pronunciation as most of the key sounds of French are present. Listen carefully to words such as trois and huit.

 **brilliant activity 3**

2.13

1.49 Listen to these conversations in various shops and write down how much each item is:

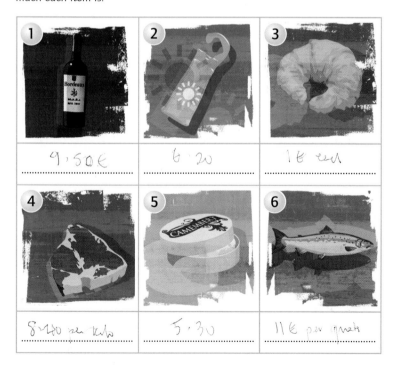

 learning tip

To improve your chances of understanding numbers, get into the habit of repeating them under your breath or out loud, as soon as you hear them. Keep saying the number to yourself and then you can slow it down in order to work out what it is.

Successful shopping is largely a matter of getting the formula right: vocabulary plus set phrases to keep the conversation moving. These kinds of exchanges soon become second nature and that gives you time to build your understanding of French by scrutinising labels for new vocabulary or eavesdropping on other people's conversations.

 activity 4

1.50 You're off to the poissonnerie to buy fish (poisson) and shell fish (fruits de mer, literally 'fruits of sea'):

un crabe   12 langoustines
6 huîtres *oysters*   un homard *lobster*

Practise the pronunciation of these words and then take part in the role play.

- Bonjour. Vous désirez?
- Say that you'd like a crab. *Je voudrais un crabe*
- Voilà et avec ça?
- Ask how much a lobster is. *Un homard c'est combien*
- Dix-huit euros vingt.
- Say fine, one lobster, please. *Très bien. Un homard s'il vous plaît*
- Avec ceci?
- Say you'd like 12 langoustines and six oysters. *Je voudrais douze lang — et six huîtres*
- Voilà, ce sera tout?
- Say yes, that's all, and ask how much it is. *Oui, c'est tout merci, c'est combien?*
- Quarante euros quatre-vingt dix, s'il vous plaît. *40,80*
- Hand the money over and take your leave. *Voilà Merci au revoir*

How many?

You'll need higher numbers in order to express quantities such as grammes. Have a go at the 100s from 100 to 900. Once you've got those fixed, add 25 and 50 (125, 250 etc) to help with weights and measures.

 **activity 5**

A **1.51** Practise by identifying what these people are buying from the prices given. Prepare yourself for a bit of mental arithmetic as they may be buying different quantities from those quoted:

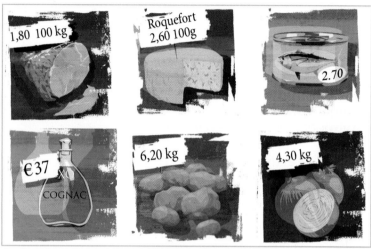

1. Deux kilos, ca fait huit euros soixante
2. Deux cents grammes, C'est trois euros soixante
3. Alors deux ca fait Soixante-quatorze euros
4. Cinq cents grammes, C'est treize euros
5. Trois kilos, dix-huit euros soixante
6. Alors huit euros dix pour les trois

B In the grid below there are examples of items you might buy in various quantities. Try saying them for yourself. Note that de (in common with ne and le) loses its e before a vowel: **un kilo d'oranges.**

une tranche *slice* de	une bouteille *bottle* de/d'	un kilo, (2, 3, 4 kilos) de/d'	100, 250, 500 grammes de	une boîte *tin* de/d'
jambon salami lard	shampooing cognac eau minérale	pommes de terre *potatoes* oignons	fraises *strawberries* saucisson	olives tomates thon *tuna*

2 kilos onions   500g Roquefort
200g ham   3kg potatoes
2 bottle cognac   3 tins tuna

C **1.52** Listen to someone checking off their shopping list and tick the items that you hear from the list on the previous page. *kilos of onions,*

cinq tranche de saucisson, un bouteille d'eau minérale

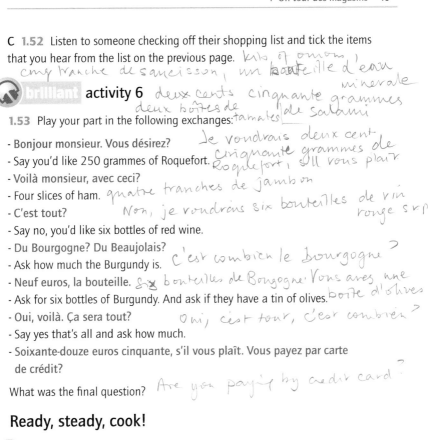

activity 6 *deux cents cinquante grammes*

deux boîtes de

1.53 Play your part in the following exchanges: *tomates de salami*

- Bonjour monsieur. Vous désirez? *Je voudrais deux cent*
- Say you'd like 250 grammes of Roquefort. *cinquante grammes de Roquefort, s'il vous plaît*
- Voilà monsieur, avec ceci?
- Four slices of ham. *quatre tranches de jambon*
- C'est tout? *Non, je voudrais six bouteilles de vin rouge srp*
- Say no, you'd like six bottles of red wine.
- Du Bourgogne? Du Beaujolais?
- Ask how much the Burgundy is. *C'est combien le Bourgogne?*
- Neuf euros, la bouteille. *Six bouteilles de Bourgogne. Vous avez une boîte d'olives*
- Ask for six bottles of Burgundy. And ask if they have a tin of olives.
- Oui, voilà. Ça sera tout? *Oui, c'est tout, c'est combien?*
- Say yes that's all and ask how much.
- Soixante-douze euros cinquante, s'il vous plaît. Vous payez par carte de crédit?

What was the final question? *Are you paying by credit card?*

Ready, steady, cook!

 **activity 7**

A **1.54** Expressing the notion of 'some' in French is slightly more complicated than in English. Look at and listen to these ingredients for making an omelette:

> Il y a des œufs, du beurre, du lait, du sel, du poivre et des herbes.
> Vous pouvez ajouter de la crème aussi.

some eggs – **des oeufs**
some salt – **du sel**
some cream – **de la crème**

You've already met **des** but there are other ways of saying 'some' which change according to the gender and number of the word that you want some of:

Masculine	Feminine	Before a vowel or h	Plural
du (de + le)	de la	de l'	des (de + les)
du sel *salt*	de la crème	de l'huile *oil*	des œufs

Du, de la and des also mean 'any', so you can put them with vous avez to ask 'Do you have any ...?'.

B **1.55** In Chapter 2 you came across un croque-monsieur. A variation of this snack is a un croque-madame. Here's a recipe for croque-madame; choose the right words to complete it and then listen to check your answers. What's the variation?

Vous prenez deux tranches (de/du/de la/de l'/des) pain. Mettez (de/du/de la/de l'/des) beurre sur les deux tranches. Sur une tranche vous mettez (de/du/de la/de l'/des) jambon et (de/du/de la/de l'/des) Gruyère et avec l'autre tranche, vous formez un sandwich. Mettez le sandwich au gril. Mettez (de/du/de la/de l'/des) œufs au plat sur le sandwich avant de servir.

C **1.56** Using the table below to help, have a go at saying what you want or asking for items. Use your dictionary or the glossary to check out gender and meaning when necessary. Listen to the audio for some sample sentences.

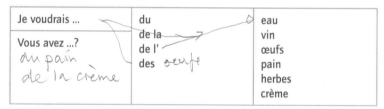

Je voudrais ...	du	eau
Vous avez ...? *du pain de la crème*	de la de l' des *œufs*	vin œufs pain herbes crème

What on earth?

Of course you will be assailed by all kinds of new experiences in French-speaking countries so arm yourself with some key questions to help you build your knowledge.

 **brilliant** activity 8

A **1.57** Read and listen to this conversation about cheese. See if you can identify two key phrases: 'What is ...?' and 'What do you have in the way of ...?'.

- Qu'est-ce que vous avez comme fromages?
- J'ai du Reblochon, du camembert et du Port Salut.
- Et qu'est-ce que c'est, le Reblochon?
- C'est du fromage de la région. C'est un fromage au lait de vache.

Qu'est-ce que means 'what'. Although composed of a number of words, the phrase is pronounced as one.

brilliant learning tip

Qu'est-ce que c'est? *What is it?* and Qu'est-ce que c'est en français? *What is it in French?* will be extremely useful for building your vocabulary on the spot.

B Work out how you might ask:

1 what Bouillabaisse (f) is.
2 what bisque (f) is.
3 what ratatouille (f) is.
4 what gratin dauphinois (m) is.

Now try to match your questions with these answers:

a C'est un ragoût de poissons.
b Ce sont des pommes de terre avec de la crème et du fromage.
c C'est un ragoût de légumes.
d C'est une soupe aux fruits de mer.

Have you spotted another way of saying 'it is':

C'est un ragoût de poissons.
C'est une soupe aux fruits de mer.

You've heard it before in this chapter in the question C'est combien?. C'est *it is* is extremely common, particularly in spoken French, both in questions and statements. The good news is that c'est does not alter as a result of the gender of the noun to which it refers, although it does have a plural form ce sont *they are*.

Qu'est-ce que c'est?
Ce sont des pommes de terre.
Ce sont des saucisses de Toulouse.
Ce sont des vins de Bourgogne.

language tip

> C'est is generally used to define or identify things, which is why it is used with Qu'est ce que c'est?. It's also used to express a view or describe a situation: C'est vrai *It's true*; C'est bon *It's good*; C'est bizarre *It's strange*; Ce n'est pas grave *It doesn't matter* (literally, 'It's not serious').

 pronunciation

1.58 The various forms of a that you have met give you a chance for a vowel workout. The sound of the letter a changes depending on the combinations it makes with other letters. This is true of all the vowel sounds. Have a go by repeating the words on the audio. The a in French is a flat sound as in:

chocolat   plat   glace

If it is combined with i it becomes 'ay' as in:
Beaujolais   voudrais   raisin

And with a u it becomes 'oh' as in:
au   aussi   journaux   eau   bureau

Now listen to the letter i. You need to stretch your mouth sideways in a grin shape and produce a short sharp 'ee' sound:
dix   pastille   cerise

Tasty morsels

 **activity 9**

A 1.59 You're in a restaurant and the waiter is explaining the plats du jour, the day's specials. Think about how these words will sound before you listen, then number the dishes as you hear them; which dish is not mentioned?

☐ la soupe aux champignons

☐ le steak au poivre

☐ la tarte aux pommes

☐ les crêpes au saumon

☐ la mousse au chocolat

☐ le bœuf au vin rouge

☐ le poulet à la crème

By the way, did you spot the words for starter, main course and dessert? Two at least will be familiar!

Now look again at how flavours are described: la mousse au chocolat *chocolate mousse*. In French you start with the food and add the flavour using au, à la, à l', aux. Which you use is determined by the gender and number of the flavour.

Masculine	Feminine	Before a vowel or h	Plural
au (à + le)	à la	à l'	aux (à + les)
au chocolat	à la crème	à l'ail *garlic*	aux noix *nuts*
au saumon	à la vanille	à l'oignon	aux pommes

B 1.60 On the audio you will hear people ordering various desserts. Listen and see if you can complete the menu below:

Les desserts

fondant .... chocolat noir

crème brûlée .... vanille

fruits exotiques flambés .... rhum

moelleux .... pommes

tarte .... banane

tarte .... fruits de saison

glace .... fraise

You can use je voudrais to make an order in a restaurant:

Vous désirez, madame?

Je voudrais la soupe à l'oignon, s'il vous plaît.

 **activity 10**

How would you order the following?

1 onion tart (**une tarte**)
2 mushroom soup
3 some vanilla ice cream
4 ham crêpe
5 cheese sandwich

 **activity 11**

A Read the extract from a French menu below.

1 If you were allergic to fish what would you avoid on this menu?
2 If you were vegetarian what might you choose?
3 What kind of bread is served?
4 What is the mayonnaise flavoured with?

PAIN À L' AIL

SALADE CÉSAR AU POULET
Tranches de poulet grillées servies sur notre salade césar

SALADE AUX ÉPINARDS
Épinards frais garnis de champignons, d'oignons rouges avec
une mayonnaise piquante au citron

SALADE AU FROMAGE DE CHÈVRE
Fromage de chèvre chaud, couvert de noisettes, tomates,
concombres, salade verte avec une vinaigrette aux herbes
fines

SALADE AU POULET ET AUX POIRES RÔTIES
Poulet, poires rôties, Gorgonzola et noix caramélisées, servis
sur salade verte mixte

SALADE AU SAUMON FUMÉ
Saumon fumé de l'Atlantique servi sur salade verte, avec
oignons rouges, olives noires, câpres, et une vinaigrette à
l'huile citronnée

B Underline all the flavours that use au, à la, à l', aux. Guess what you might be ordering for each one before checking in a dictionary.

 **learning tip**

It's often the little words that pose the greatest challenge to language learners. You will come across many different uses of à and de, so it's worth learning how they behave when combined with le (au, du) and les (aux, des) as this will remain constant. À, for example, can variously mean 'to', 'at', 'in' and 'on', as well as describing flavours and prices (un menu à 21 euros).

Test case

 **activity 12**

1.61 You call the tourist office to get some restaurant recommendations and they give you a choice of four. Listen and write down their phone numbers:

Le Pont de La Tour ....

La Bonne Bouche ....

Chez Mimi ....

Café Antigone ....

 **activity 13**

1.62 In French restaurants you can either order à la carte *from the menu* or decide to go for un menu à prix fixe *a fixed price menu*. In most restaurants there will be several fixed price options and you indicate which you'd like by reference to the price: Je voudrais le menu à vingt et un euros.

Have a go. The waiter is approaching your table to see if you've chosen:

- Vous avez choisi?
- Say yes, you'd like the 25 euro menu.
- Bon, qu'est-ce que vous prenez en hors d'œuvres?
- Say you'd like the goat's cheese salad and chicken in red wine.
- Très bien.
- Ask what desserts he has.

- Nous avons la tarte à la fraise et le clafoutis.
- Ask what le clafoutis is.
- C'est un gâteau aux cerises.
- Say no, thanks, and ask if they have any ice creams.
- Vanille, chocolat, rhum raisin.
- Say chocolate ice cream, please.
- Et pour boire, vous désirez?
- Ask for a bottle of white wine and some water.

Wouldn't it be great if all the French you needed to know was in one book? The only way for that to happen would be for you to write it yourself! Communication is an individual activity. You'll need to adapt and develop the core language in this book to gain your own French voice. You may also want to take advantage of other language-learning tools.

Languages and language-learning references have a terminology all of their own. This is not really unusual or surprising; we're very good at bestowing bespoke terms on key activities. Think about the words we use in relation to computers or the jargon generated by certain jobs. The language of language learning mostly describes grammar and when you learn on your own some understanding of the terms will help you navigate the tools at your disposal.

Key technical terms for using language references

- **Noun** – a person, name, animal, thing or concept: 'woman', 'John', 'cat', 'fork', 'freedom'. In French, all nouns are either masculine or feminine. This is called **gender**.

- A **pronoun** is used in place of a noun to avoid repeating it: 'he', 'she', 'it' etc.

- The noun or pronoun that does an action is called the **subject**, a noun or pronoun that has the action done to it is called the **direct object**. The noun or pronoun that is the recipient (i.e. the person or thing something is given, sent etc to) is called the **indirect object**.

  subject: 'She lives in Brighton.'
  direct object: 'She bought a house.'
  indirect object: 'I talk to her every day.'

- **Adjectives** describe or 'qualify' nouns. In French, they change their form to 'agree' with the gender and number of the noun. **Number** in this sense means singular or plural: 'an interesting book'; 'a long walk'; 'the green fields'.

- **Adverbs** describe or qualify verbs, adjectives and other adverbs: 'The boy goes out slowly'; 'He's a very good student'; 'He sings quite well'.

- **Prepositions** tell you where something/someone is in relation to another in time or place, or can indicate direction: 'with my friend'; 'near school'; 'before the meeting'.

- A **verb** is a word describing an action or state of being: 'Henry plays'; 'we think'; 'they exist'.

- The **infinitive** is the basic form of the verb, which you will find in dictionaries and vocabulary lists. It is *in-finite*, i.e. it is not in a **tense** or person. You could call it the verb 'in neutral': 'to travel', 'to think', 'to exist'.

- A **finite verb** is a verb which is in a **tense**. A tense relates the verb (i.e. the action) to time – past, present or future – telling you for example when the action took/takes/will take place.

- **Conjunctions** join words, phrases, and parts of a sentence to each other: 'tea and coffee'; 'firm but fair'; 'We went home because it was raining'.

Verb tables and grammar references

The idea of verb tables might remind you of multiplication tables, their Maths equivalent. They are reference guides that model the behaviour of different kinds of verbs.

Go to **www.wordreference.com**, select 'French' from the 'conjugators' ('conjugate' is the technical term for giving the different forms of a verb) and find the present tense of être, with which you are already familiar. Patterns for verbs are acquired gradually as you develop your knowledge of French; you do not need to crack them all at once.

Verb tables may form part of a larger grammar reference which describes the rules of the language. Navigation of these relies on knowing the terminology; you'll be looking for rules under headings such as 'nouns', 'verbs', 'adjectives', 'prepositions' etc.

Grammar references usually give you a definition of the term ('noun', 'adjective' etc), a description of the rules and of the exceptions to a rule.

Information is illustrated through examples. There are online grammar references too; follow this link to find out about French nouns **http://french. about.com/od/grammar/a/nouns.htm.**

The bilingual dictionary – does size matter?

A dictionary is a rich source of information that goes way beyond the simple 'translation' of words from English to French and vice versa. If you prefer a text dictionary you will need to put some thought into size. At one end of the dictionary scale you'll find the pocket version, great for carrying around or for quick reference at home, such as checking spellings. Large 'desk' dictionaries, sometimes in two volumes, provide numerous useful examples of the language at work but can be expensive and cumbersome. You'll probably be better off with something in-between. Look out for one that contains examples of new words in action. Internet dictionaries are user-friendly and often give you the sound of words. **www.wordreference.com** has a 'Forum' section where usage, tricky words and expressions are debated among learners and native speakers.

Le mot juste - French to English

Using a dictionary to work from French into English is relatively straightforward since you'll usually be searching for words to complete a picture that already makes some sense.

In this entry for château, it is relatively easy to spot that in different situations it will be the word for a castle, palace, mansion or even château:

château, pl - x (ʃato) nm (forteresse) castle; (palais) palace, castle; (manoir) mansion; (en France) château. **Bâtir des -x en Espagne** to build castles in the air; - **de cartes** house of cards; - **d'eau** water tower; - **fort** stronghold, fortified castle

(ʃato) is a representation of the pronunciation of château using the International Phonetic Alphabet (IPA). IPA symbols will be explained in the dictionary; you do not need to learn this alphabet but you might find it helpful to capture the correct pronunciation of words that are new to you.

Now look at the other information about château. 'Pl – x' tells you that the plural (pl) of château is formed by the addition of x not s, un château, des châteaux. 'Nm' informs you that château is a noun ('n') that is masculine ('m').

Grammatical clues and context will be key to making correct use of dictionaries. Look out for:

adj = adjective		**nf** = noun feminine	
adv = adverb		**nm** = noun masculine	
conj = conjunction		**vr** = verb reflexive	
prep = preposition		**vt** = verb transitive	
pron = pronoun		**vi** = verb intransitive	

(You'll come across reflexive verbs in Chapter 7.)

 **activity 1**

What are you being told about the following:

1 canal, pl - aux nm
2 être, vb
3 national, mpl - aux adj

English to French

You want an electric fan. The word 'fan' can be an adjective ('a <u>fan</u> club'; 'a <u>fan</u> belt'), a verb ('<u>to fan</u> the flames') and a noun ('<u>a fan</u>'). In this instance you will be looking for the latter but there are different kinds of fans (hand held, football, mechanical).

In order to get as close to the right word as possible:

- Look the word up in the English–French part of the dictionary.
- Choose the correct part of speech (verb, noun, adjective etc).
- Read through the translations and examples and pick the one that most closely matches your meaning.
- Check the word you have selected in the French–English part of the dictionary.

If you don't think that you've hit the nail on the head, try to find another word or phrase in English that expresses what you mean and start a new search.

Investigating verbs

When you look for a verb, you will find its infinitive. In English, infinitives are preceded by 'to' ('to be', 'to talk', 'to buy' etc), so remove the 'to' and look for 'be', 'talk', buy'. Since dictionaries deal in infinitives, it's important to be able to match parts of verbs to their infinitive form. Most of the time this is straightforward but irregular verbs may take a bit of thought and research ('I talk' from 'to talk'; je parle from parler; but 'I am' from 'to be'; je suis from être). When you meet different French verbs remember to note their infinitive forms.

In English there are rather a lot of verbs referred to as 'phrasal'. These are verbs whose meaning changes when different prepositions are attached. Think about 'to go', for example. You can 'go up', 'go down', 'go round', 'go out', 'go off', the list 'goes on'. There will be one French verb for each of these with no preposition, monter *go up*, descendre *go down* etc, so you'll need to be sure to examine the definitions carefully in order to 'go for' the correct one!

The terms transitive and intransitive simply tell you whether a verb needs a direct object (transitive) or can be used without one (intransitive). Some verbs can be used both transitively and intransitively, e.g. 'to fly':

piloter un avion (vt) – Marcel pilote un Airbus A380. *Marcel flies an A380 Airbus.* (direct object)
voler (vi) – L'hirondelle vole vers le sud. *The swallow flies towards the South.* (no direct object)

Quick tips

- Adjectives in French will be given in their masculine singular form. You'll need to apply the rules (take a look in Chapter 9) to change the adjective to fit your noun.

- If you are looking for the meaning of a phrase such as à côté de or en face de, don't try to translate word by word. Search until you find the total phrase. It's sensible to start among the longer words (côté and face).

Have a go

Look up the following words for practice. Some are ambiguous. You can only choose a meaning (and a part of speech, e.g. noun, adverb, adjective) if you know about the context in which they are to be used ('There's a strong <u>wind</u> blowing'; 'You're <u>wind</u>ing me up'). Others are colloquial expressions which don't translate literally but may have an equivalent in French.

1	wind	11	peut-être
2	but	12	maïs
3	right	13	droit
4	to be going to	14	se faire couper les cheveux
5	I have to	15	il me faut
6	they would like to	16	on voudrait
7	It's all a question of time!	17	Qu'est-ce qu'il y a?
8	broken down	18	tomber en panne
9	saw	19	serre
10	in spite of	20	en plus

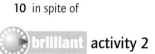 **activity 2**

See if you can work out what's gone wrong with the dictionary use in these examples:

Dans ma chambre il y a des aveugles devant la fenêtre.

Magasin caisse tu goutte!

Je supporte jambon occidentale.

Propriété privée

- Talk about families
- Learn about possession
- Familiarise yourself with avoir *to have*

Soft soap

 activity 1

1.63 You are about to enter the alternative world of La Résidence, the setting for un feuilleton *soap opera*. Get ready by listening to and repeating some words for marital status and family relationships:

marié(e) *married* (m/f)	le frère *brother*
divorcé(e) *divorced* (m/f)	la sœur *sister*
célibataire *single* (m/f)	la belle-mère *stepmother, mother-in-law*
le compagnon *male partner*	le beau-fils *stepson, son-in-law*
la compagne *female partner*	la demi-sœur *stepsister, half sister*
le mari *husband*	le grand-père *grandfather*
la femme *wife*	le cousin/la cousine *cousin* (m/f)
le père *father*	les enfants *children*
la mère *mother*	

Note that the words for 'married' and 'divorced' gain an e when applied to women: Suzanne Lefarge est divorcée; Marguerite Vouvray est mariée; Henri Leblanc est divorcé. Since célibataire already ends in e the spelling remains the same for both men and women. Take heart from the fact that most of these spelling changes are not pronounced, although the addition of the e for feminine cousine does cause the sound of the word to change, as with the word voisin(e) neighbour, which you will also meet.

Blockbuster

 activity 2

A **1.64** La Résidence is a block of flats and, in the true tradition of soap operas, almost everyone living there is related in some way. Can you work out from the information you are given the names of the residents of each of the flats, their marital status and their relationship to each other. Habiter means 'to live (in)'.

Numéro d'appartement	Nom	Situation de famille	Famille
1			
2			
3			
4			
5			

- Philippe Rocard est le compagnon de Julie Corot.
- Le monsieur avec une demi-sœur est le beau-fils d'Annette Metzger.
- La femme dans l'appartement numéro un est la demi-sœur d'Antoine Lesieur.
- Marianne Dugard est divorcée.
- Antoine Lesieur est marié; sa voisine n'est pas mariée, elle a un compagnon.
- La femme dans l'appartement numéro quatre est la cousine de Marianne Dugard.
- Annette Metzger habite l'appartement entre Philippe Rocard et Julie Corot.
- Une femme divorcée est la belle-mère d'Antoine Lesieur.
- Le monsieur dans l'appartement numéro deux est le compagnon de Julie Corot.
- Antoine Lesieur habite l'appartement numéro cinq.
- Le compagnon de Julie Corot avec l'appartement entre deux femmes divorcées est le cousin du monsieur marié.

Look again at the phrases le compagnon de Julie Corot *Julie Corot's partner* and le beau-fils d'Annette Metzger *Annette Metzger's stepson*. In French the use of an apostrophe is confined to missing letters (il n̲'est pas; un kilo d'oranges); it is never used to express possession. Instead you say la cousine de Marianne *Marianne's cousin*, literally 'the cousin of Marianne', l'appartement d'Antoine *Antoine's apartment*, literally 'the apartment of Antoine'. This rule makes the word order different in French, which will have a bearing on your understanding. You need to listen in different places to grasp the meaning.

B Now you've worked out who's who in La Résidence, how might you explain these relationships in French?

1 Julie Corot – Philippe Rocard   **3** Antoine Lesieur – Philippe Rocard

2 Marianne Dugard – Antoine Lesieur

The possessed

 activity 3

1.65 Here are the residents of La Résidence in conversation with a visitor, who is trying to unravel the relationships – you will come across three new ones: la nièce *niece,* le neveu *nephew,* les petits-enfants *grandchildren*.

1 What does the newcomer want to know about Philippe and Antoine?

2 Which family relations does Annette list in her answer?

Listening to that conversation, you will have heard three different words for 'my', mon, ma and mes. Have a look at the transcript and pick them out. The main point to remember is that the word for 'my' changes according to the person 'possessed' rather than the person doing the possessing. So whoever's talking, be it a man or a woman, they will use: mes enfants, mon neveu, ma nièce. Like les, mes is used for both masculine and feminine plural words.

The table below summarises the possessive adjectives. You will use some more than others, but have a look through them all and check out the patterns:

	masculine singular	feminine singular	plural
my	mon	ma	mes
your (tu)	ton	ta	tes
his/her	son	sa	ses
our	notre	notre	nos
your (vous)	votre	votre	vos
their	leur	leur	leurs

If a feminine word begins with a vowel or a silent h use mon, ton, son instead of ma, ta or sa to keep the flow of the sound:
une amie *female friend*: mon amie, ton amie, son amie
l'hérédité *heredity*: mon hérédité, ton hérédité, son hérédité

brilliant learning tip

You have already learnt the pattern for 'the': le, la, les. It might help to keep this in mind when learning the pattern for these possessive adjectives: mon, ma, mes; ton, ta, tes; son, sa, ses.

brilliant activity 4

1.66 Annette is now talking about her family. Using the table on page 65 for guidance, choose the correct word from the options given and then listen to the audio to check:

Je suis divorcée deux fois avec deux enfants. (Mon/Ma/Mes) fille s'appelle Marianne et (son/sa/ses) demi-frère est Antoine. (Mon/Ma/Mes) ex-mari, le père d'Antoine, est Pierre. (Son/Sa/Ses) neveu Philippe habite dans l'appartement numéro deux. La partenaire de Philippe, Julie, est (mon/ma/mes) nièce. Antoine, (son/sa/ses) femme et (leur/leurs) deux enfants habitent dans l'appartement numéro cinq. Nous sommes vraiment 'en famille' dans La Résidence!

Keeping up with the neighbours

brilliant activity 5

1.67 Of course possessive adjectives aren't just used to talk about people. Listen to the snippets of conversation taking place at a party in La Résidence. It's an exercise in one-upmanship! Number the following phrases in the order that you hear them:

☐ a swimming pool	☐ an office	☐ a garden
☐ a flat in Paris	☐ a glass	☐ a Citroën
☐ a Peugeot	☐ a house in Antibes	☐ photos of Marrakech

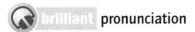 **pronunciation**

1.68 The French letter e can be pronounced in several different ways. You will need to listen closely to pick up some of the nuances but it's well worth persevering. The sounds are:

- Like the 'e' sound in 'angel' or 'angle'. This sound is often heard in single-syllable words like le and me and is created by making your mouth into a pouting shape:
petit   le   de   je

- Like the 'e' in bed. This sound is found when e has a grave accent (père) or a circumflex (tête) and when a syllable ends with a consonant sound:
mère   frère   athlète   poète   belle   sept   gilet

- Like the vowel sound in 'say' (without the 'y' sound at the end). This sound occurs when e has an acute accent (été), and in the verb endings -er and -ez: habiter, mettez. To get this right in French, stretch your mouth into a grin and, above all, remember that all French vowel sounds are shorter and sharper than you would expect them to be in English:
musée   nécessité   éternité   publicité   habiter   avez

You already know that vowel sounds change when in combination with other letters and e is no exception. Listen and practise these combinations:
bleu   cheveux   Europe   sœur   cœur   œuf

To have and to hold

 **activity 6**

A 1.69 Here is Nathalie Lesieur, Antoine's wife, talking about her family:
1 Who is her elder child?
2 What are the benefits of living in La Résidence?

B You have already met parts of the verb avoir to have. Use the text about the Lesieurs to help you complete the pattern.

j'	ai	nous	
tu	as	vous	avez
il/elle		ils/elles	

In the text you will have seen the verbs avoir and être working together. On the whole, the use of avoir and être equates to English: 'I <u>am</u> married' Je <u>suis</u> mariée; 'We <u>have</u> two children' Nous <u>avons</u> deux enfants. There is a clear exception, however, when you talk about age. 'Xavier <u>is</u> four years old' is Xavier <u>a</u> quatre ans, literally 'Xavier <u>has</u> four years'. To ask how old someone is, you use the same formula: Vous <u>avez</u> quel âge? (literally, 'You have which age?') or Il <u>a</u> quel âge? *How old is he?*

C Annette has been required to complete this **formulaire**:

Nom:	Metzger
Prénom:	Annette Rosalie
Situation de famille:	Divorcée
Âge:	Cinquante-deux
Emploi:	Serveuse à temps partiel
Famille:	Une fille, un beau-fils, deux petits-enfants

How would you describe her situation? Start with Elle s'appelle Annette Rosalie Metzger. Elle est divorcée ... (À temps partiel means 'part time'.)

Have a go

 **activity 7**

There are other commonly used phrases where avoir *to have* appears when you might expect 'to be' in English. Read these sentences and, from the context, try to guess what the phrases mean and match them with their English translations in the box below:

- Ma mère a peur des hôpitaux.
- J'ai soif. Il y a un bar près d'ici?
- Oui, c'est vrai. Tu as raison. Elle est de Paris.
- Vous avez chaud? Mais, c'est normal. Nous sommes dans un sauna!
- Il a de la chance. Il a un ticket gagnant à la loterie.
- Non, vous avez tort. La grande muraille de Chine n'est pas visible de la lune.
- Les enfants ont faim. Tu as du pain?
- Mon cousin a toujours froid en Angleterre. Il habite en Éthiopie.

1 avoir faim	**a** *to be right*
2 avoir froid	**b** *to be hot*
3 avoir raison	**c** *to be cold*
4 avoir peur	**d** *to be lucky*
5 avoir chaud	**e** *to be thirsty*
6 avoir de la chance	**f** *to be afraid*
7 avoir tort	**g** *to be hungry*
8 avoir soif	**h** *to be wrong*

Haves and have nots

 activity 8

1.70 Listen to Annette talking about La Résidence. You'll hear prendre ma retraite which means 'retire', literally 'take my retirement':

1 Why does the lack of garden not bother her?
2 What forms of transport are close by?
3 Where does Annette want to retire to?

Now look at the transcript. You will notice the phrases on a *we have* and on est *we are*. The literal translation of on is 'one' as in 'one has', 'one is'. In English 'one' is confined to the very well-spoken but in French on is widely used, in particular as a replacement for nous. Listen and look out for on and, if you want to use it yourself, it takes the same part of the verb as il and elle, as 'one' does in English.

Look at these sentences:
Nous avons un jardin.
Nous n'avons pas de jardin.

On a un balcon.
On n'a pas de balcon.

Je voudrais du Camembert.
Je ne voudrais pas de Camembert.

Vous avez des photos?
Vous n'avez pas de photos?

A new rule: if a negative verb is followed by un, une or du, de la, des these all change to de. The exception to this rule is with the verb être.

Je ne suis pas un résident.
Ce ne sont pas des brioches.

Remember that le, la, les do not change.

Il a <u>la</u> voiture. Il n'a pas <u>la</u> voiture.
On a <u>les</u> photos. On n'a pas <u>les</u> photos.

 activity 9

Choose the correct word:

1 Je n'ai pas (des/de/les) sœurs.
2 On n'a pas (un/le/du/de) piscine dans notre villa.
3 Vous n'avez pas (de/les/des) cousins?
4 Il n'est pas (le/de/un) neveu de Marguerite.
5 Je ne voudrais pas (d'/de/un) appartement. Je voudrais un hôtel.
6 Ce ne sont pas (de/des/les) photos de ta famille?

Test case

 activity 10

A family tree

A 1.71 You're trying to get to grips with the family connections of an acquaintance, Didier Louvain. You know the names of some of his relatives but not the relationships between them. Listen to Didier's interview in which he talks about Jean-Claude, Monique, Marc, Gustave, Beatrice and Chantal. Fit the information you gather into the family tree:

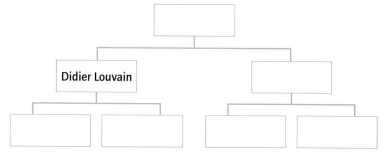

What's the word for female twins? Use a dictionary to find the masculine equivalent.

B 1.72 To double check, ask Didier who these people are using qui *who* (Qui est Jean-Claude?): Gustave; Béatrice; Marc; Monique and Chantal.

C Now try to describe his family to someone else using son/sa and ses. In French, how would you describe the relationship Marc and Béatrice have to Monique and Chantal?

 activity 11

1.73 Look at the following text and insert the correct part of avoir or être. Listen to check.

Marie-France .... mariée avec Franck. Les Legrand .... trois enfants, un fils et deux filles. Leur fils .... technicien à Paris. Il .... une fille qui s'appelle Sophie qui a deux ans. Les filles des Legrand ne .... pas mariées. Sylvie .... vingt-six ans et elle est infirmière. Sa sœur, Thérèse, ... dix-huit ans et elle .... étudiante à l'Université de Strasbourg.

 activity 12

A 1.74 Listen to the exchange between Antoine and the official and complete his formulaire.

Nom:	
Prénom:	
Situation de famille:	
Âge:	
Emploi:	
Famille:	

B People are naturally curious so it's wise to have all this information about yourself mentally prepared for when the time comes – questions and answers.

 activity 13

Here is a very brief history of one of the most famous French monarchs, Louis XIV, the Sun King (le Roi-Soleil). Without looking anything up can you answer the following questions:

1 Who was his mother?

2 Who were his paternal grandfather and his maternal grandmother?

3 What nationality were his grandparents?

4 How old was he when he became king?

Fils de Louis XIII et d'Anne d'Autriche, Louis est le fruit d'unions politiques multi-culturelles puisque ses grands-parents paternels Henri IV et Marie de Médicis, étaient respectivement français et italienne. Ses grands-parents maternels, Philippe III et Marguerite d'Autriche-Styrie étaient espagnol et autrichienne. À la mort de son père, l'enfant devient roi sous le nom de Louis XIV. Comme il n'a que quatre ans et demi, sa mère, Anne d'Autriche, devient régente.

Endgame

Match these titles of soaps to the English equivalents:

1 Urgences	a Six Feet Under
2 Je suis une célébrité, sortez-moi de là	b The Avengers
3 New York section criminelle	c Are you smarter than a ten year old?
4 À la Maison Blanche	d The West Wing
5 Chapeau Melon et Bottes de Cuir	e ER
6 Frères d'Armes	f Band of Brothers
7 Six Pieds Sous Terre	g Law and Order: Criminal Intent
8 Mariés, deux enfants	h I'm a celebrity, get me out of here
9 Êtes-vous plus fort qu'un élève de dix ans?	i Married ... with Children

le chapeau melon – *bowler hat*
les bottes – *boots*
le cuir – *leather*
élève – *pupil*

6 Bon voyage!

- Learn about catching transport and going places
- Discover days of the week and hours of the day
- Learn your ABC
- Meet a variety of prepositions

 activity 1

Travel broadens the mind

1.75 You're about to go travelling, so you'll need the words for ways to travel. Match the form of transport to the graphic and use a dictionary or the glossary to help with any you can't guess. Beware, one word is not as it seems!

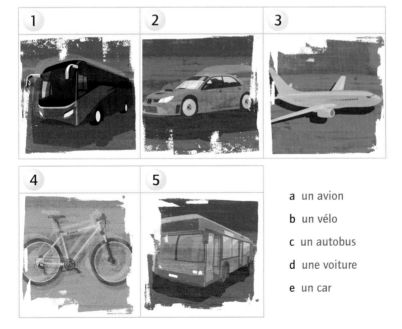

a un avion

b un vélo

c un autobus

d une voiture

e un car

You should have little difficulty translating the following: un train, un taxi, un ferry and le métro. In France you will also come across un TGV, which is an abbreviation of Train à Grande Vitesse, a high-speed train.

 **activity 2**

Trains and boats and planes

A 1.76 Listen to these people talking about their travel plans and have a go at answering the questions, then listen again and read the conversations.

1 Which mode of transport given in the previous section is not mentioned?
2 Which cities are the holidaymakers visiting?
3 What are the advantages of Sylvie's transport choice?
4 Why are the people going to England travelling by separate routes?

● Vous êtes à Paris en vacances, je crois?
● Oui, c'est vrai. Nous sommes ici pour un week-end seulement. Aujourd'hui, on prend le métro pour visiter la Tour Eiffel, ensuite un tour en autobus. Demain on prend le TGV pour Lille.

● Tu as une voiture, Sylvie?
● Moi, non, je n'ai pas de voiture.
● Alors, est-ce tu prends le bus pour aller au bureau?
● Non, j'ai un vélo, c'est écologique et il n'y a pas de problème de parking!

● Notre voyage en Angleterre? Bon, je prends un taxi pour arriver à la gare, ensuite le train jusqu'à Calais, un ferry et un autre train. Ma compagne prend l'avion de Roissy Charles de Gaulle à Heathrow; elle n'a pas le temps de prendre le train.

Pour generally means 'for', unless it's used with a verb in the infinitive when it means 'in order to' or just 'to': Tu prends le bus pour aller au bureau? *Do you take the bus (in order) to go to work?*

B The travellers are talking about transport that they intend 'to take'. They use a new verb, prendre. You'll find prendre useful in all kinds of situations. Complete the table using the transcript to help.

je		nous	prenons
tu		vous	prenez
il/elle/on		ils/elles	prennent

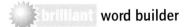 **word builder**

On prend des vacances *We're taking a holiday*; Il prend congé *He's taking leave*; Elle prend des photos *She's taking photos*; On prend le bus *We're taking the bus*.

These uses of **prendre** line up closely with English, but **prendre** has a variety of other meanings. It's a verb frequently used in relation to having drinks and things to eat:

Il prend un café. *He's _having_ a coffee.*
Vous prenez un apéritif? *Are you _having_ an aperitif?*

And sometimes to express the outcome of these activities!
Elle prend du poids. *She's _putting on_ weight.*

You'll find other uses too:
Je prends l'adresse. *I'm _taking down_ the address.*
Il prend un accent. *He's _putting on_ an accent.*

What do you think that this saying might mean? C'est à prendre ou à laisser.

 **activity 3**

Bed and board

A 1.77 Listen to what Stéphanie says about her holiday plans. You'll hear the words **le petit déjeuner** *breakfast*, **le déjeuner** *lunch* and **le dîner** *dinner*.

1 Who is she going on holiday with?
2 What are her travel plans?
3 On what terms are they staying at the hotel?
4 What advice is she given at the end?

B The person who was talking to Stéphanie is recounting her plans. Help out by inserting the right parts of the verbs:

Stéphanie (prendre) ses vacances avec son mari à Nice. Ils (prendre) le train de Lille à Paris et le TGV pour Nice. Leur hôtel (être) dans le centre de Nice. Ils (être) en demi-pension mais ils (avoir) des plans pour le déjeuner – ils (prendre) un snack à midi. Régime Low Carb après les vacances!

The term for half board in a hotel is **demi-pension**; full board is **pension complète**. Bed and breakfast is not a common deal in French hotels, where you will normally have a room (**une chambre**) and then pay a supplement for le petit déjeuner.

Coming and going

Having decided on your mode of transport you may want to narrow your travel options down.

 **activity 4**

Read the email exchange:

Robert,

Pour aller à Besançon vous avez le choix:

1. le train de 8h45 qui arrive à Besançon à 11h53 ou

2. le train de 9h03 qui arrive à 11h37.

Antoine

Antoine,

Je prends le train de 9h03 et le retour?

Robert

Robert,

Vous avez encore le choix; il y a un train qui part de Besançon à 17h13 et qui arrive à 19h46 et un qui part à 18h21 et arrive à 20h48.

Antoine

You will have spotted that the 24-hour clock is used for travel so, to start with, turn to the numbers section and brush up on numbers one to 59. The important word for talking about time in French is **heure** *hour.* To ask the time you say **Quelle heure est-il?**, literally 'What hour is it?' and to tell the time you need to insert the word **heures** between hours and minutes: 8h45 – huit heures quarante-cinq.

1.78 Listen to the times given in the email exchange and identify which one is not mentioned.

Go back to the email and check out the use of the words 'leave' (**part**) and 'arrive' (**arrive**). They turn up again in the questions you need to ask about departure and arrival times.

Le TGV pour Marseille part à quelle heure? *What time does the Marseilles train leave?*

L'autobus de Colmar arrive à quelle heure? *What time does the Colmar bus arrive?*

Notice the order of these questions, which is entirely different from English. The mode of transport begins the question and 'what time' (à quelle heure) is at the end. Note too that you use pour to ask about transport *to* and de for transport *from* (Le train pour Paris; l'autobus de Croissy).

 activity 5

1.79–1.80 First of all listen to the two questions above, then ask about the departure times of:
1 the coach to Rennes.
2 the ferry to La Corse *Corsica*.

And the arrival times of:
3 the plane from Montréal.
4 the train from Rome.

 activity 6

1.81 Listen to the rather harassed tour operator on the phone checking up on lost holidaymakers due to arrive in various ways.

1 Listen first for the modes of transport.
2 Then listen again for the departure time that is mentioned.
3 Finally, see how many times you have to listen to pick up all the arrival times correctly; the more times you listen, the more number practice you need!

Departure and arrival announcements at travel destinations can be perplexing but can also provide practice on the hoof. Next time you're travelling, use multilingual information to listen to the French and then check your understanding with the English version. Announcements have a language of their own:

Le vol à destination de Washington part à vingt et un heures trente-cinq de la porte numéro trente-deux.
The Washington flight is leaving at 21.35 from Gate 32.

Le train en provenance de Londres arrive à quatorze heures cinquante et un au quai numéro cinq.
The train from London is arriving at Platform 5 at 14.51.

In airports and stations hearing what is said can be tricky, so concentrate on spotting the name of your destination and any key words or phrases that might alert you to alterations in your plans:

en retard – *late*
dix minutes de retard – *ten minutes late*
annulé – *cancelled*

 **activity 7**

1.82 Listen to the station announcements and enter the origin/destination of the train, whether it's arriving or departing and the difficulties that you hear.

origin/destination	arriving/leaving	status

 **A to Z**

1.83 The French alphabet, when written down, looks the same as the English but from your experience of hearing the way **TGV** is said it won't surprise you to know that the letters are pronounced differently. Listen to the audio and familiarise yourself with how they sound.

Some letters such as **j** and **g** need particular attention and the vowels are great for giving your mouth a real pronunciation workout. Setting yourself random practice tasks can help fix the alphabet in your mind. Spell out street names, labels and signs as you walk around.

 alphabet activity

1.84 What about the names of friends and family? Try spelling out these names and check your answer with the audio: Jones, Griffiths, Upsall, Monique, Warren, Mary.

It's useful to be able to ask how to spell something. The phrase you need is **Ça s'écrit comment?** and it works by saying what you want spelt first: **Marseille, ça s'écrit comment?**

 activity 8

Ticket to ride

A Here is a word map that relates to buying train tickets. How many of these words can you work out without recourse to a dictionary?

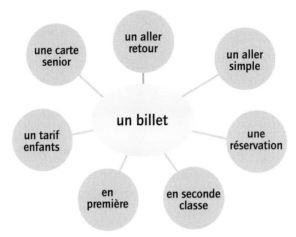

B 1.85 Buying tickets couldn't be more straightforward with the language you already have but, before you have a go, practise saying the following using the audio:

Un aller retour pour Bruxelles.
Un aller simple pour Antibes.
Un aller retour en première pour Monte Carlo.

Remember to specify destination using pour *for* – un aller retour pour Bruxelles *a return to (for) Brussels* – and that if you want first class it goes after the ticket – un aller retour en première *a first class* return.

C 1.86 Take part in the role play:

- Bonjour. Vous désirez?
- Say you'd like a return to Clermont Ferrand.
- En première ou en seconde?
- Ask how much it is in first class.
- C'est quatre-vingt-quatorze euros soixante-cinq.
- Say OK and say you have a senior travel card.
- Bon, le tarif est soixante-seize euros soixante-cinq.
- Say thank you and ask what time the train leaves.

- À dix heures trente-cinq et il arrive à quatorze heures vingt. Voici votre billet.
- Say thank you and take your leave.

How much did you pay and what time will you be in Clermont Ferrand?

Going walkabout

If you want to talk about travelling by a certain mode of transport you will be using different prepositions, summarised in the grid below:

Prepositions are the words in a sentence like 'in', 'at', 'on', 'to', 'for', 'by', 'until', 'before'. They relate a noun or pronoun to another part of the sentence in terms of place, time or purpose.

en	à	par
voiture avion ferry autobus car métro taxi	vélo pied	le train le TGV NB par avion is used with reference to mail, not people.

 **activity 9**

1.87 Have a go at completing these sentences then listen to the audio to check:

1 Je vais à Paris .... le train.
2 On va à Saint Tropez .... vélo.
3 Elle ne va pas en autobus, elle préfère aller .... taxi.
4 Ils vont .... car entre Lille et Bruxelles
5 Vous allez en Angleterre .... le TGV ou .... avion?

brilliant learning tip

By and large motorised forms of transport and boats use **en**, trains and their variations use **par** followed by **le, la, les** etc and transport that has two wheels (or legs) uses **à**!

 **activity 10**

A If your powers of recall are working well you will have recognised the word **allez** from the phrase you met in Chapter 1, **Comment allez-vous?**, literally 'How are you going?'. If you look at the statements on the previous page you will see other parts of the verb **aller** *to go* in action. It's irregular, so use the transcript to complete the pattern.

je		nous	allons
tu	vas	vous	
il/elle/on		ils/elles	

B **1.88** Aller is a very useful verb for elaborating on your travel plans. Listen to the exchanges on the audio and number the destinations in the order that you hear them. You will hear the word **souvent** meaning 'often'.

Guadeloupe ☐   Canada ☐   Guyane ☐   Nouvelle Calédonie ☐
Seychelles ☐   Martinique ☐

Listen again and answer the following questions:
1 What special occasion is one holiday for?
2 Which words for family relationships did you hear?
3 Who is not travelling and why?
4 Which destination requires a connecting flight?
5 Why is someone visiting Guadeloupe?

C Look at the transcript of the exchanges and note how you say 'to' a country. There are two possibilities: <u>au</u> Canada, <u>en</u> Guyane. If a country is masculine (**le Canada**) you say **au** and if it's feminine (**la Guyane**), use **en**. Countries that end in **e** are usually feminine, so which would you use for the following?

.... France   .... Belgique   .... Luxembourg

.... Suisse   .... Andorre   .... Vietnam

✳brilliant cultural tip

As you may already know, French is the official language of 29 countries as well as of United Nations agencies and a large number of international organisations (you will have heard of Médecins sans Frontières, for example). It's the third most spoken second language in the European Union (after English and German). To find out more about the extent of French, research Francophonie, the term used to describe the community of French speakers.

D **1.89** When you go to a town or a city the preposition you need is à.

Example: Je vais à Québec, au Canada. *I'm going to Quebec, in Canada.*

(À and en with places can also mean 'in'.)

Use the example to talk about the following and listen to check:

1 (je) Besançon – France
2 (on) Lausanne – Suisse
3 (Luc et Sylvie) Papeete – Polynésie française
4 (M. Cornouet) Bruxelles – Belgique
5 (Xavier) Hanoï – Vietnam

✳brilliant language tip

If you look back through this chapter you will notice that the word à has a number of different meanings. You've just used it for 'at' or 'to' a place, Je vais à Québec au Canada *I'm going to Quebec in Canada.* Earlier it meant 'at' Il arrive à dix heures *It arrives at ten* and 'by' a mode of transport à vélo *by bike.* French also uses it to talk about distance: La gare est à environ deux kilomètres *The station is about 2km away.*

The meaning of en depends on the context too, en France *in France*, en voiture *by car.*

Diary dates

 activity 11

A 1.90 Talking about travel plans often includes days of the week. If you're not familiar with the days of the week in French, you might like to listen to how they're pronounced first.

lundi   mardi   mercredi   jeudi   vendredi   samedi   dimanche

The French week begins with Monday not Sunday. When days and months are written down they don't generally start with a capital letter.

B 1.91 Here's an excerpt from a diary. Louis Dumont is describing his week; listen to the audio and enter his activities in English in the correct spot.

Le matin is 'the morning' or 'in the morning', 'l'après-midi', 'the afternoon' or 'in the afternoon' (no word for 'in' necessary); you have already met the word for 'evening' (soir) in the expression bonsoir.

jour	matin	après-midi
lundi		
mardi		
mercredi		
jeudi		
vendredi		

Did you spot that mercredi matin means 'on Wednesday morning'? When you talk about doing something 'on Monday' you don't need a word for 'on' in French; just lundi will do.

Location location

 activity 12

1.92 Listen to this description of Louis' Normandy gîte. In it you will find some more useful prepositions: 'in', 'on', 'under', 'near' 'next to', 'in front', 'behind' and 'opposite'. Compare the the text to the picture and see if you can underline them.

Le gîte se trouve dans le centre du village près de la place principale. À côté de la maison, il y a un garage et devant, un jardin. Derrière, vous avez une terrasse et une piscine. Sur la terrasse, il y a un barbecue et des chaises longues. Sous la maison, il y a une cave où il y a des vélos à votre disposition. Si vous avez des problèmes, ma mère habite en face.

✷ brilliant learning tip

Thinking back to any French songs you know can be a great help with remembering vocabulary. Are you familiar with either of these?

Sous les Ponts de Paris *Under the Bridges of Paris* – a famous Tino Rossi song

Sur le pont d'Avignon *On the Avignon Bridge*

Some prepositions are made up of one or more words plus de, and de will need to change for the masculine and plural as usual. If no noun follows, leave out de:

en face (de) *opposite*
près (de) *near*
à côté (de) *next to*

(Le barbecue est à côté de la piscine *The barbecue is next to the swimming pool*; La maison est à côté du parc *The house is next to the park*.)

 **activity 13**

1.93 One of Louis' friends is borrowing the gîte for a weekend and phones for extra information. Make a note of what the numbers on the diagram correspond to.

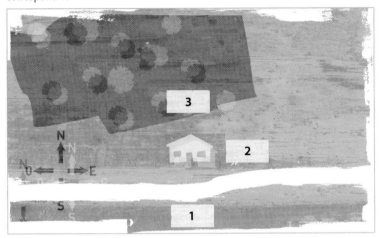

1 ....

2 ....

3 ....

activity 14

On the next page are brochure extracts for three gîtes. Use them to build up vocabulary for rooms, outside space, facilities and services on offer. This exercise will require you to do some dictionary research; make sure that you check the gender of the nouns that you find. Note differences in word order, e.g. le chauffage électrique *electric heating*.

Rooms	Outside space	Facilities	Services
example: un séjour	une terrasse	un lecteur DVD	les draps en location

En pleine campagne, maison traditionnelle en pierre située dans un grand jardin. Maison indépendante. Séjour. Cuisine. 2 chambres. 1 lit 140. 2 lits 90. 1 lit bébé. Salle de bains. WC. TV. Lecteur DVD. Lave-linge. Sèche-linge. Draps en location. Chauffage électrique. Terrain clos privé. Terrasse. Salon de jardin. Barbecue.

Entrée dans un grand salon/ salle à manger avec cheminée, cuisine américaine avec lave-linge, lave-vaisselle et four électrique. 1 ch (2 lits 1 pers.). 1 salle d'eau avec WC. Location avec chauffage, ménage, draps et linge de toilette offerts.

Gîte duplex de 50 m² dans une construction de 1794. Salle à manger/salon (avec canapé convertible 1 pers.) cuisine indépendante, salle d'eau avec WC. Draps fournis et lits faits à l'arrivée. Linge de toilette. Jardin privatif et parking clos (100m²). Connection Internet.

Getting your bearings

 activity 15

A 1.94 You've arrived at your holiday **gîte** and the owner is explaining where things are. Make a note of what she says in readiness to complete activity C.

B 1.95 You're wanting some extra information so play your part using questions that begin **Où est** ... *Where is ...*, **Où sont** ... *Where are ...* or **Il y a** ... *Is/are there ...*

- Ask if there's an internet connection.
- Oui, oui c'est gratuit.
- Ask where the shops are.
- Alors vous avez une boulangerie en face et un supermarché dans la ville

à côté.

- Ask if there are bikes.

- Oui, ils sont dans le garage, sous la maison.

- Ask if there's a station near the gîte.

- Oui pas trop loin. À environ cinq kilomètres.

C You've dropped the notes you've been making in the swimming pool. Can you reconstitute them by filling in the blanks?

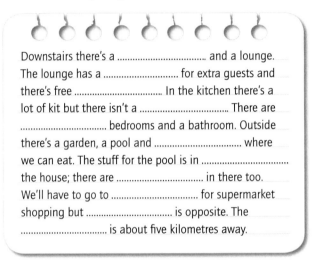

Downstairs there's a .... and a lounge.
The lounge has a .... for extra guests and
there's free .... In the kitchen there's a
lot of kit but there isn't a .... There are
.... bedrooms and a bathroom. Outside
there's a garden, a pool and .... where
we can eat. The stuff for the pool is in ....
the house; there are .... in there too.
We'll have to go to .... for supermarket
shopping but .... is opposite. The
.... is about five kilometres away.

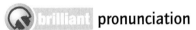 **pronunciation**

1.96 As a general rule, the o in French is pronounced like the 'o' in lot:

olive   tomate

unless it is the last sound of a word or has a circumflex, when you need to make your mouth into a rosebud shape, tongue near the roof of your mouth, so that the sound is expelled through nose and mouth:

hôtel   hôte   mot   euro

Now listen to the oi combination of letters in these words:

au revoir   voilà   poisson   trois

Oi is pronounced 'wa'. How do you think the following words might sound? Try them out and then listen and repeat:

une poire   un oiseau   une boîte   droite

Here's a tongue twister (un virelangue) to really challenge you:

Il était une fois, un homme de foi qui vendait du foie dans la ville de Foix.
Il dit ma foi, c'est la dernière fois que je vends du foie dans la ville de Foix.

*Once upon a time, there was a man of faith who was selling liver in the town
of Foix. He said, my faith, this is the last time I sell liver in the town of Foix.*
(Foix is a town in the Pyrenees mountains in the south of France.)

Test case

 activity 16

1.97 Play your part in the following conversation where you run into a friend
on the way to the station.

- Greet your friend Sabine and ask if she's OK.
- Salut, oui ça va bien merci. Tu vas où?
- Tell her you're going to the station.
- Ah bon, tu vas en vacances, n'est-ce pas?
- Say yes, you're going to Deauville.
- Tu ne vas pas en voiture alors, tu prends le train?
- Say yes, you're taking the train. It leaves at 10.45.
- Tu restes dans un hôtel à Deauville?
- Say no, you have got a gîte opposite the casino.
- Bonnes vacances!
- Thank her and say goodbye.

 activity 17

What kind of town is Deauville? Read the extract below. Why is there such a
high percentage of second homes? What do you think pour cent means?

Deauville est reliée à Paris par l'autoroute A13. La ville est à environ
deux heures de la capitale. Il y a quatre mille Deauvillais et un nombre
important de parisiens venant passer leurs week-ends ou leurs vacances
dans la ville. La ville comprend environ cinq mille résidences secondaires
pour un peu moins de sept mille deux cents habitations (environ soixante-
dix pour cent de résidences secondaires).

En avant!

- Talk about the present
- Talk about likes, dislikes and preferences
- Discover the benefits of regular verbs

Searching for the right word ...

Cherchons les mots!; Je cherche à comprendre; On cherche un restaurant
Let's look for words!; I'm looking to understand; We're looking for a restaurant

 **activity 1**

A Chercher is the French verb for 'to look for' and, if you say it out loud, you
will realise that it sounds a bit like 'search', which it also means. Can you work
out what the following verbs might be in English: préférer, arriver, admirer,
fixer, explorer, tourner, détester, habiter, voyager, accepter, commencer?

learning tip

> Think laterally to unravel meanings. English synonyms may help
> breach any gaps: chercher *to search* → *to look for*; voyager *to voyage*
> → *to travel*; habiter *to inhabit* → *to live*; commencer *to commence* →
> *to start*

B Look again at the verbs above, which all end in -er. There are many
examples of verbs that correspond directly to English with the simple addition
of this ending. Guess what the following might be in French and look your
answers up in a dictionary to check:

to invite	to consult	to confirm	to continue
to compare	to exist	to change	to transform
to vote	to imagine		

C Knowing that so many words in French and English are similar gives you
carte blanche to have a guess. Very occasionally, you will come across a

faux ami, or 'false friend', a word that looks as though it might have a close English equivalent but actually means something else entirely. Look these words up in your dictionary or the glossary:

| rester | embrasser | travailler | assister |
| blesser | quitter | attendre | demander |

The part of the verb that you have seen so far in this chapter is called the *infinitive*. This is the basic form which in English is often preceded by 'to' ('to do', 'to be'). It's what you will find in the dictionary (remember to ignore the English 'to' when looking for verbs).

Giving it some verbal

It's all very well being able to conjure up infinitives but, as you already know, you do need to learn the different forms of the verbs too so that you can say what different people, including you, are doing ('I live'; 'we love'; 'John works').

 **activity 2**

A Read the text below and answer the following questions.

1 What's attracted Madeleine to the South?
2 What are her favourite times of year?
3 What sporting activities are mentioned?
4 Who goes to the beach with Madeleine?

> Je suis Madeleine Dugard – vétérinaire. Mon compagnon, Christophe et moi nous habitons un appartement à Nice. On travaille ensemble à Cannes; Christophe est vétérinaire aussi. Je suis du nord, mes parents habitent à Strasbourg, mais j'aime bien le sud: le climat, le style de vie et la cuisine. Je voyage beaucoup mais je reviens toujours ici.
>
> Christophe adore Nice, sa famille habite Lyon mais il préfère être au bord de la mer.
>
> Ici, il joue au tennis et il nage. On se promène sur la plage tous les jours avec notre chien, Roger. On s'amuse bien ici.
>
> On aime l'été quand les touristes arrivent et la région se transforme; mais nous préférons le printemps et l'automne, c'est plus calme.

B Now go through the text highlighting all the verbs you can see, together with their subjects (the words that indicate who or what the verb relates to – e.g. je, Christophe, les touristes, la région). Three of the verbs have a se before them (like on se promène). These are called reflexive verbs and you will read more about them later in this chapter. The se is the equivalent of the English 'self' ('himself', 'herself', 'itself', 'ourselves') but isn't generally translated.

C Among the verbs you highlighted will be:

on travaille
nous habitons
je voyage

You met the infinitives of these verbs in the section above. What are they?

A regular delight

French verbs are divided into groups. So far you've met largely what are known as *irregular* verbs (avoir, être, prendre, aller etc) as these are often the most commonly used.

Many irregular verbs have developed unique patterns through this extensive use, but the majority of verbs in French are *regular*, which means that they all conform to a pattern that is common to their particular family. This is good news because it means that you only have to learn one pattern for each of the family groups and all the other verbs in that group will behave in the same way.

Family groups of regular verbs are identified by the final two letters of the infinitive. So, as well as '-er verbs', there are also '-ir verbs' (finir, choisir) and '-re verbs' (attendre, descendre).

 activity 3

Can you complete this table using the patterns that you've already met?

travailler	je travaille	il travaille	nous travaillons
aimer	j'aime		
adorer		il adore	
habiter	j'habite		nous habitons
jouer		il joue	

brilliant learning tip

Dictionaries only deal in infinitives so you won't find travaillons if you look it up. Getting back to the infinitive is straightforward since patterns are usually formed directly from it (travailler, travaillons). Even if you can't guess the ending of the infinitive, the stem travaill- will give you enough information to find it. Searching for irregular verbs like être can present a few problems since their various parts bear little or no relation to the infinitive (je suis, ils sont). If it's any consolation, it's exactly the same in English ('to be': 'I am', 'he is'). Fortunately, there aren't many verbs in this category, and you can learn them individually as you go along.

Putting words together

brilliant activity 4

2.01 Listen to these people talking at work and answer these questions:

1 Why isn't M. Martin available?
2 Does the designer work for Dupont or Peugeot?
3 How many languages does Mlle Lefarge speak (parler)?
4 How are the delegates arriving on 3rd May?
5 What is preferable about the centre of Bordeaux?

brilliant pronunciation

2.02 Have you spotted the pronunciation of words that end in -ail, -aille or -eil, -eille? The l is pronounced as a 'y' so le travail sounds less like its English counterpart 'travail'

Listen and repeat these words:

Je travaille   le travail   ail *garlic*   un conseil *a piece of advice*
Marseille

Compare with the pronunciation of these words where l sounds as you might expect:

la ville   le village   un collège   un million

Pattern making

 activity 5

You've met the patterns of the -er family in the previous conversations. Look at the transcripts and work out what goes into the blank boxes in the table.

	arriver	chercher	parler	rester
je/j'		cherche		
tu				restes
il/elle/on			parle	reste
nous	arrivons			
vous		cherchez		
ils/elles	arrivent			restent

The first step in creating the pattern of -er verbs is to remove the -er from the infinitive, chercher → cherch, for example. Cherch is the stem to which different endings must be added according to the person or people who are doing the searching (-e, -es, -e, -ons, -ez, -ent).

Les tweets

 activity 6

The following people have forgotten to put the verbs into their Twitter contributions. Can you complete the tweets using the verbs below?

Je .... au tennis dans le parc. Belle matinée!

Ils .... les céréales; moi, je .... le pain

Journée importante, les parents .... Attention!

Bizarre! Elle .... anglais avec Sophie. Pourquoi?

On .... le régime aujourd'hui. Pas de chocolat!

Mon compagnon .... une augmentation de salaire
– bonne chance!

Nous .... la ville pour la campagne. À bientôt!

préfère, joue, arrivent, demande, quittons, mangent, commence, parle

Reflexive verbs

You have come across a few reflexive verbs in this chapter: on s'amuse, la région se transforme and je me promène. You met another very common reflexive verb in Chapter 1: Vous vous appelez comment? Je m'appelle ...

Reflexive verbs indicate that the subject of the verb is performing the action upon himself, herself, or itself, even if it is not always explicitly stated in English: 'We enjoy ourselves'; 'The region transforms itself'; 'I take myself for a walk'.

The distinguishing feature of reflexives is that they gain a pronoun: je m'appelle; vous vous appelez; on se promène. Their infinitives are always preceded by se (s' before a vowel or h): se promener, s'appeler, s'amuser.

The reflexive verbs you have met so far end in -er so the endings will be the same as those you already know.

s'amuser

je	m'amuse	nous	nous amusons
tu	t'amuses	vous	vous amusez
il/elle/on	s'amuse	ils/elles	s'amusent

Spelling quirks

There are a few verbs, reflexive and non-reflexive, that have quirks of spelling in certain forms. They are called stem-changing verbs. The je, tu, il, elle, on, ils, elles forms will have similar spellings, either with an added grave accent or with a doubled consonant, while the nous and vous forms mirror the infinitive: se promener, je me promène, nous nous promenons; s'appeller, je m'appelle, nous nous appelons.

Sometimes spelling changes are made to preserve a particular sound. Manger *to eat* and nager *to swim* gain an e in the nous part: nous mangeons, nous nageons. The e ensures that the preceding g keeps the soft sound of the other parts of the verb. If it were not there the g would be hard as in the English 'gone'. For the same reason commencer *to begin* gains a cedilla in the nous form to keep the c soft: nous commençons. Watch out for other stem spelling changes as you meet more verbs.

More verbs

 activity 7

A **2.03** Listen to a student talking about what's happening after he leaves college. What parts of France will he visit in the next few months? From the context of the conversation, what do you think a stage pratique might be? You'll hear une vie which means 'a life'.

- Quand vous finissez vos études, vous retournez à la maison?
- Si je réussis à mes examens, non. J'attends les résultats et ensuite je descends dans le sud pour les vacances. En octobre je commence mon stage pratique chez Michaud à Paris.
- Vous choisissez une vie bien loin de Rennes alors?
- Oui, mais mes parents comprennent l'importance de ce choix.

B Look back over the transcript of the dialogue and underline all the verbs. Can you spot any other patterns?

The verbs finissez (finir), choisissez (choisir), réussis (réussir), attends (attendre) and descends (descendre) come from the two other major families, the verbs ending in -ir and -re. Here is a completed pattern verb for each of the three main verb families.

	retourner → retourn	finir → fin	attendre → attend
je	retourne	finis	attends
tu	retournes	finis	attends
il/elle/on	retourne	finit	attend
nous	retournons	finissons	attendons
vous	retournez	finissez	attendez
ils/elles	retournent	finissent	attendent

Have you noticed that there are cross-family similarities? All of the groups end in -ons, -ez and -ent for the nous, vous and ils/elles forms. -ir verbs acquire a rather exciting -iss- as well in their plural forms!

The -er family is the largest of the regular group so you will soon become very familiar with its pattern. Don't overlook -ir and -re patterns in your learning, however; they open doors to a great deal of communication.

Métro, boulot, dodo

 **activity 8**

A Most of us have 'stuff' that has to be done regularly. These people are talking about their regular habits. Complete the routines with the correct part of the verb (attendre means 'to wait' and 'to wait for'):

1 Ma journée de travail (finir) à dix-huit heures.
2 À six heures on (se promener) avec les chiens.
3 Elle (attendre) son collègue à la gare tous les jours.
4 Nous (arriver) toujours au bureau à huit heures.
5 Les week-ends, je (rendre) visite à mes parents.
6 Je (passer) tous les soirs dans le jardin.
7 On (se baigner) dans la mer le jour de Noël.

B **2.04** Listen to the descriptions on the audio and see if you can work out what jobs these people do. Then listen again while reading the transcript.

1..

2..

3..

C **2.05** Now imagine that you are the third woman. How would you describe your morning? Change the verbs to the je form to personalise the text. Make the changes orally and then listen to the audio to check. Remember to change son and sa to mon and ma. Note how similar the verbs in the two versions sound, except for the reflexive verb. Make the changes in writing. The rules about verb endings are much more obvious in writing than in speech.

Making sense of what you hear

When you listen to -er verb patterns you only hear a really noticeable difference in the nous and vous forms with the -ons and -ez endings. Attendre and descendre share some common pronunciation features with the -er family but the d in ils attendent is pronounced because it comes before a vowel, whereas you don't hear it in j'attends.

The je, tu, il/elle parts of -ir verbs tend to sound the same and, although the -ent of ils/elles is silent, the ss becomes very apparent (as in réagissent), letting you know that the subject is plural ('they', not 'he' or 'she').

With verbs beginning with a vowel, or with a silent h, you will hear the s (sounds like a z) of ils and elles: ils‿attendent, elles‿aiment.

 activity 9

2.06 Look at these pairs of verbs and tick the version you hear on the audio. Highlight those pairs where you don't hear a difference. Make a note of the infinitives of the verbs once you have listened. (Elle réagit means 'she reacts', elle vend 'she sells' and elle s'habille 'she gets dressed', literally, 'dresses herself').

il arrive	ils arrivent
il descend	ils descendent
ils parlent	il parle
elles aiment	elle aime
elle mange	elles mangent
elle réagit	elles réagissent
il se promène	ils se promènent
ils entendent	il entend
elle vend	elles vendent
elle s'habille	elles s'habillent

Eats shoots and leaves

Most of the verbs you have met so far are in the present tense, enabling you to talk about events that are happening now ('I'm working') or things that happen habitually ('I work every day'). Both of these can be expressed by je travaille in French. Remember too that when you're asking questions in French, or saying something negative, there's no equivalent of 'do': 'Do you work?' Vous travaillez?; 'I don't work' Je ne travaille pas.

Tense is a grammatical term that describes the time during which the verb occurs (i.e. past, present, future). In French the word is temps, which is linked more closely to the Latin 'tempus' *time*.

 activity 10

A 2.07 Listen to the description of the build-up to a football match; as you listen, replace the verbs in the gaps using the selection below to help. Look up any vocabulary you're unsure of first but try to guess any words you don't know from the context before looking them up. Obviously, meaning will help you choose which verb goes in which gap, but look also at the noun or nouns that are the subject of each verb, as these will tell you whether you need a singular or a plural verb form.

Ça .... tôt. Petit à petit, des hommes, des femmes, des jeunes, des enfants même .... les rues. C'est une armée en uniforme bleu qui .... vers le stade. Ils .... dans les cafés et les bars; ils .... ; ils .... un verre; ils .... le match. Une queue .... ; un par un ils .... dans le stade; ils .... leur place. D'abord, un murmure de milliers de voix; ensuite, ils .... ; ils .... ; ils .... les noms des joueurs. À trois heures, on .... un coup de sifflet; le match .... Qu'ils .... ou qu'ils ...., on .... chaque semaine pour encourager l'équipe.

> gagnent, donne, mangent, se dirige, commence, entrent, applaudissent, s'arrêtent, retourne, remplissent, prennent, trouvent, crient, perdent, discutent, se forme, chantent, débute

B Now imagine that you are among the supporters. How will you say:

1 I stop in a bar.
2 We discuss the match.
3 I go into the stadium.
4 We sing.
5 We applaud.
6 I go back each week.

Likes, dislikes and preferences

There are quite a few verbs from the -er family that will help you to give your opinion: aimer, adorer, détester, préférer, admirer, respecter, apprécier.

 **activity 11**

A **2.08** Listen to these people talking about likes and dislikes. The French for most sports is similar to the English but listen out for le catch *wrestling*. Remember that the word may be spelt similarly, but will be pronounced very differently.

Circle the sports that you hear:

> rugby tennis badminton cycling basketball wrestling
> swimming hockey motor racing football golf trekking boxing

B Listen again. What are the phrases for 'not much' and 'not at all' that you hear?

Pas tellement and pas trop both mean 'not much' or 'not a lot' and can be used on their own (Tu aimes le sport? Pas trop *Do you like sport? Not much*) or with a verb (Je n'aime pas tellement le sport *I don't much like sport*). Pas du tout means 'not at all' (Vous aimez le cyclisme? Pas du tout *Do you like cycling? Not at all*; Je n'aime pas du tout le cyclisme *I don't like cycling at all*).

You'll have heard the word mais meaning 'but'. Mais is a 'conjunction' or a 'connective', a word that joins two ideas together. Connectives help you to create longer utterances which contribute to greater fluency.

 **activity 12**

Look at this grid. You'll notice that it's necessary to include the word for 'the' when you are talking of generalisations: J'aime <u>le</u> jazz *I like jazz*. In order to express 'I like doing/to do' something you add an infinitive to j'aime: J'aime danser *I like dancing/I like to dance*. In negative sentences ('I don't like dancing'), the ne and pas go around the first verb only: Je n'aime pas danser.

J'aime Je n'aime pas Je préfère J'adore Je déteste	le shopping/faire les achats en ligne aller au cinéma/au théâtre parler français/allemand la poésie/les romans les documentaires/les feuilletons regarder la télé/écouter la radio la musique pop/le jazz/le rock le vin/la bière

A **2.09** How would you talk about the fact that you:

Example:
hate shopping but like buying online.
Je déteste le shopping, mais j'aime faire les achats en ligne.

1 like wine but prefer beer.
2 like going to the cinema but don't like going to the theatre much.
3 don't much like pop music; you prefer jazz.

4 don't like watching TV but hate listening to the radio.
5 don't like novels but appreciate (**apprécier**) poetry.
6 loathe watching documentaries but like soap operas a lot.

Listen to check your answers.

B Use these sentences to fashion statements that you might make about yourself.

Keep repeating and reworking sentences until you've run out of ideas. Remodelling is one way of getting to the point where you can speak without thinking too hard about what to say.

Change the verb to ask about other people's opinions:
Vous aimez les chansons d'Edith Piaf? Oui, elles sont formidables!
Il aime le football ou le rugby? Le rugby, je crois.
Tu préfères le sud ou le nord? Le nord.
Elle préfère le bus ou le métro? Elle déteste le bus.
Ils admirent les hommes et les femmes politiques? Non, pas du tout.

Note the use of **ou**, which means 'or' and is very useful when asking about preferences.

C Using **vous**, how would you ask someone if:

1 they like watching TV or listening to the radio?
2 they prefer speaking French or German?
3 they like jazz or rock?
4 they prefer living in Paris or London?

D What questions containing the verb **aimer** might have generated the following answers?

1 Non, il n'aime pas tellement le sport.
2 Oui, j'adore la cuisine française.
3 Nous admirons Monet, mais nous préférons Cézanne.
4 Non, je déteste les films de science fiction.

Test case

 activity 13

A **2.10** Remember **La Résidence** and its inhabitants from Chapter 5? The director is setting a scene for a forthcoming episode. He describes the scenario; make notes on the characters' actions in the relevant apartment.

Appartement 1	Appartement 2	Appartement 3	Appartement 4	Appartement 5

B Now complete the text to discover the action at 8pm.

Plus tard …

Dans l'appartement numéro quatre Philippe (téléphoner) à la police. Sa compagne Julie (pleurer).
Madeleine (manger) avec sa mère. Elles (entendre) les pleurs de Julie à côté, mais elles (continuer) à manger.
Antoine, les enfants et les chiens (rentrer). Ils (remarquer) la porte ouverte au numéro quatre mais ils n' (entrer) pas.
Natalie (se reposer) dans le salon. Elle (choisir) un magazine sur la table.

Although some of the verbs in the brackets are new, you should have no difficulty working out the parts that you need if you follow the rules in this chapter.

 activity 14

2.11 Play your part in the following conversation:

- Qu'est-ce que tu fais?
- Say you're having a rest; you are watching TV.
- Qu'est-ce tu regardes?
- Say you're watching a documentary.
- Tu aimes les documentaires?
- Say you prefer soap operas but you like documentaries too.
- Tu travailles demain?
- Say no, you're not working, you're staying at home (à la maison), you're waiting for a delivery (une livraison) but you're working on Wednesday.
- Bon, à mercredi alors!

Sing us a song

Look out for verbs not just in what people say but also when you read French. Song lyrics provide an opportunity to study the mechanics of language more closely. Take a look at Comme d'habitude, a song by Michel Sardou, on YouTube and concentrate on the verbs. For some light relief why not listen (and even sing) along as you read?

Reading such as this provides an opportunity to observe the different ways in which new language can work. Do you recognise the verbs that are being used? Which parts of the patterns can you see? How many are regular verbs? A little grammatical research of this nature can expand your knowledge and confirm what you know and what you need to check up on.

8 Points d'interrogation

- Learn about different ways of asking questions
- Discover how to ask for help and invite people to do things
- Add to your irregular verb bank
- Talk about what you never do

Displaying a healthy interest

Asking questions, as well as helping you get what you need, lets you get under the skin of another culture so it's a skill worth cultivating. You'll recall that changing the tone of your voice is the most simple, and a very common way, of asking questions in French.

 activity 1

A 2.12 Listen to the audio and identify whether the following are questions or statements:

	question	statement
1 Tu restes à Bordeaux		
2 Il habite Edimbourg		
3 Vous allez au cinéma		
4 Vous avez des croissants		
5 Ça va		
6 Elle est chef des achats		
7 Ils travaillent à l'université		
8 On voyage en avion		

There are, however, other question forms which are worth learning, because even if you don't want to use them yourself, you will need to understand them. Look at these three ways of asking for the same information.

Vous avez des enfants?
Est-ce que vous avez des enfants?
Avez-vous des enfants?

Vous êtes professeur?
Est-ce que vous êtes professeur?
Êtes-vous professeur?

Vous parlez français?
Est-ce que vous parlez français?
Parlez-vous français?

Est-ce que literally means 'is it that', which would be rather an odd way of asking questions in English: 'Is it that you speak French?'. In French, the use of est-ce que is very common and has the advantage of giving you a little extra time to marshal your thoughts before you speak.

In the third question the order of the verb and its subject alters, vous avez to avez-vous. This process is called inversion and, although not quite as frequently used as the other forms, is something that you will hear.

When you use question words such as où *where*, comment *how*, quand *when* and à quelle heure *what time*, you have the same three options.

Add est-ce que:
Où est-ce que vous allez? *Where are you going?*
Comment est-ce que vous arrivez? *How are you arriving?*

Or change the order of the question:
Vous allez où?
Vous arrivez à quelle heure?

If you start with a question word and don't use est-ce que you need to invert the verb and its subject:
Où allez-vous?
Quand arrivez-vous?

B 2.13 Try out these different question forms by asking someone if they have:

1 some brioches.

2 a garden.

3 the time (l'heure).

Listen to see whether you have got the questions and intonation right.

C Now use the est-ce que and changed word order options to ask:

1 Where do they live?

2 When does the conference begin?

3 How is he arriving?

4 What time does the plane go?

 activity 2

Speed dating

A You've agreed to go with a friend to a speed dating event. Before you set off you want to work out some questions to ask. In the grid below one question has been completed in each category. Can you create another way of asking the same thing so that you can vary your questions at the event?

1 le travail	Vous travaillez?
2 le domicile	Habitez-vous Calais?
3 les sports	Est-ce que vous faites du sport?
4 les passe-temps	Aimez-vous le théâtre?
5 les vacances	Vous voyagez souvent à l'étranger?

B 2.14 Now put your questions and make a note of the answers you are given. Could this be a relationship made in heaven?

 activity 3

Voulez–vous

A 2.15 Once you've identified like-minded people through close questioning, the next step is to fix a date. Listen to the exchanges and work out which invite is accepted and which declined.

	oui	non
prendre un pot		
aller au cinéma		
faire une promenade sur la plage		
manger au restaurant		
venir chez moi		

Vous voulez and tu veux are useful ways of finding out what people want (Veux-tu une bière ou un vin blanc? *Do you want a beer or white wine?*) and also a means of issuing invitations (Tu veux venir chez moi? *Do you want to come to my place?*). Je veux bien *I'd like to very much* is part of the same verb, vouloir *to want.* Did you spot the use of désolé(e) and je regrette to soften the blow of a refusal?

B Issuing invitations using vous voulez or tu veux usually involves adding another verb in the infinitive form: Vous voulez manger ...? *Do you want to eat ...?*; Tu veux voir ...? *Do you want to see ...?*. How might you invite people to do the following? Use a dictionary or the glossary to research any infinitives you don't know; there are clues to help you decide between vous and tu.

1 go to the theatre (friend)
2 visit your office (work contact)
3 come to your place (chez moi) (mates)
4 travel by train (work contact)
5 eat at the Brasserie Flo (friend)
6 have a drink (new colleagues)
7 meet Marie-Claire (family member)

C You'll be aware by now that the verb you're dealing with is irregular. See if you can complete the grid.

je		nous	voulons
tu		vous	
il/elle/on	veut	ils/elles	veulent

Just occasionally irregular verbs such as **vouloir** have 'friends', other verbs that, although irregular themselves, share characteristics. Did you notice the phrase **je ne peux pas** *I can't* in the previous conversations? Read on to discover more about **vouloir**'s partner, **pouvoir**.

 activity 4

Anything you can do ...

A 2.16 Listen to these exchanges where people are seeking assistance. Complete the grid as you listen. What do people want help with and do they get the help they need?

Help to do ...?	Help received?

Did you notice **Pouvez-vous m'aider** *Can you help me*? If you say **m'aider** out loud you will realise that it's a phrase that's passed into English nautical language: 'mayday, mayday'. **Pouvez-vous m'aider** is a useful set phrase, helpful in starting a conversation. Have a look at the position of **me** in **Pouvez-vous m'aider**. In the transcript you will find other examples that follow this pattern:

Pouvez-vous me conseiller ...? *Can you advise me ...?*
Vous pouvez m'indiquer ...? *Can you show me ...?*
Vous pouvez m'appeler ...? *Can you call me ...?*

Me loses its **e** in front of a vowel. Its grammatical name is 'object pronoun' and these go in front of the verb, hence the change in order of words between the French and the English. There'll be more about object pronouns in the next chapter.

B You will have noticed that **pouvoir**, like **vouloir**, is usually followed by another verb in the infinitive. Have a go at asking the receptionist in your hotel if she can:

1 recommend a restaurant for you.
2 call a taxi for you.
3 help you; you want to go to the station.

As well as asking people to do things for you, you'll need other parts of the verb **pouvoir** in order to be able to check that it's OK for you to take action.

Examples:
Je peux stationner la voiture ici? *Can I park here?*
Est-ce qu'on peut visiter les caves de Champagne? *Can we visit the Champagne cellars?*
Nous pouvons laisser nos bagages avec vous? *Can we leave our luggage with you?*

C 2.17 So how would you ask whether you can do the following? Try out je, on and nous questions and check your answers with the audio

1 Entrer dans le château (je)
2 Réserver les billets (nous)
3 Déguster les huîtres (on)
4 Choisir les vins (on)
5 Voir la chambre (je)

Do you know what you've just enquired about? Check out the meaning of new words and unravel the faux ami; déguster is not as disgusting as it sounds!

D Complete the pattern for **pouvoir** and compare it with **vouloir**:

je		nous	
tu	peux	vous	
il/elle/on		ils/elles	peuvent

Double entendre

Think about how you use 'can' in English. It expresses both a sense of 'being able to' do something ('I can come on Tuesday') as well as 'knowing how to' do something ('I can dance a tango'). **Pouvoir** only expresses the first of these meanings. If you want to talk about 'knowing how' you need another verb, savoir *to know*.

You'll come across je sais *I know* and je ne sais pas *I don't know* frequently in conversation, so much so that je ne sais pas may be pronounced ché pas, much as 'I don't know' has become 'I dunno'.

To help fix the difference between **savoir** and **pouvoir** in your mind, think of the skills that people might have. Compare these examples using **savoir**, which are concerned with whether people know how to do something, with those below using **pouvoir**, which are concerned with making arrangements:

On sait jouer au tennis. *We can play tennis.*
Je sais faire une omelette. *I can make an omelette.*
Il sait conduire une moto. *He can drive a motorbike.*
Vous savez créer une base de données? *Can you create a database?*
Vous pouvez jouer au tennis mardi? *Can you play tennis on Tuesday?*
Tu peux me faire une omelette pour mon déjeuner? *Can you make me an omelette for my lunch?*
Je peux conduire ta moto? *Can I drive your bike?*
On peut créer la base de données la semaine prochaine. *We can create the database next week.*

These subtleties demonstrate again that you have to go beyond word-for-word translation and think about what you actually mean to say. At the start, this process demands that you stop and think, but with practice the correct choice will become second nature.

 activity 5

2.18 Vous pouvez or vous savez?

1 Vous .... venir dimanche?
2 Vous .... télécharger *download* la musique?
3 Vous .... changer un pneu *tyre*?
4 Vous .... partir à seize heures?

 prounciation activity

2.19 It's worth spending a little time perfecting the sound of the French vowel **u**. Listen to these words on the audio:

u	ui	ou
une du vue fracture brûlure	huit suis huilc	cousine Anjou chou-fleur

The **u** in the first column is probably the most challenging sound to produce. You need to form your mouth into a tight rosebud, tongue clenched between teeth; you should be able to feel a pull on the muscles in your cheeks as you produce this very sharp sound. Repeat the words in the first column for practice. When u combines with other vowels its sound changes. Ui as in **huit** sounds more like an English double 'e' ('feet', 'sheet'), although tighter, and ou is similar to 'oo' ('boot', 'loot').

Have a go at these words then check to see how you did:

tu   vous   nuit   dessous   dessus

 activity 6

Getting to know you

2.20 The speed dating has been a success and conversation blossoms. Listen to these people talking about time off. You'll hear the verb **faire**, which means 'to do' or 'to make'. It's an irregular verb:

je	fais	nous	faisons
tu	fais	vous	faites
il/elle/on	fait	ils/elles	font

Complete the grid with activities that you hear. You may need to listen a few times. All the activities mentioned look very like their English equivalents, but, of course, they won't sound much like them:

sports	leisure pursuits

 **language tip**

Faire is one of the few verbs whose **vous** form doesn't end in -**ez**. This feature is shared by être (vous êtes) and dire (vous dites). It is also unusual in that its ils/elles form doesn't end in -ent, a characteristic it shares with être (ils sont), aller (ils vont) and avoir (ils ont).

Faire also features widely in French idioms: faire de la place *to make space*, faire des affaires *to do business*, faire des études *to study*, faire des histoires *to make a fuss*. Keep your eye out for this verb and make a mental note to jot down interesting examples.

 **activity 7**

A **2.21** Use the grid to help you play your part in the role play on the audio. Check any meanings you can't guess in a dictionary or the glossary:

Qu'est-ce que vous faites ...?	à la maison	les sports
Je fais On fait Nous faisons	la cuisine la sieste la vaisselle du bricolage du jardinage	de la natation du ski du vélo du golf du jogging

- Vous aimez le sport?
- Say not much but you do go jogging.
- Vous faites d'autres sports?
- Say yes, you ski.
- Votre compagnon fait du sport?
- Say yes, he swims and cycles.
- Vous avez d'autres passe-temps, tous les deux?
- Say we garden and your partner likes DIY.
- Et c'est vous qui faites la cuisine à la maison?
- Say no, your partner cooks and does the washing up too.

Of course, should you be a 'couch potato' (**un pantouflard**), you will probably want to say:

Je ne fais rien. *I don't do anything/I do nothing.*
Je ne fais rien à la maison.
Je ne fais rien dans le jardin.
Je ne fais rien le week-end.

B Or you could comment on the fact that:

1 your partner does nothing in the garden.
2 your children do nothing about the house.
3 you and your partner do nothing at the weekend.

Ne ... rien, as you may have noticed, is a negative that behaves just as ne ... pas does, by wrapping itself around the verb.

C On the same theme, these people are talking about things they never do (ne ... jamais) or don't do any more (ne ... plus). Remember that, as with ne ... pas the words un, une, du, de la and des all become de after the negative.

Je ne fais jamais de jardinage.
On ne fait plus de ski.
Il ne fait plus la cuisine.
Elle ne fait jamais le ménage.

D Make the following statements negative:

1 On fait du bricolage. (ne ... jamais)
2 Elle fait de la musique. (ne ... plus)
3 On fait de la conversation. (ne ... jamais)
4 Nous faisons du golf. (ne ... plus)

Decisions, decisions

 **activity 8**

Read the email message to get the gist of Pierre's dilemma. What does he ask in relation to the cinema, the restaurant and match?

1 cinema ....

2 restaurant ....

3 match ....

Salut Sophie,

Peux-tu sortir ce soir? Si oui, qu'est-ce que tu veux faire? Le cinéma,
mais quel film? Un restaurant, peut-être? Tu préfères quelle sorte
de cuisine, la chinoise, l'italienne, la vietnamienne? Aller à un
match, mais tu aimes quels sports? Dis-moi quelles sont tes
préférences?

Bisous,

Pierre

There are a number of different ways of translating 'what' in French. You've
used qu'est-ce que in this chapter and elsewhere; note that it is usually
followed by a phrase with a verb in it: Qu'est-ce que tu veux faire? In order
to ask what someone is called you need comment: Comment vous appelez-
vous? When you were travelling you asked 'what time': Le train part à quelle
heure? Choosing the right 'what' in French is a question of saying what you
mean rather than translating what you say.

If you can replace an English 'what' by 'which' and the question still makes
sense, the chances are that you'll need quel rather than qu'est-ce que.

It won't have escaped your notice when reading the email that quel has a
number of different forms. That's because it is accompanied by a noun and so
agrees in gender and number with the noun to which it refers:

Quel film? (m)
Quelle cuisine? (f)
Quels sports? (mpl)
Quelles préférences? (fpl)

All the different forms sound the same which makes life easier when it comes
to speaking.

 activity 9

2.22 Work out how you would ask the following questions then listen to the
audio and decide which of the answers below are true and which are false:

- Ask which wine the person prefers. (use vous)
- Ask what flavours (parfums) the person likes. (use vous)
- Ask which house they like? (use vous)

- Ask which regions they prefer. (use **tu**)

	True	False
1 The person likes red but prefers white wine.		
2 They like vanilla and chocolate but not pistachio.		
3 They like the house with three bedrooms.		
4 They love the Jura and Languedoc.		

If you feel you need some more practice in the different forms of **quel**, write down the questions you asked.

 activity 10

Your turn to email now. Complete the draft with the right 'what' and if you use **quel** make sure you make the agreement.

> Salut Didier,
>
> (Qu'est-ce que/Quel) tu fais mardi? Tu peux m'aider? Je veux changer ma voiture mais je ne sais pas quoi faire? (Qu'est-ce que/Quel) marque préfères-tu? (Qu'est-ce que/Quel) concessionnaires? (Qu'est-ce que/Quel) tu suggères? Je peux venir à ton appartement à douze heures si tu es libre. Sinon, tu peux proposer (Qu'est-ce que/Quel) autre journée? (Qu'est-ce que/Quel) est ton numéro de portable?

Once you have completed the exercise, look again at the text. There's yet another word for 'what' in the phrase **Je ne sais pas quoi faire** *I don't know what to do*. What is that certain **je ne sais quoi** that makes you stand out from the crowd?

Quoi is used if 'what' comes after the verb rather than before it as with **qu'est-ce que**. In very informal speech, it can be used to replace lengthier or more complicated structures:

Tu veux quoi? as an alternative for **Qu'est-ce que tu veux?**
What do you want?
C'est quoi, ça? for **Qu'est-ce que c'est que ça?** *What's that?*

Test case

 activity 11

Une blind date

2.23 You're the compère of a game show and your job is to grill contestants. You can prepare for the event by taking some time to think of the questions you might ask. Follow the prompts.

Messieurs, dames, bonsoir. Voici notre premier participant.
- Over to you. Say good evening and ask the name of the person.
- Je m'appelle Olivier David.
- Ask how old Olivier is.
- J'ai vingt-six ans.
- Ask if he works (use est-ce que).
- Oui je suis plombier.
- Ask where he lives.
- J'habite chez mes parents à Toulouse.
- Ask what Olivier does when he's not working.
- Alors, je ne sais pas, pas grande chose.
- Say 'you do nothing?' Ask him if he likes sports (est-ce que).
- Oui, oui.
- Ask what sports he likes.
- Le rugby, le football.
- Ask him if he can play rugby.
- Mais non, je regarde les matchs a la télé!
- Ask if he travels much.
- Un peu, en vacances.
- Ask which countries he wants to visit.
- Je voudrais bien aller au Vietnam et en Chine.
- Thank him and wish him good luck (bonne chance!).

 activity 12

Read about leisure time in France. Without resorting too often to a dictionary, can you work out:

1 What reputation the French have gained *vis-à-vis* work?
2 What the rules for working hours and time off are?
3 What happens to enable people to faire le pont?

4 Annually what the average working times are?
5 What older adults can look forward to?

La France a la réputation d'être un paradis pour les travailleurs qui y travaillent moins que dans d'autres pays. Les Français ont aussi la réputation de ne pas aimer le travail, d'aller souvent en vacances. Il est préférable de dire que la plupart des Français sont attachés à leur vie en dehors du quotidien professionnel et qu'en France la législation du temps de travail est très règlementée: trente-cinq heures de travail par semaine, cinq semaines de congés payés par an, onze jours fériés, congés de maternité pour les femmes (seize semaines, dont six avant l'accouchement), congés de paternité pour les hommes (deux semaines).

Il existe en France une tradition qui permet d'augmenter les jours de congé: lorsqu'un jour férié 'tombe' un jeudi ou un mardi, les entreprises ferment souvent leurs bureaux le vendredi ou le lundi pour permettre à leurs employés de 'faire le pont' pour un week-end allongé. Malgré toutes ces vacances, les Français travaillent mille sept cents heures en moyenne par an, soit environ deux cent quarante jours sur trois cent soixante-cinq. Enfin, la retraite, à partir de soixante ans, constitue une réserve de temps libre presqu'infinie, et beaucoup de 'seniors' aujourd'hui apprécient et profitent de ce moment important de la vie.

(Edited from the original text *Temps Libre* by Denis C. Meyer, University of Hong Kong **www.hku.hk/french/dcmScreen/lang2043/tempslibre.htm**)

Learning strategies

You already know pretty much all there is to know about learning language; you've done it before with your mother tongue. You're in the habit of keeping communication up to date; you do that using a variety of ways that have become second nature. Now you've decided to learn French it's helpful to reflect on and recycle some of the language-learning strategies you use or have used in the past.

The words

How did you manage to assimilate words like 'computer', 'email', 'twitter'; what about 'the green pound' or 'the grey vote'? The process is: exposure to the word or phrase; getting to grips with its meaning, usually from the contexts in which it appears; understanding the kind of word or phrase it is (formal, informal, verb, adjective etc); making a decision about whether it's useful for you; trying it out for yourself; being corrected or self-correcting its use.

A further development may involve adaptation of the original word or phrase: creating different parts of speech ('an email' (noun), 'he emails' (verb) and 'email message' (adjective)) or changing elements of a phrase to suit different circumstances ('the pink pound'). All in all, you have a natural tendency to play with language and that's how you both learn and create your own 'voice'.

Increasing your word power

Your mother tongue happens all around you in different formats on a daily basis. As a learner of French you need to try to recreate some of that exposure in order to 'fix' new words (and new grammar) in the mind. The internet is an invaluable source of contexts in which to pin down meaning, as are radio, TV, DVDs, films, music, newspapers, magazines, books, and French speaking family and friends.

There are any number of ways to put yourself in the way of French without having to travel or resort to a more academic route via dictionaries, glossaries or grammar references.

See how much you can learn about colours in French by using a search engine to track down the background and meaning of the following song titles and phrases: La vie en rose by Edith Piaf; Rouge by Michel Sardou; le vignoble de Bordeaux; les pages jaunes; éminence grise; rouge et noir.

Making it up as you go along

When you do use a dictionary, get into the habit of looking further than single words. You're researching a noun; does it have various meanings? Does it have an accompanying verb or adjective? Store these words in family groups:

Example:

un voyage *a journey*
un voyageur *a traveller*
un voyageur fréquent *a frequent traveller*
voyager *to travel*
une agence de voyages *a travel agency*
Le mal des transports *travel sickness*

Develop a family group from le travail *work*.

A little knowledge

Don't get stuck with using the same old words. Look for alternatives and opposites to expand your vocabulary and help you remember, e.g:

une maison *a house* – une demeure, un foyer, un logis, un domicile, un gîte, un appartement

noir – blanc *black – white*
heureux – malheureux *happy – unhappy*
grand – petit *big – small*
riche – pauvre *rich – poor*
certain – incertain *certain – uncertain*

Quick fixes

French, like English, makes great use of prefixes and suffixes to alter the meaning of words or to make new ones. Removing them helps you identify the core of the word, which you may then recognise. Conversely, learning how they correspond to English prefixes and suffixes will also help you increase your vocabulary.

- The prefix dé- in French is either 'de-' or 'un-' in English:
  débloquer *unblock*

décoder *decode*
démystifier *demystify*
déréguler *deregulate*
débrancher *unplug*
défaire *undo*

- The French prefixes re/ré/res/r- can be added to hundreds of verbs to make new ones:
  remarier *to remarry* (added to marier *to marry*)
  revenir *to come back* (added to venir *to come*)
  ressortir *to go out again* (added to sortir *to go out*)
  réapparaître *to reappear* (added to apparaître *to appear*)
  rentrer *to return home* (added to entrer *to enter*)
  rouvrir *to reopen* (added to ouvrir *to open*)

- The prefixes in-/im- equate to the English prefixes: incorrecte, impossible

- Adding -age to the stem of a French verb can provide the equivalent of a noun ending in '-ing' in English. Nouns ending in the suffix -age are masculine:
  jardiner *to garden* → le jardinage *gardening*
  balayer *to sweep* → le balayage *sweeping, scanning*
  raser *to shave* → le rasage *shaving, shearing*
  badiner *to gossip* → le badinage *gossip*
  assembler *to assemble* → assemblage *assembling, assembly*

- Other common suffixes include:
  -able: confort → confortable
  -ment: avancer → avancement
  -eux: joie → joyeux

Take time to check up on how your vocabulary building is going. Look around you; how many items can you name in French? What actions do you routinely undertake? How many of these do you know the French for? What do you particularly enjoy doing? Have you got the vocabulary to talk about it?

My memory isn't what it was

Memorising language is a process of understanding and learning the basics, and constant (or at least very regular) practice of different kinds to ensure that, alongside all the other learned skills you have (driving a car, cooking, using a computer), French remains a current and usable talent.

We all learn in different ways, and most of us use a combination of methods without realising it: visual learners learn by seeing, auditory learners by hearing, and kinaesthetic learners by doing. Help yourself by thinking about how you learn best. Here are some suggestions for learning vocabulary which combine different learning styles:

- Copy word lists in French and English in two columns. Say each word aloud, then cover up one column and try to say the word in the other. After a time doing something different, see how many words you can remember.

- Set yourself a target of a number of words, or a word family, each day or week. Check your list to see how many words you know already; tick them off. Write out a list of those you didn't know, and set yourself a target number and timescale in which to learn them. Use colours to pick out, for example, verb endings, genders and odd spellings. Stick your list on the wall next to your mirror, and learn them while brushing your hair, shaving or just getting ready (this does not take time from other work!).

- For objects in the house, write the word on a sticky note and attach it to the object.

- Find an 'association' for words, e.g. similarities to an English word or a word in any other language.

- 'Picture' words or what they represent, perhaps even linking them with situations you have experienced.

- 'Undress' long words to get at their core meaning, by removing prefixes and suffixes.

- Before you look up a word, always try to guess its meaning and what type of word it is (noun, verb etc) based on the context.

- Make a point of trying out words in different contexts.

- Music is a good aid to memory, and French songs can provide not only the words but even grammar points!

- Take every opportunity to reinforce words and structures. You need to review them many times and at regular intervals to get them to stick.

Making experience count

Use what you already have to develop your command of French. If you can't come up with the exact words for what you want to say, think of alternative ways of getting the message across that might be more 'translatable'.

Who's that woman over there? → Elle s'appelle comment? (while gesturing in the right direction)

Do I need a password to send emails? → (Envoyer) un email, c'est possible?

You have to make compromises in the beginning, simplifying what you would normally say to fit the French that you know. Speak without worrying too much about correctness or style. Engaging in conversation is the best way of spotting and rectifying your mistakes and increasing your word power.

The rules of the game

Learning the grammar of a language is crucial in order to move from the 'me Tarzan, you Jane' mode of communication to something that resembles normal speech. The most effective way of gathering rules is to observe them in action and to mimic what is going on, but there is room for some old-fashioned learning too.

You have already met a number of grammatical structures that have manifested themselves as set phrases:

Je voudrais ...
Qu'est-ce que vous avez comme ...?
Pouvez-vous m'aider ...?

You use these phrases as they are without needing to change any of the elements. Since this is the case, they can simply be learned using the same strategies that you would use for vocabulary. You might find it useful to collect phrases under topics or themes.

I did it my way

There are other rules that you need to internalise in order to be able to manipulate French to your own ends and chief among these are verb patterns. The chanting of verbs evokes memories of a bygone age but regular repetition remains an effective way of drilling information into your brain. You need to reach the point where you have a reflex response to producing the correct part of a verb. Muttering verb patterns is an activity that lends itself to association with other reflex actions: gardening, housework, the gym. Learning of this sort needs organisation:

- Choose a sample verb for each of the regular families: parler for -er verbs, finir for -ir and attendre for -re, for example.
- Learn each of the irregular (avoir, être) patterns separately.
- Pick a couple of reflexive verbs for good measure; s'appeler and se promener will give your pronunciation a good workout too.

- Don't be over ambitious; set yourself a reasonable target number of verbs to learn per week.
- As you progress, come back to your week-one verbs at regular intervals to see how much you can still recall.
- Set yourself challenges. Come up with the **nous** part of all the verbs you can remember; try making whole patterns negative (**je ne suis pas**).
- Once you have the sample regular verbs off pat, diversify into different verbs from each family.
- Write patterns down from memory.

The verb treatment will be useful for other fundamental rules you will come across, such as:

- adjectives
- possessive adjectives (**mon, ma, mes**)
- **du, de la, des**
- this (**ce, cette, ces**)
- the immediate future (**je vais acheter**)
- the past tense

You will have already developed your own learning style. Once you have identified how you learn best, you just need to make sure that you learn in that way, making a bit of extra effort to give yourself the necessary 'memory hooks' to store the information away in such a way that you can drag it out again when you need it!

And remember that even a short period of learning can give results.

9 Parler de la pluie et du beau temps

- Talk about the weather
- Meet adjectives
- Learn about direct object pronouns
- Engage in small talk

What's the weather like today?

The title of this chapter alludes to 'rain' (la pluie) and 'fine weather' (le beau temps). Having an opinion about the weather is an expectation of the British. Look out for faire, the verb that you met in the previous chapter, as you embark on meteorological small talk.

 activity 1

2.24 Practise these weather phrases using the audio to help with pronunciation:

Il fait beau.	Il fait mauvais.	Il fait chaud.	Il fait froid.
		+30°C	–5°C
Il fait vingt degrés.	Il fait du soleil.	Il fait du vent.	Il fait du brouillard.
20°C		20	
Il pleut.	Il neige.		

What's the weather like today? **Quel temps fait-il aujourd'hui?** Remember, you need **quel** because of the accompanying noun **temps** *weather*. **Temps** is a versatile word, which also means 'time' (**de temps en temps** *from time to time*) and 'tense' (of a verb).

brilliant activity 2

A **2.25** Passing comment about weather conditions can be a useful conversational gambit. Listen and tick off the phrases you hear:

☐ Il fait froid.	☐ Il pleut.
☐ Il fait du brouillard.	☐ Il fait chaud.
☐ Il fait beau.	☐ Il fait du soleil.
☐ Il neige.	☐ Il fait du vent.

1 What temperature was mentioned?

2 What is each of the two people in the third exchange going to do as a result of the weather?

Did you hear **n'est-ce pas** in two of the conversations? It is the equivalent of 'isn't it?' and helps the flow of conversation. **Il fait chaud, n'est-ce pas?** *Hot, isn't it?*

Remember **n'est-ce pas** for future use. It is a very handy way of inviting people to agree with what you are saying. **Je parle bien français, n'est-ce pas?** ought not to get any other answer than **oui**!

B Using **n'est-ce pas**, what might you say for a day that is:

1 sunny

2 windy

3 unpleasant

Passing comment on the weather brings you face to face with the use of idiomatic French where words acquire unexpected meanings (e.g. **faire**) and are used in unusual ways. Deal with this by treating descriptions of weather conditions as set phrases to be learned as whole utterances. **Il pleut** and **il neige** are impersonal verbs and, in the context of weather, **il fait** is an impersonal verb too.

An impersonal verb is a verb form that doesn't relate to people or things and generally starts with 'it', e.g. 'It's snowing'.

Waxing lyrical

Among the words used above to describe the weather you will find some useful adjectives: beau, mauvais, chaud, froid.

 activity 3

2.26 Take a look at the following and spot the rules for the use of adjectives:

le lait froid	la bière froide
du chocolat chaud	de la nourriture chaude
un costume régional	une cuisine régionale
le vin français	la langue française
un musée intéressant	une vie intéressante
un centre commercial	une entreprise commerciale

Listen to the audio and check out the pronunciation. The addition of e in the feminine form means that you will often hear the last consonant.

You may have already noticed that, unlike in English, most adjectives follow the noun they describe: la langue française *the French language*, une bière froide *a cold beer*. French adjectives 'agree' in gender with the noun they describe: un centre commercial, une enterprise commerciale. As you will have seen from the examples above, you generally create feminine adjectives by adding an e to the masculine word.

> An adjective describes a noun in some way: shape, colour, size, nationality, for instance.

 cultural tip

The Norman invasion of 1066 had a massive influence not only on French words coming into English, but also on the structure and grammar of English. Generally, it's the rule in English that adjectives go before the noun, but there are some set expressions that are a hangover from the Norman conquest: 'mission impossible', 'princess royal', 'governor general'.

Gender wars

 activity 4

Complete these phrases by changing the adjectives:

Example: un homme important   une femme importante

1 un musée contemporain   une peinture ....

2 un ami amusant   une amie ....

3 un obstacle évident   une question ....

4 un paysage charmant   une vue ....

In the case of contemporain the change in sound affects more than the final letter: contemporain, contemporaine.

 pronunciation

2.27 The letters n and m in French deserve a closer look since their sound changes depending on the letters that surround them. If they are preceded by a vowel they develop a nasal tone, unless they are doubled (comment, australienne) or followed by another vowel (contemporaine). It's the kind of sound you make when you have a light head cold! Listen to these words:

un   en face   maison   indépendante   grand   jardin   plein
faim   impossible   simple   employée   temps

Have you noticed the tone? Your mouth makes a cave shape, tongue at the bottom with lips apart so that the sound that is produced through the nose is amplified. Have a go!

Now compare this nasal sound with that of the following words where the n and m sounds are much closer to their English equivalent:

cousine   minérale   omelette

How should these words sound? Check your answers with the audio.

Londres   train   vendredi   sang-froid   important
un bon vin blanc   jambon   américain   américaine

 **activity 5**

A **2.28** Listen to this description of a house on the Mediterranean coast. As you listen match the adjectives with their nouns:

petite	moderne	belle	spacieuse	grand	méditerranéenne
	ombragée	spectaculaire	charmant		

- une .... maison
- la côte ....
- un .... salon ....
- une cuisine .... et ....
- une vue ....
- une .... piscine
- une terrasse ....

Take a close look at your list of phrases. When there are rules there are usually exceptions!

B Which three adjectives are in front of the words they describe?

A small number of very commonly used adjectives go before the noun. One way to memorise them is to use the acronym 'BAGS':

Beauty: beau, joli *pretty*, vilain *ugly*
Age: jeune *young*, nouveau *new*, vieux *old*
Good and bad: méchant, bon, mauvais
Size: grand, petit, long, gros, vaste

Examples: une jolie maison *a pretty house*; un jeune homme *a young man*; une nouvelle voiture *a new car*; un bon repas *a good meal*; un petit problème *a small problem*.

 **learning tip**

Sometimes a common phrase that is used in English will help to fix this rule in your mind:

Bon appétit!	Grand Prix	Belle Époque
nouveau riche, nouvelle cuisine		petits fours

 activity 6

A **2.29** Listen to this woman talking about her sister, Annie, and her sister's boyfriend, Yves. First of all, see if you can work out whether she approves of him. You'll hear the verb se marier, which means 'to get married'.

B Now familiarise yourself with the adjectives below (which are all in the masculine form), then listen again and say which of the adjectives refer to Annie, which to Yves and which to someone or something else. Make any agreement changes to the adjective that are necessary.

petit   sympathique   gros   pas gentil   vieux

C Finally, look at the transcript and, using a dictionary, find the opposites of these adjectives in the text:
1 sale   2 désagréable   3 mauvaise   4 laid

The exception proves the rule

 activity 7

A What would the masculine versions of charmante and the feminine of grand be?

Now look at these adjectives again, plus a new one, cher *expensive*:

masculine	feminine
spectaculaire	spectaculaire
moderne	moderne
cher	chère
méditerranéen	méditerranéenne
bon	bonne
sportif	sportive
spacieux	spacieuse
beau	belle

Adjectives may vary in the way that the feminine form is created.

- Those that already end in -e do not add another (sympathique (m), sympathique (f)).
- Adjectives that end in a vowel plus -l or -n become feminine by doubling the consonant before adding -e (gentil, gentille; italien, italienne).
- Those that end in -x change to end in -se (merveilleux, merveilleuse).
- Those that end in -if in the masculine change to -ive in the feminine (excessif, excessive).
- Some have a completely different feminine form (beau, belle; vieux, vieille)!

A few adjectives that precede the noun also have an extra version for masculine nouns that begin with a vowel or silent h.

(This is to maintain the characteristically fluid sound of French by avoiding the pause that would be created between one word ending in a vowel sound and another beginning with a vowel sound.)

masculine	masculine + vowel	feminine
beau – un beau jardin	bel – un bel hôtel	belle – une belle vue
nouveau – un nouveau restaurant	nouvel – un nouvel appartement	nouvelle – une nouvelle idée
vieux – un vieux château	vieil – un vieil homme	vieille – une vieille femme

B **2.30** Complete the travelogue by selecting the correct adjective before you listen to it on the audio:

Je suis au sommet d'un (grand/grande) volcan (éteint/éteinte) dans la (beau/bel/belle) région de l'Auvergne. La vue est (fabuleux/fabuleuse); là bas un (petit/petite) village avec son église (ancien/ancienne), les champs, les forêts, une (vieux/vieil/vieille) habitation (fermier/fermière). En effet une image (idéal/idéale) de la France (rural/rurale).

word builder

As you will have seen, a large number of English adjectives share a background with French. You should have had no trouble in guessing the meanings of spectaculaire, moderne and spacieux. So rural and fabuleux won't tax your understanding either.

Many adjectives ending in -able, -ible, -ant, -ent and -al are the same: notable, variable, respectable, possible, horrible, extravagant, important, constant, innocent, prudent, urgent, régional, national, commercial

Some common English endings have French equivalents, illustrated in the grid. This is not the definitive list. Look out for further similarities as you continue to read and develop your vocabulary.

-ic → -ique	-ous/-ious → -eux	-ive → -if	-al → -el
athlétique	merveilleux	négatif	artificiel
artistique	fabuleux	actif	traditionnel
économique	joyeux	agressif	universel
diplomatique	vigoureux	impulsif	criminel
électrique	mystérieux	excessif	personnel

Number crunching

French adjectives also agree in number, that is to say they have plural forms for both masculine and feminine versions. Generally speaking, the way to create the plural is to add an s, except if the adjective ends in s or x, in which case it doesn't change:

un jour gris	des jours gris
une jupe grise	des jupes grises
un repas délicieux	des repas délicieux
une pomme délicieuse	des pommes délicieuses

 **language tip**

Rules for making adjectives feminine and plural are very similar to those for nouns. Even the exceptions to the rule behave in the same way:

mon vrai ami; ma vraie amie; mes vrais amis; mes vraies amies
un comédien italien; une comédienne italienne
un journal national; des journaux nationaux
un prix fabuleux; des prix fabuleux

Up for sale

 **activity 8**

A **2.31** You've seen a property for sale and are calling the estate agent to find out more. Make a note of the details as you listen to his responses. In this kind of conversation you may want to check quantities, of rooms, for example. You have already learnt the word for 'how much/many' in combien. When it's followed by a noun, you need de: Il y a combien de pièces? *How many rooms are there?*

living room	bedrooms	kitchen

- Allô, Agence Belle Maison.
- Say good morning. Say you'd like some details (des détails) for the house in rue de la Fontaine.
- Qu'est-ce que vous désirez savoir précisément?
- Ask how many bedrooms there are.
- Il y a trois grandes chambres.
- Ask if the house is modern.
- C'est une maison traditionnelle et typique de la région. Ancienne à l'extérieur mais avec un intérieur contemporain.
- Ask if there is a big kitchen.
- Oui, c'est une nouvelle cuisine et il y a une salle de séjour magnifique à côté.
- Ask if you can visit the house.
- Oui, bien sûr. C'est une maison charmante dans un village très populaire.

B Here are some of the adjectives that you heard the estate agent use: populaire, magnifique, grandes, contemporain, grande, typique, charmante, traditionnelle, sympathique. Can you fit them into the description below?

Située dans un village .... cette maison .... est
.... de la région. Avec une salle de séjour .... ,
trois .... chambres et une .... cuisine la maison
est .... Son intérieur .... est surprenant mais
d'un style .... N'hésitez pas à visiter cette excellente propriété.

Flattery will get you everywhere

brilliant activity 9

A 2.32 We're used to estate agent hyperbole but a little flattery comes in handy for everyone. Listen to these people praising services and facilities at a hotel. What is described as:

1 marvellous ....

2 comfortable ....

3 perfect ....

4 amazing ....

5 unbelievable ....

B How would you say the following in French:

1 The view is beautiful.
2 The meal is marvellous.
3 The white wines are amazing.
4 Your (use **vous** form) house is charming.

Moans and groans

brilliant activity 10

A 2.33 You may also experience things that do not go so well. These people are complaining about various things. See if you can identify what is wrong with the:

1 room ....

2 wine ....

3 tee shirts ....

4 dimensions ....

When you're saying something that is not so complimentary you may wish to add Je regrette, mais ... to take the edge off!

B 2.34 Your turn to find something wrong. Take part in the following conversation:

- Bonjour. Je peux vous aider?
- Say yes, you're sorry but your room is too small.
- Désolé, mais c'est une de nos chambres les plus populaires.
- Say you understand but you'd like to see a different room (une autre chambre).
- Très bien.
- And you want a room with a spacious bathroom.
- Voici les clés de la chambre numéro cinq.
- Return the keys. Say the bed is old and uncomfortable and there isn't a television in the room.
- Alors, nous avons seulement la chambre numéro huit. C'est une suite. Voici les clés.
- Say the room is perfect; ask how much it is.
- Cent euros par nuit.
- Say it's too expensive and take your leave.

 learning tip

One of the interesting things that will no doubt happen as you wrestle with adjectives is that your control over the other rules you've learnt slips a bit. Have you remembered how to use the verbs you've needed? Have you got your nouns right? How's your pronunciation?

It's important to know how a language works so that you can make it work for you but you don't have to be word perfect to get your meaning across. Qui ne risque rien, n'a rien, as the proverb says ('nothing ventured, nothing gained').

What's your opinion?

 activity 11

A 2.35 Listen to these people giving their opinions about various things. Match objects with the correct description.

1 tennis	a pleasant
2 train journeys	b beautiful
3 the Côte d'Azur	c complicated
4 working in Paris	d energetic
5 steak and chips	e favourite
6 detective novels	f exciting

B Now fill in the adjectives with the correct agreements:

1 J'aime le tennis. C'est si .... (énergique).

2 Les voyages en train, ils sont .... (agréable).

3 Pour les vacances je préfère la Côte d'Azur qui est très
.... (beau).

4 J'aime travailler à Paris. C'est une ville ....
(passionnant).

5 J'adore le steak frites. C'est mon plat .... (favori).

6 J'aime les romans policiers, surtout s'ils sont ....
(compliqué).

C 2.36 Listen to the question and answer session. There are six adjectives that closely resemble their English counterparts. Can you hear them? Listen a couple of times then look at the transcript to check. You will also hear the words **les romans**, which means 'novels', and **ennuyeux**, which means 'boring'.

D The answers included the words for 'it' and 'them' ('I like them'; 'I find it'). Can you identify them in the sentences?

They are familiar words (**le, la, les**) but they mean something different from usual here. They have a dual role in French as the definite article, 'the', and the direct object pronoun ('it'/'them').

Direct objects are the people or things in a sentence which receive the action of the verb, e.g. *I like* <u>*snails*</u> (snails are on the receiving end of my appreciation). *Direct object pronouns* are the words that replace the direct object, 'I like snails. Do you like <u>them</u>?'

Object pronouns

Vous aimez <u>les films</u> de François Truffaut?
Oui, je <u>les</u> trouve admirables.

Que pensez-vous de <u>la presse</u> anglaise?
Je <u>la</u> trouve de temps en temps trop intrusive.

In the examples above you can see how a noun in the question influences the answer by dictating the gender and number of the direct object pronoun. Understanding how these rules work will help you make sense of what you hear and what you read.

Unlike in English they are placed before the verb: Je les aime *I like them*. When they are before a verb that begins with a vowel, le and la become l': Je l'apprécie.

When you use them with a negative like ne ... pas, it sandwiches the object pronoun and the verb: Je ne les aime pas; Il ne la fait plus.

 **activity 12**

Practise substituting the nouns in these sentences with pronouns.

Example: J'aime les chansons de Trenet. → Je les aime.

1 Il déteste la politique.
2 Vous regardez les feuilletons?
3 Je trouve les restaurants vietnamiens magnifiques.
4 Il ne donne jamais son adresse.

Sharing your thoughts

As you have seen above, the regular verb penser followed by de is the one you need to ask what people think of something.

Remember that de changes according to the gender and number of what follows (du, de la or des):
Qu'est-ce que vous pensez des escargots?
What do you think of snails?
Qu'est-ce que vous pensez du Château de Versailles?
What do you think of the Château of Versailles?

 **activity 13**

A 2.37 You're going to hear some people talking about their opinions. Before you listen, read through the questions and see if you can predict which is the correct answer to each. Use the subject and object pronouns as clues (was the question about a singular or plural noun, a masculine noun or a feminine one?).

Listen to see if your predictions were correct.

1 Qu'est-ce que vous pensez du football?	a Je les aime beaucoup.
2 Qu'est-ce que vous pensez de la décision?	b Je le déteste.
3 Qu'est-ce qu'elle pense des plans?	c Je ne l'aime pas, c'est trop abstrait.
4 Qu'est-ce qu'ils pensent de la nourriture?	d Ils la trouvent acceptable.
5 Qu'est-ce que vous pensez des magasins?	e Je l'aime bien, je le prends.
6 Qu'est-ce que tu penses du dessin?	f Elle ne les aime pas du tout.
7 Qu'est-ce que vous pensez du vase bleu?	g Je ne l'aime pas, elle est trop impulsive.

B 2.38 How would you ask someone's thoughts about:
1 sport
2 the view
3 the euro
4 soap operas

Test case

 **activity 14**

2.39 Play your part in this conversation at the local store. You might want to take a few minutes to think of some of the things you could say before you start.

- Bonjour madame.
- Return the greeting and make a comment about the weather, which is cold.
- Oui, il fait très froid. Vous restez dans le gîte de Monsieur Colbert?
- Say yes, you like it very much.
- Qu'est-ce que vous pensez de la région?
- Say that you love it. You like the little villages and the mountains (les montagnes).
- Vous faites du ski?
- You don't, you prefer to visit in October when it's nice weather.
- Qu'est-ce que vous faites aujourd'hui?
- Say that you are going to St. Germain, a really pretty town. You want to take some photos and have lunch (déjeuner) in a traditional restaurant.
- Alors, bonne journée, madame.

 activity 15

Reading is a really helpful way to focus on adjectives. Look at the following extract, which describes the new season's fragrances for men and women in suitably flowery language.

There will be new vocabulary for you to look out for: se dévoilent *are unveiled*, oublier *to forget*, vitrines *shop windows*, tenues *outfits*, chatoyantes *sparkling*.

There are other words that you might be able to work out:

- Épicées: remember that if you replace an e with an s you get something very close to an English word.

- Regard: you've met the verb regarder *to look at*; regard is a noun, so what do you think it means?

- Boisées: un bois is 'a wood', boisées is an adjective.

Which word are the following adjectives describing:

1 fleuries
2 gris
3 vives

How would the title change if parfums were to replace fragrances?

Les nouvelles fragrances ensoleillées arrivent

Fruitées, fleuries et légères pour les femmes, ou marines, boisées ou épicées pour les hommes, les nouvelles fragrances se dévoilent.

Déjà un rayon de soleil nous fait oublier le ciel gris et bas, et espérer des températures plus clémentes.

Pour nous remonter un peu le moral et nous faire patienter encore un peu, les vitrines des boutiques commencent déjà à exposer des tenues plus légères aux couleurs chatoyantes. Dans les vitrines des parfumeries et dans les grands magasins, c'est la même chose, les flacons toujours beaux se parent de belles couleurs gaies et vives pour attirer nos regards.

(Source: France Soir www.francesoir.fr/divers/nouveaux-parfums-les-fragrances-ensoleillees-arrivent)

10 La réglementation

- Be instructed and directed
- Talk about illness
- Say what you must do
- Get people to help you out

Streetwise

You need to develop magpie tendencies when you are in a French-speaking environment. It's remarkable how much easier vocabulary and phrases are to retain when you have heard or seen them *in situ*. There's a wealth of information to be had from just reading signs, labels, adverts, notices, leaflets and so on. The context will usually help you guess the meaning.

brilliant activity 1

Here are a few signs to get you started, with some clues to help:

1 · POUSSEZ ·   · TIREZ ·

on a door to a shop or office

4 ALLUMEZ VOS PHARES

on driving into a tunnel

2 *Roulez à droite*

on leaving a ferry port by car

3 Attachez vos ceintures

on a plane

5 Appuyez sur le bouton vert

to open a safety locked door

Some may be more obscure: Compostez votre billet (in a railway station).

Which part of the verb can you see in use here? Verbs ending in -ez are, of course, the easily identifiable vous form. When you're giving instructions or advice, you're effectively saying 'you do' something.

If you want to issue orders to someone you know well, use the **tu** form (minus the **s** for -er verbs).

Parle français. *Speak French.* (Tu parles français.)
Mange ton gâteau. *Eat your cake.* (Tu manges ton gâteau.)
Choisis un livre. *Choose a book.*
Attends, j'arrive. *Wait, I'm coming.*

The grammatical term for the way in which you order someone to do something using verbs is the 'imperative'.

Sometimes an infinitive is used for a more general audience – in instruction manuals and recipes, for example:

Mettre toujours la ceinture de securité. *Always wear your seatbelt.*
Vérifier l'huile avant de démarrer. *Check the oil before starting up.*
Mélanger le beurre et le sucre. *Mix the butter and sugar.*

You are more likely to be on the receiving end of instructions than giving them out.

 activity 2

A 2.40 Listen to these direction words. Be careful with the pronunciation of à droite *right* and tout droit *straight on*. You risk a number of blind alleys!

à gauche　　　　à droite　　　　tout droit

You will need ordinal numbers for directions too. 'First', 'second' and 'third' are premier/première, deuxième and troisième. You can easily identify them because, apart from premier, they are largely formed by taking the number and adding -ième. Go to page 187 for a list of 'first' to 'tenth'. If you see ordinal numbers written down, they are commonly abbreviated to 1er, 2e, 3e and so on.

B 2.41 You're about to hear some directions which correspond to the following diagrams. See if you can number them in the order they occur.

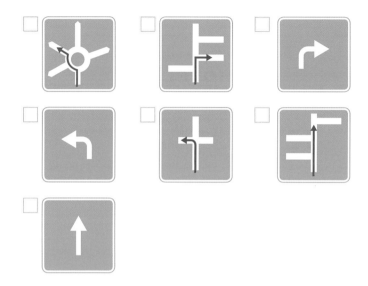

C **2.42** Follow these sat nav directions. As you listen, identify which of these instructions are incorrect – they are in the order you'll hear them:

1 At the end of the road turn left. ☐
2 In 200m cross the roundabout, first exit. ☐
3 In 500m keep right. ☐
4 Take the motorway. ☐
5 In 500m, take the exit. ☐
6 At the roundabout, second exit. ☐
You've arrived at your destination!

 **learning tip**

> If you're a driver with a sat nav and know pretty much where you're going, turn it to French mode for additional practice with directions.

 **activity 3**

A **2.43** You can get disorientated in buildings too. You're in reception listening to various people asking for directions to: **le bureau du directeur financier, la cantine, le bureau du PDG (président directeur général), la salle de gym, le service du personnel, les salles de réunion** and le restaurant panoramique. See if you can place them on the correct floor in the grid below:

HÔTEL UNIVERS	
sixième étage	
cinquième étage	
quatrième étage	
troisième étage	
deuxième étage	
premier étage	
rez de chaussée	
sous-sol	

As you can see, 'to the first floor' is **au premier étage** and **au** is also the way to express 'on the' when talking of floors: **Le PDG est au cinquième étage** *The CEO is on the fifth floor*. Note that **premier** has a feminine form (**première**), the only ordinal number that does (**le premier étage, la première rue**).

B Put these instructions on how to get to a business meeting in the correct order:

☐ Mon bureau est en face de l'ascenseur, c'est la salle numéro huit.
☐ Descendez la ruelle et vous arrivez sur la Place du Marché.
☐ Entrez et montez au quatrième étage.
☐ Traversez la place et vous voyez un grand bâtiment blanc.
☐ Dans la rue Rabelais cherchez une petite rue à gauche, La Ruelle de la Fontaine.
☐ En sortant de la gare prenez la Rue Rabelais à droite.

language tip

The language of directions is useful for other walks of life. Watch out for the fact that droit can be a noun, an adjective or an adverb. When used to give directions it is an adverb with just one form: à droite. As a noun it can be both masculine and feminine: la droite ('the Right' of political parties); un droit ('a right' as in a legal right). As an adjective it agrees with the noun to which it refers (l'aile *wing* droite; un défenseur droit).

la politique	le sport
le premier ministre	la première division
la droite	l'aile droite
la gauche	un défenseur gauche
les partis de l'extrême droite	un avant-centre

 **activity 4**

The Wikipedia extract below explains why in France the terms 'left' and 'right' are used in politics. It has something to do with physical space and the position of the President, but what?

La distinction politique gauche/droite a été établie au XIXe siècle. On a pris l'habitude de parler de partis de droite et de partis de gauche dans les pays où les assemblées nationales élues siègent dans une salle en demi-cercle.

À la gauche du président de l'Assemblée parlementaire, quand il regarde la salle, siègent les partis socialistes, social-réformistes et radicaux, les partis sociaux-démocrates au centre, à sa droite les partis conservateurs et libéraux, et au fond à droite, les partis d'extrême droite.

In sickness and in health

For all of us, keeping well involves occasional visits to a doctor or chemist, where we'll receive another barrage of instructions.

 **activity 5**

A How do these lozenges work? How often do you need to take them and what do you need to do if the symptoms don't go away?

Sucez une pastille trois fois par jour.
Ne dépassez pas la dose.
Consultez un médecin si les symptômes persistent.

At the chemist's you may well want to ask for advice. **Qu'est-ce que vous avez contre ...** is the question 'What have you got for ...'. **Contre** actually means 'against' (think of pros and cons).

B **La toux** is a cough. What do you think these common ailments might be?

1 la diarrhée
2 un coup de soleil
3 des piqûres d'insecte

C **2.44** Now ask for something for each of these problems using **Qu'est-ce que vous avez contre ...?**; what is the advice you are given? You'll hear the verb **gratter** *to scratch*. You will also hear two words for 'tablet': **comprimé** and **cachet**.

symptom	cough	diarrhoea	sunburn	insect bite
cure				

(If **ciel** is 'sky', what do you think **un gratte-ciel** might be?)

In order to explain what is wrong, you will need the phrase **avoir mal à** *to have something wrong with*. It's not very scientific but it will get you to the seat of the problem. It's accompanied by parts of the body: **J'ai mal à la tête.** *I've got a headache.*

 activity 6

A 2.45 Look at the diagram. Practise the pronunciation of some parts of the body using the audio to help. You will also hear the very irregular plural of l'oeil *eye*, les yeux.

B 2.46 Now listen to these people and identify what is wrong. Tick off the parts of the body you hear on the diagram.

Avoir mal à is the equivalent of a number of different expressions in English ('I've got a headache/a sore throat'; 'my knee hurts' and so on). You'll have noticed the preposition à at work again, together with its variations, à la, à l', au, aux.

C 2.47 Have a go with the following and then check how you did with the audio:
head   ears   stomach   throat

Use avoir too for winter scourges such as colds and flu: avoir un rhume *to have a cold*; avoir la grippe *to have the flu*.

Should you have overindulged, you can describe the consequences by saying J'ai mal aux cheveux *I'm hungover*, literally 'my hair hurts'.

D 2.48 Play your part in the exchange at the doctor's:

- Bonjour, asseyez-vous, s'il vous plaît.
- Respond accordingly.
- Comment est-ce que je peux vous aider?
- Say you've got earache and a sore throat.
- Vous souffrez?
- Say yes, you can't eat and you can't sleep.
- Bon, voici un antibiotique. Vous devez prendre deux comprimés trois fois par jour. Finissez la bouteille.

---

 pronunciation activity

2.49 As in English, q is usually followed by u in French where it is always pronounced 'k' as in 'plaque'. Listen to these words:

quiche   quart   quarante

The letter 'q' was only imported into English as a result of the Norman invasion, so you will often find words that are spelt qu in French being rendered with a 'c' in English: 'communicate', communiquer; indicate, indiquer etc.

The letter c has two sounds in French, as in English: 'soft', like in the English 'centre', when it is in front of e, i or y and 'hard', like in the English 'cat', when it is before a, o, u and all other letters, or when it comes at the very end of a word. It is always soft if it has a cedilla:

cafard *cockroach, depression*   comment   d'accord
ça va   cent   ciel *sky*   ceinture *belt*

Ch is always pronounced like the English 'sh' in 'shop':

chaise *chair*   chaleur *heat*   chouette *super*

Problem solving

Did you notice how the doctor told you that you 'must' take two tablets? **Vous devez prendre deux comprimés.** You'll find **vous devez** again in the reading passage on the next page.

 **activity 7**

Help is at hand for a variety of gardening problems posed by the readers of this magazine. Read the extract about planting a shrub (**un arbuste**) in the ground or in a container; use the cognates and your gardening knowledge to work out what you should do:

Planter un arbuste. Vous devez d'abord creuser un trou suffisamment large pour installer confortablement la plante dans un mélange de terre de jardin et de compost. Dans les terres lourdes, vous devez mettre une couche de graviers au fond du trou pour améliorer le drainage. Pour les plantes en conteneur, vous devez décompacter la motte à l'aide d'un outil à dents. Comblez avec le mélange de terre et compost et arrosez.

Vous devez comes from the verb devoir, which has two meanings:

Je vous dois combien? *How much do I owe you?*, a useful alternative to C'est combien?
Je dois aller au supermarché. *I must go to the supermarket.*

 **activity 8**

A **2.50** Listen to this person running through the preparations for a visit. As you listen, fill in the gaps in the text with the appropriate part of devoir chosen from the list below. Bear in mind that devoir is irregular and use your experience of how verbs behave to make the correct choices: devons, doivent, dois, devez, dois, doit.

Je .... téléphoner pour un taxi pour nos visiteurs. Ils arrivent à la gare à neuf heures trente et ils .... être dans la salle du conseil à dix heures quinze pour la présentation qui commence à dix heures trente. Madeleine .... organiser les rafraîchissements et le technicien .... vérifier la connexion Internet. Toi, tu .... préparer un discours. Nous .... être totalement préparés pour cette visite; vous .... remuer ciel et terre pour assurer un succès.

Have you spotted the idiom 'moving heaven and earth'?

B Complete the table below for the full pattern for devoir:

je		nous	
tu		vous	
il/elle/on		ils/elles	

 **word builder**

The word confortablement *comfortably* and totalement *totally* are adverbs – words that describe verbs, adjectives and even other adverbs ('really slowly'). To build up your stock of adverbs, remember that English adverbs ending in '-ly' often have French equivalents ending in -ment.

The -ment ending is added to the feminine form of the adjective: lent *slow* → lente → lentement *slowly*. English also uses adjectives as a basis from which to create adverbs: 'comfortable' (adjective) → 'comfortably' (adverb).

A What adverbs can you create from the following:

normal   fondamental   rapide   régulier   heureux

There are exceptions. In the magazine text you met suffisamment *sufficiently*. Adjectives ending in -ant (suffisant *sufficient*) become -amment (suffisamment *sufficiently*) and those ending in -ent become -emment (évident, évidemment).

B So what will the adverbs derived from these adjectives be?

constant   récent   fréquent   courant

Is that really necessary ...?

As an alternative to **vous devez**, French has a very common expression, **il faut** *it's necessary; you should*. **Il faut** is an impersonal verb; like **il pleut** and **il neige** that you met in the previous chapter, it only exists in the **il** form.

brilliant activity 9

A Do the matching exercise on the next page to give people the help they need:

1 Je cherche une chambre pour la nuit.	a Il faut aller à la jardinerie.
2 Je voudrais un avis médical.	b Il faut regarder les horaires sur internet.
3 Quelles sont les heures du train?	c Il faut trouver un garage.
4 Nous cherchons des plantes pour le jardin.	d Il faut téléphoner à l'office de tourisme.
5 La voiture est en panne.	e Il faut aller à la pharmacie.

B **2.51** At the hotel reception a number of people are in need of help. They ask the question Qu'est-ce qu'il faut faire (pour) ...? to get advice. Listen and number the requests in the order you hear them:

☐ pay the bill   ☐ hire skis

☐ send a parcel   ☐ contact Monsieur Legrand

☐ visit the wine cellars   ☐ reserve tickets for the match

☐ book a room

Qu'est-ce qu'il faut faire pour contacter Monsieur Legrand? in English might be: 'What must I do to contact M. Legrand?'; 'How should I go about getting hold of M. Legrand?'; 'What do we need to do to contact M. Legrand?'

Look again at the question: Qu'est-ce qu'il faut faire pour visiter les caves? It's bristling with verbs! Il faut is usually followed by another verb in the infinitive: il faut faire, il faut contacter, il faut demander. The people at the hotel reception are all asking for instructions 'in order to do something'. How do they say 'in order to' and what follows?

C Once you've got to grips with the pattern, find out how to:
1 hire a car.
2 have an international driving licence (un permis de conduire).
3 organise a doctor's appointment.
4 go to the airport.

D Il faut is a handy phrase for giving advice and instruction. It's not quite so brusque as the imperative route that you met above but ought nevertheless to encourage people to action or stop them from making gaffes.

Sort the following into dinner party and business etiquette rules:

	Dinner party	Business
1 Il ne faut pas arriver tard pour le dîner.		
2 Il ne faut pas offrir des chrysanthèmes ni du vin de qualité inférieure.		
3 Il ne faut pas utiliser un prénom si vous ne connaissez pas la personne.		
4 Il ne faut pas mettre les coudes sur la table quand on mange.		
5 Il ne faut pas être impatient dans les réunions d'affaires.		
6 Il ne faut pas enlever la veste ni la cravate au bureau.		
7 Il ne faut pas fumer à table.		
8 Il ne faut pas entrer sans frapper.		

What social gaffes might you warn French friends and colleagues of when visiting the UK?

Test case

 **activity 10**

Play your role in these exchanges:

A 2.52
- Ask if the restaurant is on the fourth floor.
- Non, c'est est au cinquième. Vous pouvez prendre l'ascenseur ou l'escalator. En sortant, tournez à gauche.
- Ask if it's necessary to reserve a table in the restaurant.
- Normalement vous devez téléphoner à l'avance, mais aujourd'hui il y a des tables de libre.

B 2.53
- Ask what you have to do to hire a car.
- Vous devez aller à notre bureau à l'aéroport.
- Ask if you need to have an international driving licence.
- Non, vous devez avoir seulement votre permis de conduire anglais.
- Ask if you have to return (ramener) the car to the airport.

- Non, vous pouvez la ramener à notre agence en ville, si vous voulez.

C **2.54**

- Bonjour, je peux vous aider?
- Tell her you've got a sore arm and ask if they have anything for insect bites.
- Vous êtes allergique aux antihistaminiques?
- Say no, but you prefer to have a cream.
- Bien, voici, vous devez appliquer la crème trois fois par jour et si ça persiste, allez voir le médecin.
- Say thank you and double-check the dosage by saying what you think you must do.
- Oui, c'est ça.

 activity 11

A Recipes make good reading for imperatives. Here's one for un tartare de saumon:

Ingrédients:
150g de saumon
1 échalote
1 jus de citron
quelques brins de persil
quelques câpres ou cornichons
1 pointe de tabasco

Recette du Tartare de saumon:
Enlevez la peau du saumon.

Coupez en cubes le poisson et ajoutez une échalote finement hachée.

Mélangez puis incorporez le jus d'un citron, un peu de persil, un peu de gingembre, du cornichon haché ou des câpres.

Assaisonnez avec une pointe de tabasco, du sel, et du poivre du moulin.

Servez sur des toasts grillés.

Use a dictionary to work out what verbs these imperatives come from and what they mean: servez, assaisonnez, coupez, enlevez, mélangez.

B You began this chapter looking at instructions that you might see when in France or other French-speaking countries. There are two more expressions that are useful to know in order to stay on the right side of the law. Défense de and interdit are the equivalent of the English 'no' as in 'no parking' or 'don't' as in 'don't feed the ducks'.

What are you not permitted to do?

1 Défense d'entrer
2 Défense de marcher sur la pelouse
3 Stationnement interdit
4 Baignade interdite
5 Défense de fumer
6 Pique-nique interdit

11 Équilibre travail–vie

- Talk about future plans
- Learn how to say 'this'
- Meet **pourquoi** and **parce que**
- Make comparisons

So far you have used the present tense of verbs to talk about things that are going on now, but communication, of course, involves talking about the future and past too. In this chapter we'll look at ways in which you can say what you're going to be doing tomorrow, next week or next year.

 activity 1

Take a look at the time line below; it shows the words that help locate your plans.

today	tomorrow	next ...
aujourd'hui	demain demain matin demain après-midi demain soir	la semaine prochaine le mois prochain l'année prochaine

1 What gender is **mois**?
2 Where have you met **soir** before?
3 What kind of word is **prochain**?
The question word when asking about time is **quand** *when*.

Years and years

There are two words for 'year' in French, **un an** and **une année**. The distinction is quite subtle, so just remember that if you're using 'year' with an adjective ('this year', 'next year' etc) use **année** and when you're talking about age use **an** (il a dix ans). **Bonne année** is the standard greeting on **le premier janvier**.

Back to the future

 activity 2

Look at these newspaper headlines:

Le président part demain pour le Moyen-Orient

Une nouvelle famille va arriver dans 'La Résidence'

Les ministres vont discuter l'euro

Une vedette de la télé va aller en prison

Les Bleus vont aller en finale en juin

La France va gagner la coupe du Monde!

They all refer to future actions. Underline the verbs in the headlines to see how they go about doing this. The answer is ... in exactly the same way as in English! Use either the present tense, Le président part demain pour le Moyen-Orient *The president is leaving tomorrow for the Middle East*, or the present tense of aller plus a verb in the infinitive, La France va gagner la coupe *France is going to win the cup*. As in English, you can have two allers together: La vedette de la télé va aller en prison *The TV star is going to go to prison*.

 activity 3

A 2.55 Listen to a group of people talking about their plans for the future days, weeks and months. Two of the following activities are not mentioned by anyone. Which two?

Going to the cinema	Going to play tennis
Going out for dinner	Going to watch a match
Going to take the TGV	Going to leave for the States
Going to the theatre	Going to go on holiday
Going to meet a friend	Going to go to a meeting

B 2.55 Now listen again and choose which version of the verb was used to talk about the future activity:

1 je (joue/vais jouer)

2 je (vais/vais aller); je (rencontre/vais rencontrer); on (dîne/va dîner)

3 elle (est/va être) ; elle (assiste/va assister)
4 je (vais/vais aller) voir; il (part/va partir)
5 il (va/va aller); il (prend/va prendre); il (rentre/va rentrer)
6 nous (partons/allons partir); le mariage de notre fille (est/va être)

Find the time expressions that were used to reinforce the sense of 'future':
'this afternoon', 'tomorrow evening', 'next week', 'next year', 'in June', 'in
September'.

This and that

Look again at the words for 'this'.
Now that you are sensitised to
gender, it probably won't come as a
surprise that 'this' must agree with
the noun to which it refers. There's
an extra masculine form to look
out for, cet, which is used before
masculine words beginning with a
vowel or silent h.

Ce, cet, cette and ces are
demonstrative adjectives,
sometimes referred to as
'determiners' since, along with
words such as le, la and les,
they determine what you are
actually talking about.

masculine	feminine	plural (m & f)
ce matin cet après-midi	cette semaine	ces hommes ces femmes

 activity 4

A **2.56** Listen to the exchange between two women planning a shopping
trip. What does each woman want to buy? You'll hear the colours rose *pink*,
vert *green* and noir *black*.

B **2.56** Listen again, this time looking at the transcript of the dialogue. Fill
in the blanks with the appropriate version of ce.

● Qu'est-ce tu fais .... après-midi?
● Je vais faire du shopping.
● Je ne suis pas libre .... matin mais .... après-midi
ça va, je peux venir?
● Mais oui, bien sûr. Je cherche une tenue pour le mariage de ma fille.
Qu'est-ce que tu penses de .... tenue? Regarde la photo.
● Euh, ... photo n'est pas tellement facile à voir. De quelle
couleur est la tenue?

- On peut l'avoir en plusieurs couleurs. Voici. J'aime bien la rose mais qu'est-ce que tu penses de .... verte?
- Je préfère la rose. .... créations sont vraiment chic. Je vais voir s'il y a un pantalon. Tu vois .... pantalon noir, parfait pour le bureau!
- On va dépenser de l'argent, nous! On y va?

C How would you say:

1 This afternoon he's going to Paris.
2 I'm not working this week.
3 This October we're going to visit Marrakech.
4 She doesn't like these photos.
5 Are you going to catch this train?
6 They're going to be at the restaurant this evening.

To make sentences using aller plus an infinitive negative, the ne and pas go round the aller part only:

Je ne vais pas être à la maison ce soir.
I'm not going to be at home this evening.
Il ne va jamais aller à l'université.
He's never going to go to university.
Nous n'allons plus acheter cet appartement.
We're not going to buy this flat any more.

D 2.57 How would you say:
1 I'm not going to catch this train.
2 They're not going to be at the restaurant this evening.
3 We're not going to do anything this afternoon.

Listen to check your answers.

Diary dates

 activity 5

2.58 Here is your diary for next week. Your colleague has filled in a number of appointments that you don't yet know about. Listen as he explains what you are going to be doing and complete your diary with the details:

	lundi 1 avril	mardi 2 avril	mercredi 3 avril	jeudi 4 avril	vendredi 5 avril
le matin			Visite à Concourès	Au bureau	
l'après-midi	Réunion du service personnel		Au bureau		
le soir	Salle de gym			Cinéma 21h00	

Did you notice the dates? **Vendredi le cinq** can mean both 'Friday the 5th' and 'on Friday the 5th', and **le deux avril** 'the 2nd of April' and 'on the 2nd of April'. Unlike English, French uses cardinal numbers for dates (**deux, trois, quatre**), except for the first of the month (**le premier avril, le premier juillet**).

 activity 6

2.59 Listen and fill in the dates for the French public holidays (**un jour férié**):

La fête nationale	
la fête du travail	
le jour de l'an	
l'Armistice	
la Toussaint	
Noël	

Whilst France and England share some public holiday dates, there are others that are uniquely French. Use an online encyclopaedia to research public holidays further.

 activity 7

2.60 Now listen to a conversation about Morocco.

In the following list there is one activity that the traveller does not take part in. Which one is it? **visiter la médina; étudier la culture; aller au jardin botanique; passer deux jours à Casablanca; faire un périple à la montagne; essayer la cuisine**

What reflexive verb do you hear?

 activity 8

A Imagine that you are going on holiday to Tunisia. Make sentences from the key words below about your forthcoming trip using aller plus the verbs listed. The first one is done for you as an example.

1 aller/Tunisie/au mois de mai
Je vais aller en Tunisie au mois de mai.

2 visiter/les ruines romaines/Carthage
3 choisir/hôtels traditionnels
4 manger/restaurants pas touristiques
5 prendre/train et car

B **2.61** Now listen to an interview with someone who is going to Tunisia, and answer the following questions:

1 Why isn't this traveller flying to Tunisia?
2 How were the booking arrangements made?

You'll notice that the question word **pourquoi** *why* can generate a response beginning with **parce que** *because*. Parce que can begin a sentence or connect two parts of a sentence together:

Pourquoi la Tunisie?
Pourquoi est-ce que vous allez en Tunisie?
Parce que je veux voir Tunis.
Je vais en Tunisie parce que je veux voir Tunis.

The e from **que** is replaced with an apostrophe in front of a vowel:
Il prend le bateau parce qu'il déteste les avions.

Cause and effect

 activity 9

2.62 Match the questions and answers and then listen to check:

1 Pourquoi est-ce qu'il va voyager en Tunisie?	a Je vais les prendre en mai parce qu'il va faire moins chaud.
2 Vous allez choisir des hôtels traditionnels, pourquoi?	b Ça va être plus rapide et plus facile.
3 Pourquoi est-ce que vous allez prendre vos vacances en mai?	c Parce qu'il va y aller l'année prochaine.

4 Vous allez réserver par internet, pourquoi?	d Il va y aller pour connaître la culture.
5 Pourquoi est-ce qu'il ne va pas visiter le Maroc?	e Parce que nous recherchons une expérience culturelle.

Note the use of pronouns in the answers, in particular their position. When you use aller and the infinitive to express the future the pronouns are placed before the infinitive: Je vais les prendre. Did you spot y meaning 'there'? Y is a pronoun too, so follows the same placement rules: il va y aller.

Pros and cons

The Tunisian traveller has decided to go in May quand il fait moins chaud *when it's less hot/cooler* and is booking online because it is plus rapide et moins cher *quicker and less expensive/cheaper*.

Making plans involves weighing up options. You can add '-er' to English adjectives to make a comparative adjective (one that allows you to compare two things): 'quick', 'quicker'; 'cool', 'cooler'. Or you can add 'more' or 'less' ('more expensive'). French adjectives become comparative through the use of plus *more* or moins *less*: plus facile, moins chaud. There is a common exception to the rule in both French and English: 'good' → 'better'; bon → meilleur.

 activity 10

A 2.63 Listen to these people talking about factors that might impact on their holiday choices. What comment is made about:

1 travelling by boat ....

2 holidaying in May ....

3 mountain climbing ....

4 Brittany ....

5 the train ....

In these exchanges you will have heard:

L'alpinisme est plus dangereux que la plongée sous-marine.
Cette région est moins intéressante que la Bretagne.

They demonstrate how to say something is 'more' or 'less' (interesting, dangerous) 'than': plus/moins ... que.

Example:
La ville médiévale est plus pittoresque que la ville moderne.
Ces hôtels sont moins traditionnels que les riads.
Il fait plus froid dans le nord.

You'll note that the plus/moins and que wrap themselves around the adjective, which still must agree in number and gender with the noun it describes. You don't have to have something to compare with: 'it's colder in the North'. The position of the adjective doesn't change; if it normally goes after the noun, it stays there with plus/moins in front of it:

une plus grande ville
une ville plus pittoresque
un moins joli hôtel
un hôtel moins convenable

B How would you say:

1 This hotel is less convenient than the Hotel Mercure.
2 This square is bigger than the Place de la Concorde.
3 It's colder here than in Belgium.
4 Holidays in France are more popular.
5 I'm going to visit the souk because it's more interesting.
6 Is this train faster?

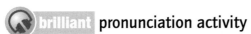 **brilliant language tip**

> Collect phrases and sayings that include plus and moins for future use. Use a dictionary to discover what they mean:
>
> de plus en plus
> de moins en moins
> plus ou moins
> ni plus ni moins
> Plus ça change, plus c'est la même chose.

brilliant pronunciation activity

2.64 As in English, the letter **g** has a hard and a soft sound, but the soft sound is like the 's' in the English word 'treasure'. Listen to this soft sound before an e or an i:

gentil   village   ombrage *shade*   gîte

Compare it with:

golf   gaz   guide

Gn, on the other hand, sounds like the 'ny' sound in the middle of the English word 'onions':

oignon   champignon   Dordogne

The letter j always sounds like the soft version of a g:

je   jeune   bijou   jaune *yellow*

Test case

 activity 11

Play your part in the dialogues. Take a few minutes beforehand to check up on your vocabulary:

A 2.65

- Parlez-moi un peu de vos projets de vacances.
- Say that you're going to spend two weeks in Madagascar (à Madagascar).
- Quand est-ce que vous allez visiter Madagascar?
- Say you're going to go there on June the 14th.
- Pourquoi en juin?
- Say because it's cooler and it doesn't rain.
- Qu'est-ce que vous allez faire?
- Say that you're going to see the plants and animals in the national parks (all of these words are similar to the English).
- Vous vous intéressez à l'écotourisme alors?
- Say yes, and you prefer more active holidays. This trip is perfect.

B 2.66

- Ask your friend what he's going to do this weekend.
- Je vais passer le weekend en Normandie.
- Ask why he's going to Normandy.
- Parce que je vais assister au mariage de mon cousin.
- Ask what time he's going to leave.
- Je vais quitter Paris ce soir à environ dix-neuf heures. Je dois être à la mairie à dix heures demain matin. Et toi, qu'est ce que tu fais ce week-end?
- Say you're going to spend it at home with a good book!

- Alors, tu vas bien t'amuser! Bon week-end.
- Wish him a good weekend.

 activity 12

Read this travel piece on Marrakech and answer the questions below.

Arriver à Marrakech, c'est franchir les portes du temps. Vous allez cheminer dans les ruelles pittoresques de la vieille ville médiévale, la médina. Les souks offrent tout ce que le voyageur attend: couleurs, ambiances, parfums, visages souriants et accueillants. Celui de Semmarine est consacré aux vêtements. Dans les petites rues qui le bordent, vous allez trouver de nombreux vêtements typiques réalisés selon les procédés traditionnels. Quelques échoppes y proposent aussi des bijoux ou des antiquités. Et sur la fameuse place Jemaa El Fna, vous allez entrer dans un univers médiéval où conteurs, commerçants et charmeurs de serpents rivalisent pour capter l'attention des passants. À portée de regard se dresse l'emblème de la ville: le splendide minaret de la mosquée de la Koutoubia. Un rêve pour ceux qui aiment flâner et apprendre, sentir et ressentir. Prenez le temps de regarder et d'écouter ...

1 What is the emblem of the city ?
2 What could you expect to see in the Jemaa El Fna?
3 From which period in history does the city date?
4 Marrakech has a long history of trade. What is for sale these days?
5 What are you instructed to do at the end of the passage?

Brush up on your adjectives, underline them in the text and check out any that you don't recognise or can't guess.

12   Je suis venu, j'ai vu, j'ai vaincu ...

- Talk about the past
- Describe a series of events

Past master

Up to now you have been concentrating on talking about the present and planning for the future. Learning about how verbs behave in the present tense (regular, irregular, verb families, negatives, questions) will stand you in good stead for talking about the past. Have a look at these questions:

Qu'est-ce que <u>vous avez visité</u> hier? *What <u>did you visit</u> yesterday?*
<u>Vous avez mangé</u> où samedi dernier? *Where <u>did you eat</u> last Saturday?*

Here is one possible reply:
<u>J'ai visité</u> le quartier Latin et <u>j'ai trouvé</u> un restaurant vietnamien où <u>j'ai mangé</u> du pho. *<u>I visited</u> the Latin Quarter and <u>I found</u> a Vietnamese restaurant where <u>I ate</u> pho.*

If you're unfamiliar with 'pho' you'll find a recipe on the following French website: www.saveursdumonde.net.

Note that in English **J'ai visité le quartier Latin** could mean 'I <u>have</u> (I've) visit<u>ed</u> the Latin quarter' or 'I visited the Latin quarter' depending on the context – two for the price of one in French! And, therefore, the question **vous avez visité?** can mean 'have you visited?' and 'did you visit?'.

 **activity 1**

A **2.67** Listen to someone describing their first encounter with pho. Translate the text into English and underline the verbs:

On a goûté le pho pour la première fois dans un restaurant à Hanoï. Nos amis ont visité le Vietnam en janvier dernier et ils ont parlé de sa cuisine délicieuse. Nous avons mentionné le restaurant au réceptionniste dans notre hôtel. Il a proposé un taxi pour y aller. Au restaurant on a demandé un pho traditionnel. On a très bien mangé!

B Work back from the verbs you've underlined to their infinitives:

on a goûté → ....

nos amis ont visité → ....

ils ont parlé → ....

nous avons mentionné → ....

il a proposé → ....

on a demandé → ....

on a mangé → ....

When you create **present** tense patterns in French you do so by changing the endings of the verb (je visit<u>e</u>; nous visit<u>ons</u>). In the **perfect** (the name of this past tense) you create the pattern by using an auxiliary verb and a past participle, which equates directly to the structure in English:

auxiliary verb	past participle
I have j'ai	*visited* visité

An auxiliary verb is sometimes referred to as a 'helping verb'. The past participle is the verb form used with auxiliaries to create the perfect tense. In English these often end in '-ed', but there are many irregulars: 'seen', 'taken', 'drunk' etc.

Look again at the verbs you have met and you will notice that, as in English, only the auxiliary changes; the past participle remains the same: <u>j'ai</u> visité; <u>on a</u> visité; <u>vous avez</u> visité and so on. You are in fact using the present tense of avoir as your auxiliary verb.

 **activity 2**

How should these sentences look?

1 Tu .... regardé le match à la télé?

2 Mes parents .... voyagé aux États-Unis en vacances.

3 Marie-Claire n'........................ pas aimé le film.

4 Samedi, nous .... joué avec la Xbox toute la journée.

5 Qu'est-ce que vous .... pensé de ce camping?

6 J'ai trouvé une tenue, mais je n'........................ pas trouvé les chaussures.

Happy endings ...

How is the past participle created? Once again, verb families play a part and influence how past participles are formed. For -er verbs, remove the er and add é; for -ir verbs, remove the -ir and add i; and for -re verbs remove the -re and add u.

-er	-ir	-re
travaillé	fini	répondu
acheté	choisi	attendu

 activity 3

A What would the past participles of these verbs be? aimer, perdre, réagir *to react*, vendre, changer, rendre, saisir *to seize*, entendre.

B 2.68 Complete the following description by inserting the correct participles and listen to check your answers.

Mercredi, j'ai .... (travailler) au bureau le matin. J'ai .... (réussir) à contacter notre nouveau client. J'ai .... (finir) mon travail à midi et j'ai .... (déjeuner) au restaurant avec Christine. Elle m'a .... (attendre) dans le bar. On a .... (discuter) du match et on a .... (décider) d'acheter des billets pour le prochain. L'après-midi j'ai .... (rencontrer) Monsieur Dufour à seize heures. Le soir, j'ai .... (passer) un appel Skype à ma compagne avant d'aller au lit. Je n'ai pas bien .... (dormir).

When you use a negative, the ne ... pas wraps around the bit of avoir, not the past participle: Marie-Claire <u>n</u>'a <u>pas</u> aimé le film; je <u>n</u>'ai <u>pas</u> bien dormi.

 activity 4

2.69 Listen to the grumpy old woman and work out why she is about to miss out on something and what that something is.

Irregular goings on

Take a look at these phrases:
j'ai fait *I've done/I did*
j'ai mis *I've put/I put*
j'ai pris *I've taken/I took*

Faire, mettre and prendre all end in -re so these past participles are irregular.

Many verbs that were irregular in the present tense will continue to be irregular in the perfect:

infinitive	past participle
être	été
avoir	eu
pouvoir	pu
vouloir	voulu
devoir	dû
voir	vu

There's a theme developing with the past participles of verbs that have -oir in the ending. Look at **pouvoir, vouloir** and **devoir**. What might the past participles of the verbs **recevoir** and **savoir** be?

 **brilliant** activity 5

2.70 Here's someone talking about a recent trip. Which Paris landmarks do you hear mentioned? Tick them off:

☐ Eiffel Tower ☐ Musée d'Orsay ☐ Notre Dame cathedral
☐ Arc de Triomphe ☐ les Halles ☐ Grande Arche
☐ Montmartre

1 When was the visit?
2 What two forms of transport were used?
3 Did you hear the verbs? Which parts of **avoir** did you hear?

brilliant learning tip

There are shortcuts to learning irregularities. New verbs created by adding a prefix will follow the pattern of the original verb.

prendre: comprendre to understand, **apprendre** to learn, **surprendre** to surprise
mettre: promettre to promise, **compromettre** to compromise, **remettre** to put back
tenir: retenir to retain, **appartenir** to belong, **contenir** to contain
venir: revenir to return, **devenir** to become, **convenir** to suit
Present tense: Je prends le bus. J'apprends le français.
Perfect tense: J'ai pris le bus. J'ai appris le français.

Shaggy dog stories

 activity 6

A 2.71 It's been a disastrous day. Listen and get the events in the correct order.

☐ Wanted to phone for a cab.
☐ Searched for my mobile.
☐ Missed the bus.
☐ Left my umbrella at my parents'.
☐ Ran.
☐ Didn't hear the alarm.

Why was all the fuss pointless?

B 2.72 Play your part in the conversation:

- Ask if your partner has had a good day.
- **Pas tellement.**
- Ask why it hasn't been good.
- D'abord j'ai dû faire une présentation, ensuite j'ai passé la journée avec des clients très difficiles. Je n'ai pas eu le temps de manger à midi. J'ai entendu que ma collègue a été promue et moi, je n'ai pas eu de promotion. Finalement, pas de trains ce soir et j'ai pris un taxi pour rentrer. Et toi?
- Tell him that you're OK. You sold a painting. You took the bus to go into town and went to the sales (**faire les soldes**). You bought some shoes.
- Alors, pour certains la vie est belle. On dîne à quelle heure? J'ai vraiment faim.

1 Why was the day dismal for your partner?
2 What do you think the English equivalent of **pour certains la vie est belle** might be?

Déjeuner du matin

 activity 7

A The disasters are mounting up! Read the first part of the poem **Déjeuner du matin**, published in 1946 by Jacques Prévert, and work out which two actions are being described.

Déjeuner du matin

Il a mis le café
Dans la tasse
Il a mis le lait
Dans la tasse de café
Il a mis le sucre
Dans le café au lait
Avec la petite cuiller
Il a tourné
Il a bu le café au lait
Et il a reposé la tasse
Sans me parler

Il a allumé
Une cigarette
Il a fait des ronds
Avec la fumée
Il a mis les cendres
Dans le cendrier
Sans me parler
Sans me regarder

When he wrote his poem, Jacques Prévert could not possibly have guessed how useful it would be for people trying to make sense of the perfect tense. Here are some other exercises based on the poem for you to try:

B

1 Recount the story from a first person point of view, e.g. 'I made the coffee' and 'without talking to her' (**sans lui parler**).

2 Nothing happened so tell the story in the negative.

3 Work out all the infinitives of the verbs used in the text.

Not to be ...

 activity 8

Here's the final part of **Déjeuner du matin**. Enjoy the emotion of the finale and then look for the way in which Prévert says 'he got up' and 'he left'.

Il s'est levé
Il a mis
Son chapeau sur sa tête
Il a mis son manteau de pluie
Parce qu'il pleuvait
Et il est parti
Sous la pluie
Sans une parole
Sans me regarder

Et moi j'ai pris
Ma tête dans ma main
Et j'ai pleuré

(Source: **Paroles** © Éditions Gallimard)

Il s'est levé *he got up* and il est parti *he left* are still clearly actions that are in the past but you will notice that the auxiliary verb has changed. In order to create the perfect tense, French uses either the present tense of être or of avoir as the auxiliary verb. You'll have worked out that se lever is a reflexive verb and all reflexive verbs use être as their auxiliary. Now might be a good time to check up on the present tenses of both avoir and être to fix them in your mind and to double check the pronunciation of each.

Gossip

 activity 9

2.73 La Résidence continues to be a source of anecdote and drama. All is not well in Apartment 1. Listen to the latest exchange between neighbours. Complete the past tense with the right parts of either être or avoir as you listen.

- Salut, Marianne, ça va aujourd'hui?
- Oui, ça va bien, mais tu .... entendu la dernière d'Antoine?
- Non, dis-moi, qu'est-ce qui s'..................... passé?
- Il .... quitté Nathalie! Il .... tombé amoureux d'une fille de dix-huit ans. Il .... allé à la fête d'anniversaire de Philippe. La fille y .... venue avec un autre.
- Non, ce n'est pas vrai. Il n'est plus à la maison alors?

● Non, il .... parti lundi dernier. Il .... allé chercher du pain le soir et il n'..................... pas rentré.

● Et Nathalie, comment va-t-elle?

● Je ne sais pas, elle n'..................... pas sortie de l'appartement. Sa mère .... arrivée hier mais nous, on n'..................... rien appris ...

1 What has Antoine been up to?

2 When did he leave?

3 What's the news about Nathalie?

There's a useful question in this exchange. Qu'est-ce qui s'est passé? means 'what's happened?' As you can see, it involves a reflexive verb and so uses être in the past: s'est passé. If you want to ask what *is* happening you would say Qu'est-ce qui <u>se passe</u>?.

In the exercise you've just done you have met some of the other verbs that use être as an auxiliary in the past. What are they?

There are actually only thirteen verbs to learn, plus a few more that are created by the prefix route described earlier

brilliant learning tip

There are different ways of memorising these être verbs. They are mostly verbs that indicate some kind of movement: descendre *to go down*; entrer *to go in*; partir *to leave*. Mnemonics are popular: **MR VANS TRAMPED** represents the first letters of each of the verbs and in **ADVENT** each letter stands for one of the verbs and its opposite, plus one extra!

<u>a</u>rriver – partir

<u>d</u>escendre – monter

<u>v</u>enir – aller

<u>e</u>ntrer – sortir

<u>n</u>aître – mourir

<u>t</u>omber – rester

retourner

Remember that, as an auxiliary verb, être changes meaning from 'to be' to 'to have' so je suis allé means 'I <u>have</u> gone' not 'I <u>am</u> going'.

Agreeing to disagree

 **activity 10**

2.74 Listen to the conversation. You will hear a useful expression avoir besoin de which means 'to need' (literally 'to have need of').

1 What did the man do before he met his wife?
2 And afterwards?
3 What pick-me-up do the two men choose?

Look at these sentences:

Nous sommes allés au château.
Elle est venue me chercher au restaurant.

Something has happened to the past participles of these être verbs. You can't hear the change so you won't need to worry about it when you're speaking. Think about adjectives and work out what is going on. The past participles 'agree' with the people (or things) doing the action: Elle est venue; nous sommes allés. You add an e if the person is feminine, s if there is more than one person and es if those people are all feminine.

Note that the negative is still formed by wrapping the être part in ne ... pas: Ils ne sont pas restés dans un hôtel; Je ne suis jamais allé(e) en Suisse.

 **activity 11**

A Complete the following account by changing the infinitive in brackets to the perfect tense:

La semaine dernière Corinne (aller) à Clermont Ferrand. Elle (avoir) un rendez-vous d'affaires dans la ville, mais elle a des amies là-bas aussi. Après le rendez-vous elle (rencontrer) ses amies et elles (aller) déjeuner ensemble. Claudine et Nathalie (proposer) une visite de la ville. Elles (partir) du restaurant à quatorze heures et la visite (finir) à dix-sept heures. Elles (décider) de prendre des cocktails à dix-neuf heures dans un bar avant d'aller manger le soir. Elles (sortir) du restaurant et (finir) la soirée avec un digestif. Corinne (quitter) Clermont-Ferrand très contente de son voyage d'affaires!

B 2.75 On her way to meet her friends Corinne witnessed a minor accident. Listen to her description; which statements are true and which false?

	True	False
1 Elle a quitté le bureau à douze heures trente.		
2 Elle n'a rien entendu.		
3 Elle a vu une voiture et un camion.		
4 Le chauffeur de camion a eu le temps de s'arrêter.		
5 L'automobiliste a crié et a accusé le chauffeur du camion de rouler trop vite.		

Travellers' tales

 activity 12

Below is the prequel to the Paris visit. Read it and note down the words that help you join sentences together; you'll be able to use them in the next exercise:

next ....

first ....

then ....

so ....

> D'abord je suis arrivé tard à l'aéroport pour le vol pour Roissy Charles de Gaulle. J'ai dû courir jusqu'à la porte de départ. Ensuite mon voyage est allé de mal en pis. L'avion a été en retard donc je suis arrivé à la Gare du Nord à vingt-deux heures, puis je n'ai pas trouvé la station de taxis et j'ai dû marcher jusqu'à l'hôtel – deux kilomètres avec ma valise!

 activity 13

A 2.76 Now select from the columns in the grid on the next page to make sentences up about your own trip. Put what you choose into a sequence that describes the trip from start to finish as per your diary entries (use the connectors that you've just discovered to help). Don't forget, if you're a woman doing this you'll need the extra **e** on some of the past participles!

J' je	ai suis	visité voyagé fait pris regardé dîné allé(e) parti(e) arrivé(e) resté(e) rentré(e)	dans un hôtel au centre dans un restaurant vietnamien la Tour Eiffel au restaurant de l'hôtel le quinze avril le dix-neuf avril les peintures au Musée d'Orsay un tour en bateau mouche Château de Versailles en avion la Grande Arche

Thursday	Arr. 15th – plane. Stayed centrally.
Friday	Visited Eiffel Tower and went on bateau mouche tour. Evening – dinner in Vietnamese restaurant.
Saturday	Musée d'Orsay, saw paintings. Metro to Grande Arche.
Sunday	9am left for Versailles by train. Returned at 6pm. Dinner in hotel restaurant.
Monday	Dep. Paris – plane 14:05.

B 2.77 You've been sharing holiday reminiscences with two friends. What questions might you have asked to get the following answers? Listen to check.

1 Nous avons visité Paris en août.
2 Non, pas par le train, on y est allé en avion.
3 Non, on n'a pas fait le tour en bateau mouche, on a pris le bus.
4 L'avion est parti à vingt et une heures quarante-cinq.
5 Oui, nous nous sommes promenés sur les Champs-Elysées et un peu partout.
6 Oui, on s'est très bien amusé.

What might you now be able to say about your own past holidays or weekend breaks?

 pronunciation activity

2.78 The combination th is not as regular a feature of French as it is of English. In French it sounds a bit like the 't' in 'table' and is made by expelling the sound from the front of your mouth with the tip of your tongue behind your front teeth. Think about the sound you make when you 'tut' at someone or something.

thé   théâtre   théorie

When t occurs before io it's not pronounced 'sh' as in English, but like 's' plus 'y':

nation   station   addition *bill*

S has two sounds – at the beginning of the word it is like the 's' of 'sit':

saumon   super   sport

If it appears within a word, it is generally pronounced like the 's' in 'rose':

expositions   musée   voisin

À la recherche du temps perdu

You should take every opportunity to look at how the perfect tense is used in French. Grasping its relationship with other ways of speaking in the past is all part of the process and something we've only touched on here!

It will help you to know that it is the tense you need to talk about:

An action *completed* in the past:
Vous avez fait du jogging dimanche?
An action repeated and *completed* a number of times in the past:
J'ai fait du jogging cinq fois la semaine dernière.
A series of actions *completed* in the past:
Il a fait du jogging, a nagé et a fait du vélo samedi.

Look again at the exercise about Corinne and you will see that the account covers a number of activities that she and her friends undertook one after the other. Each action was completed before the next happened.

Because the perfect tense expresses actions that are over and done with, it's often accompanied by a reference to a specific moment in time: Hier, j'ai vu un film *Yesterday I saw a film*; J'ai visité le Maroc il y a deux ans *I visited Morocco two years ago*; En août dernier je suis allé(e) aux États-Unis *Last August I went to the United States*.

Bearing this in mind, have a look at these sentences:

J'étudie le français depuis janvier. *I've studied French since January.*
J'étudie le français depuis deux ans. *I've studied French for two years.*

In English the perfect tense is used in both situations but in French you must use the present. The logic behind the use of the present is that the action *is still going on*, even though it may have started some time ago. (Depuis means both 'since' and 'for'.)

Back to the future

 activity 14

Complete the timeline below with the expressions for last month, last year, yesterday afternoon, yesterday evening:

la semaine dernière	hier hier matin	aujourd'hui

 activity 15

2.79 Play your part in the conversation:

- Vous apprenez le français depuis combien de temps?
- Say you've been learning it since March.
- Vous parlez très bien! Vous avez appris d'autres langues?
- Say that you learnt Spanish ten years ago.
- Vous parlez espagnol encore?
- Say no, last year you went to Spain but did not speak the language. You have forgotten the essential words (les mots essentiels).
- Dommage! Vous avez déjà visité la France?
- Say no, you've never been (use aller) to France but you did spend a weekend in Brussels last May.

 learning tip

As with English, past participles also function as adjectives. When they're used as adjectives the usual rules of agreement apply: du pain grillé, une porte fermée *a closed door*, les objets trouvés *lost property* (literally 'found objects'), des pommes de terre sautées.

Dwelling on the past ...

 activity 16

A 2.80 Listen to the description of a holiday in Brittany and answer the questions:

1 What did the holidaymakers think of Brittany?
2 What time did they get to their destination?
3 Where did they stay?
4 What did they do on their first night?
5 Where did Luc want to go?
6 What day did the holidaymaker go back to work?

B Look at the perfect tense verbs in the transcript.

1 Were the travellers men? Women? A man and a woman? How do you know?
2 Why is it **nous sommes revenus** and not **nous avons revenus**?

Can you spot two occasions when the perfect tense is *not* used?

La Bretagne, c'était formidable! *Brittany was fantastic!*
Le monastère était magnifique. *The monastery was magnificent.*

The monastery at Mont St Michel was magnificent well before the travellers arrived, not just on the day they chose to visit, and Brittany too was a fantastic place before, during and after the trip. In neither case can you use the perfect, so you have a sneak preview of the *imperfect* tense of être!

For now, treat c'était as a useful phrase meaning 'it was'. It's handy when you want to comment on something you have done or an experience you have had. It allows you to say what something was like rather than simply recount the events that took place:

La Tour Eiffel, c'était une expérience inoubliable *unforgettable*!
On a vu le dernier film de Luc Besson. C'était incroyable!
J'ai mangé de la choucroute. C'était délicieux!
Elle a reçu des fleurs de son mari. C'était une surprise!

 activity 17

2.81 Following the examples above, how might you say:

1 You've visited the Palais des Papes in Avignon and it was extraordinary!
2 You've tasted wine in Beaujolais. It was an unforgettable experience!

3 You've skied in the Alps. It was wonderful!
4 You went to Martinique. It was very, very good!

Can you find another example of the imperfect tense in Prévert's poem? It's to do with describing what the weather *was* like.

Test case

 activity 18

2.82 Play your part in the exchange. As you do, take time to celebrate how far you've come in learning French:

- Salut, comment vas-tu?
- Return the greeting and respond to the enquiry positively.
- Qu'est-ce tu fais ici?
- Say that you have come to visit Nathalie.
- Tiens, moi aussi. As-tu vu Nathalie avant son départ en vacances?
- Say no and ask where she's gone.
- Elle et ses enfants sont partis passer le mois de juillet en Provence.
- Ask why Nathalie went to Provence.
- Tiens, tu n'as pas entendu? Son mari a quitté la maison en mai. Il est parti vivre avec une fille de dix-huit ans! C'était tragique!
- Say no and ask if he is still (toujours) living with the girl.
- Non, elle a décidé d'aller travailler à l'étranger, en Afrique je crois.
- Ask if Antoine has returned to his flat.
- Non, pas encore, il attend le retour de Nathalie, mais il ne va pas être content. Elle a trouvé un nouveau copain.
- Say he must accept the situation. He left and Nathalie has changed.
- Oh, je dois partir maintenant. Je suis contente de t'avoir vu. A bientôt.
- Say 'yes, me too, see you soon.'

Blogging

 activity 19

Here's an extract from a blog. The woman is talking about having made her weekend better by providing a special treat.

1 What did she decide to make?
2 Which recipe did she use?
3 When did she do the cooking?

4 How did she test the results?

5 Who else benefited?

6 What did he think of them?

> Quel meilleur moyen d'oublier les mauvais moments du week-end que de s'offrir une douceur? Puisque nous sommes en période de Chandeleur, j'ai décidé de faire des crêpes. Hier, j'ai préparé une pâte à crêpes en suivant la recette de mon amie Aude. En fait, j'ai fait cuire les crêpes pendant la sieste des filles. J'ai mangé la dernière pour goûter. Hum, c'est bon une crêpe toute chaude! Les crêpes mettent tout le monde d'accord, surtout lorsqu'elles sont fourrées au chocolat. En fin d'après-midi, nous en avons apporté à Jacques, notre voisin. Il vient de m'envoyer un email: les crêpes étaient 'succulentes'! Merci Aude pour ta recette!
>
> (Source: One Thing in a French Day: **http://onethinginafrenchday. podbean.com/**)

The four skills

You will have gathered by now that learning French on your own will take you beyond the pages of this book. That's just as it should be since a single text can't possibly embrace everyone's motivations and needs. A degree of independence in learning is both necessary and healthy.

Trade secrets

The professionals often speak of 'the four skills': speaking, listening, reading and writing. Effectively these encompass what you can do with language once you've learned it. Although these skills interact, you can, for the purposes of learning, consider each separately.

Speaking

There are a number of tricks to adopt to ease yourself into speaking French.

Forward planning

Getting started in a conversation is often the most challenging step. Gather together some opening gambits to get you going. Greetings are always a good idea, as are expressions to catch someone's attention: Pardon; S'il vous plaît, monsieur; Pouvez-vous m'aider?; Je suis anglais(e), irlandais(e) etc.

If you have time, put a little thought into what you might say or what might be said to you. No conversation is entirely predictable but if you have some idea of what you want to say it frees you up to listen more closely to the person you're talking to. This strategy works particularly well in the day-to-day exchanges that you might have with people offering services and goods.

Set pieces

Don't undervalue the set phrase. You've met a number already that are appropriate to certain contexts (e.g. shopping: Je voudrais; C'est combien?) or to certain functions (slowing down the French spoken to you: Parlez plus lentement, s'il vous plaît). Learn these to the point where you can produce them almost without thinking.

 **activity 1**

Develop a bank of useful interjections to help keep a conversation going. Match French and English up to start your collection:

1 D'accord.	a *I don't believe so.*
2 Bon.	b *It's very good.*
3 Je ne sais pas.	c *OK.*
4 C'est pas vrai.	d *I think so.*
5 Tiens …	e *Good.*
6 Désolé(e).	f *Well …*
7 C'est très bien.	g *It's not true.*
8 Je ne crois pas.	h *I don't know.*
9 Je pense que oui.	i *Sorry.*

Make a point of looking out for exclamations that are particularly French, such as: **Bah non!** *Rubbish!*; **Euh … Er …**; **Mince!** *Drat!*; **Santé!** *Cheers!*; **Voyons!** *Really!*; **Zut!** *Blast!* You'll find more interjections and colourful expressions here: **www.bbc.co.uk/languages/french/cool/interjections.shtml**.

Train your brain to use what is said to you in order to form a response:

- Il habite Paris, votre fils?
- Oui, oui, il habite Paris.

Make time to think by reusing parts of conversation:

- Qu'est-ce qu'elle fait? Elle lave la voiture.
- Elle lave la voiture? Je dois faire ça aussi.

Putting the words together

So you know what you should have said but what came out of your mouth was less than perfect! This is quite common at the start of language learning and the best advice is to persevere. The more you speak, the more you improve your ability to do so.

Practice in speaking when you are learning on your own needs some thought and may take you down avenues of concern for friends and family! Develop the habit of talking to yourself as you go about daily routines. Download some French music and sing along. Look for online opportunities to engage in role play (among the BBC's French courses for example, **http://www.bbc.co.uk/languages/french/**).

It's quite remarkable how quickly you will develop a second sense about right and wrong. If you get stuck for something to say or if you feel that you haven't quite hit the nail on the head, store the moment up for research and revision later.

Make a point of having the audio in your car to brush up on rules and fix language in your mind. Say set phrases and new vocabulary out loud as many times as it takes to memorise them. Use questions and statements as models of useful language, repeat them and change them until word perfect.

Example:
Je voudrais un kilo de pommes et deux cent cinquante grammes de cerises, s'il vous plaît.
Je voudrais un kilo d'oignons et deux cent cinquante grammes de champignons, s'il vous plaît.
Je voudrais un demi-kilo de carottes et cinq cents grammes de poireaux, s'il vous plaît.

Making sense of what you hear

The understanding part of listening can be challenging. 'They all speak so fast' is a common complaint. Any new language sounds like a continuous stream before you have developed enough vocabulary and structural knowledge to isolate individual words. But as a beginner, you don't need to try to understand every word. Even in your own language, you naturally block out 'white noise' (words irrelevant to understanding) in order to concentrate on the relatively small amount of language that conveys meaning.

The art of undertaking this process in French lies in knowing where the key words are likely to occur. This means having a working knowledge of the rules and being able to predict vocabulary to listen out for.

Example: You're enquiring about train departure times:

- Le train pour Marseille part à quelle heure, s'il vous plaît?
- Bon, voyons, euh il part à quatorze heures quarante-sept du quai numéro cinq.

The only thing of real interest to you is the time. You know that you need to listen for numbers and that you'll hear the word heures. Use that information to navigate the response and to jettison the rest of the 'irrelevant' information. If you feel that the answer might have something else to offer, check by repeating what you've heard or by asking additional questions: Il part du quai numéro cinq?

Set aside time to watch TV online or for real if you have access. Visual clues contribute significantly to understanding. Body language, facial expression and the physical context of a conversation combine with language to convey meaning. Select from a video archive such as the one belonging to TV5 **www.tv5.org**, or visit **http://plus-belle-la-vie.france3.fr/** to get a taste of the popular soap opera Plus Belle la Vie.

Above all, keep practising your listening skills; little and often is the rule.

Reading and writing

Being able to read and write does not mean developing a lifetime passion for the novels of Alexandre Dumas (although it might), nor does it mean weekly essay writing. As well as taking pleasure in reading and writing, there are good learning reasons for tackling the written word.

The great divide

At first, you will find that you can understand much more of what is written than what you hear. The apparent similarities between French and English on the page become pronounced differences as the rules of spoken French apply.

From the outset, link the written word with how it sounds. Reading while listening will help you to associate sound with script, assisting with word order and liaison as well as the pronunciation of individual words. Work towards being able to visualise French as you say it and to 'hear' it as you read.

What to read

Don't discount anything! Signage, labelling, adverts, hoardings, leaflets, posters, timetables, promotions, newspapers, magazines, circulars, books; any reading matter is packed with potential. The internet has revolutionised our ability to access real French reading materials. From online newspapers to tourist information office sites, you can dip into a wide variety of material created for the French-speaking market.

 activity 2

Without resorting to a dictionary, discover more about Médecins sans frontières. What kind of organisation is it and where is its headquarters? What does it do? How has its work been recognised?

> Médecins sans frontières, abrégé MSF, est une organisation non gouvernementale internationale à but humanitaire d'origine française mais dont le Bureau International siège à Genève (Suisse).
>
> Elle offre une assistance médicale d'urgence dans des cas comme les conflits armés, les catastrophes naturelles, les épidémies et les famines. MSF offre aussi des actions à plus long terme lors de conflits prolongés ou d'instabilité chronique, dans le cadre de l'aide aux réfugiés ou à la suite de catastrophes. Elle a reçu le prix Nobel de la paix en 1999.

Just as you listen for key words in order to make sense of what you hear, so you look for them in what you read. In your own language skimming and scanning texts is natural. You glance at newspaper headlines, you cast your eyes over a menu and you scan travel information displays. You don't read every word.

Develop the practice of never using a dictionary when first tackling reading. Never try to translate what you read, just aim for the sense.

Once you have got the gist of a reading passage, go back and see what interesting language is to be found.

Look for cognates (organisation, humanitaire); look for the genders of new words (assistance, prix); test yourself grammatically (why does the second paragraph begin with elle?); look up words you can't guess and decide if they are of long-term interest to you (but, siège, à la suite); set yourself some revision (française is in the text; brush up on adjectives of nationality by studying the grid of langues officielles of the Union Européenne.

This specialised kind of reading is a language-learning skill. Link a reading activity to a particular piece of learning (look for the way verbs are used, for example) or use a reading passage to discover and develop vocabulary for things that are of particular interest to you.

The creative urge

Writing has the same dual function for the language learner as reading. You can write for pleasure or to communicate something and write to learn or practise what you've learnt.

Many of us have a natural inclination to write when we are studying; it's part of our learning style to record what we want to memorise. It's a strategy that works but one that comes with a health warning! Don't make speaking French into a paper-based exercise. Although the association of writing with speech is a practice to be encouraged, it should never lead to a situation where you can only say what you have worked out on paper first. Get into the habit of speaking first and writing later.

Author, author ...

Think about what you might need or want to be able to write in French. As you might expect, there are conventions for different kinds of writing. The opening and closing of informal and formal letters and emails, for example:

	informal letter	formal letter	email
opening	Cher Philippe Chère Nathalie	Monsieur/ Madame	Cher, chère
closing	Affectueusement	Veuillez agréer, Monsieur/ Madame, mes salutations distinguées.	Cordialement

 activity 3

What cards might contain the following messages?

1 Joyeux Noël.
2 Mes souhaits pour un heureux anniversaire.
3 Bonne année.
4 Avec nos sincères condoléances.
5 Félicitations pour votre mariage.
6 Joyeuse Saint Valentin.
7 Toutes mes félicitations pour la naissance de votre bébé.

Reference

 **numbers**

1.98 Learning numbers in another language is a really satisfying task to undertake but you need a strategy. Think about how numbers occur. If you're talking about dates you'll need the numbers 1 to 31 for the days and the thousands for years; for time you'll need 1 to 59. For food shopping 1 to 20 will be useful and then the 10s between 20 and 100, so that you can cope with euros and cents. Set yourself daily challenges to learn number blocks. You might also memorise numbers that are important to you: the number of your house; your date of birth; your mobile and land-line numbers. In French you give phone numbers two at a time not in single digits: 01 22 59 43 62 (zero un, vingt-deux, cinquante-neuf, quarante-trois, soixante-deux).

Although you might get real satisfaction from being able to count from one to a million in French, you are not usually called on to do so. You are more likely to need to give and understand random numbers. Get ready by turning everyday encounters into French. What's the number of that bus? What's your favourite lottery combination? And, of course, prices in shops, even in pounds sterling, give you plenty of opportunities to practise.

Here are the numbers from 1 to 20 in French.

1	un	11	onze
2	deux	12	douze
3	trois	13	treize
4	quatre	14	quatorze
5	cinq	15	quinze
6	six	16	seize
7	sept	17	dix-sept
8	huit	18	dix-huit
9	neuf	19	dix-neuf
10	dix	20	vingt

Listen to the audio and repeat, paying attention to the sounds. You'll notice that 17, 18 and 19 are compound numbers (10 + 7 etc).

You'll find more compounds as you count higher:

21	vingt et un	31	trente et un
22	vingt-deux	32	trente-deux
23	vingt-trois etc	33	trente-trois etc

40	quarante	50	cinquante	60	soixante

The forties, fifties and sixties all behave like the twenties and thirties. Listen and practise the twenties and thirties and the words for 40, 50 and 60.

After 69 things get a bit more complicated. You're still dealing with compounds but not the ones you might expect!

Look at the 70s. Can you work out what's happening?

70	soixante-dix	75	soixante-quinze
71	soixante et onze	76	soixante-seize
72	soixante-douze	77	soixante-dix-sept
73	soixante-treize	78	soixante-dix-huit
74	soixante-quatorze	79	soixante-dix-neuf

The compound for 70 is 60 + 10, so logic dictates that 71 should be 60 + 11, and so on.

80 translates literally as 'four twenties' (quatre-vingts), and counting up to 99 follows the sequence of adding the numbers 1 to 19 onto this, so:

81   quatre-vingt-un (vingt loses its s after 80)
82   quatre-vingt-deux etc.
90   quatre-vingt-dix
91   quatre-vingt-onze

Can you carry on? You are bound to feel a sense of triumph as you finally hit 100, which is cent.

Here's a selection of words from 100 to 1,000
101 cent un
112 cent douze
200 deux cents
500 cinq cents
1,000 mille

You may encounter variations in French numbers in francophone countries. Most notably there are alternatives for seventy, eighty and ninety (**septante**, **octante** and **nonante**) that enable you to avoid complex compound numbers and revert to the more straightforward pattern of the 20s and 30s.

Ordinal numbers

premier/première *first*
deuxième *second*
troisième *third*
quatrième *fourth*
cinquième *fifth*
sixième *sixth*
septième *seventh*
huitième *eighth*
neuvième *ninth*
dixième *tenth*

Months

janvier *January*
février *February*
mars *March*
avril *April*
mai *May*
juin *June*
juillet *July*
août *August*
septembre *September*
octobre *October*
novembre *November*
décembre *December*

 survival phrases 1.98

- Je regrette, je n'ai pas compris. *I'm sorry, I didn't understand.*
- Désolé(e), je ne comprends pas. *Sorry, I don't understand.*
- Voulez-vous répéter, s'il vous plaît. *Would you repeat that, please?*
- Qu'est-ce que c'est en français? *What's that in French?*
- Ça s'écrit comment? *How do you spell that?*
- Vous avez dit …? *Did you say …?*
- Je ne parle pas très bien français, je suis anglais/anglaise/irlandais/
  irlandaise/écossais/écossaise/gallois/galloise.
  *I don't speak French very well, I'm English (m/f)/Irish (m/f)/Scottish
  (m/f)/Welsh (m/f).*

French–English glossary

This glossary contains the words found in this book, with their meanings in the contexts used here. Most verbs are given only in the infinitive, but parts of some French irregular verbs are also included. Regular adjectives are listed in the masculine singular version; for irregular adjectives, the feminine endings are also listed. Abbreviations: (m) masculine, (f) feminine, (sing) singular, (pl) plural, (adj) adjective, (pp) past participle.

A

à at, in, to
absolument really
abstrait abstract
accepter to accept
accord: d'accord OK
achat (m) purchase
　faire les achats to shop
acheter to buy
acteur (m) actor
actif/ive active
actrice (f) actress
adorer to adore
adresse (f) address
aéroport (m) airport
affaires (f pl) business
Afrique (f) Africa
âge (m) age
agence (f) de voyages travel agent's
agir to act
agréable nice, pleasant
aider to help
ail (m) garlic
aile (f) wing
aimer to like
ajouter to add
allemand German
aller to go
aller retour (m) return (ticket)
aller simple (m) single (ticket)
allergique allergic
allô hello (on phone)
allumer to light
alors well, so
Alpes (f pl) Alps

alpinisme (m) mountain climbing
ambiance (f) atmosphere
ami(e) (m/f) friend
amoureux
　tomber amoureux to fall in love
amusant amusing
s'amuser to enjoy oneself
an (m) year
ancien(ne) old
anglais English
Angleterre (f) England
animal (m) animal
animateur (m) host, compère
année (f) year
anniversaire (m) birthday
annulé cancelled
Antilles (f pl) West Indies
août (m) August
appartement (m) flat
appel (m) phone call
appeler to call, phone
s'appeler to be called
appliquer to apply
apporter to bring
apprécier to appreciate
apprendre to learn
après after
après-midi (m) afternoon
architecte (m/f) architect
argent (m) money
armoire (f) cupboard
arrêt (m) bus stop
s'arrêter to stop
arriver to arrive, happen
ascenseur (m) lift

asseyez-vous sit down
assister to attend
attendre to wait (for)
augmentation (f) de salaire pay rise
aujourd'hui today
aussi too, also
autobus (m) bus
automne (m) autumn
automobiliste (m/f) motorist
autoroute (f) motorway
autre other
avance advance
　à l'avance in advance
avant (de) before
avant-centre (m) centre forward
avec with
avenir (m) future
avion (m) plane
avis (m) opinion
avocat (m), avocate (f) lawyer
avoir (pp eu) to have
avril (m) April

B

bagages (m pl) luggage
baie (f) bay
se baigner to swim, bathe
balcon (m) balcony
banque (f) bank
bar (m) bar
bas/basse low
base (f) de données database
bateau (m) boat

bateau-mouche (m) sightseeing boat
bâtiment (m) building
beau/belle beautiful
beaucoup (de) a lot (of)
beau-fils (m) son-in-law, stepson
bébé (m) baby
Belgique (f) Belgium
belle beautiful
belle-mère (f) mother-in-law, stepmother
beurre (m) butter
bien well, a lot
bien sûr certainly, of course
bientôt soon
à bientôt see you soon
bienvenue welcome
bière (f) beer
billet (m) ticket
bisou (m) kiss
blanc/blanche white
bleu (adj) blue
bœuf (m) beef
boire (pp bu) to drink
boisson (f) drink
boîte (m) tin, can
bon(ne) good
bonjour good morning, good day, hello
bonsoir good evening
bord (m): bord de la mer seaside
bouche (f) mouth
boucherie (f) butcher's
bouger to move
bouillon (m) stock
boulangerie (f) baker's
bouleversé upset
boulot (m) work (slang)
bout (m) end
bouteille (f) bottle
boxe (f) boxing
bras (m) arm
Bretagne (f) Brittany
bricolage (m) DIY
brin (m) sprig
brouillard: il fait du brouillard it's foggy
Bruxelles Brussels

bureau (m) office
but (m) goal
buvez *from boire* (you) drink

C

ça, cela that
ça va how are you?, is everything OK?; I'm fine, everything's OK
cachet (m) tablet
café (m) cafe, coffee
café crème (m) white coffee
calme quiet
camion (m) lorry
campagne (f) countryside
camping (m) campsite
canapé convertible (m) sofa bed
cantine (f) canteen
câpre (f) caper
car (m) coach
carrefour (m) crossroads
carte (f) menu, card
à la carte from the menu
carte (f) de crédit credit card
catch (m) wrestling
cave (f) cellar
ce/cet/cette this, that
ceci this
cela that
célibataire (m/f) single
cendrier (m) ashtray
cent hundred
cerise (f) cherry
ces these, those
c'est it is, this/that is
chambre (f) bedroom, room in a hotel
champ (m) field
champignon (m) mushroom
chance (f) luck
avoir de la chance to be lucky
changer to change
chanson (f) song
chanter to sing
chapeau (m) hat
chapitre (m) chapter
chaque each

charcuterie (f) cold meats, delicatessen
charmant (m) charming
château (m) castle
chaud warm
chauffage (m) heating
chauffeur (m) driver
chaussure (f) shoe
chef (m) boss
cher/chère dear, expensive
chercher to look for
cheval (m) horse
cheveux (m pl) hair
cheville (f) ankle
chèvre (f) goat
chèvre (m) goat's cheese
chez at the house of
chien (m) dog
Chine (f) China
chinois Chinese
chocolat (m) chocolate
choisir to choose
choix (m) choice
chose (f) thing
chou (m) cabbage
chou (m) de Bruxelles Brussels sprout
choucroute (f) sauerkraut
ciboulette (f) chives
ciel (m) sky
cinéma (m) cinema
citron (m) lemon
clé (f) key
climat (m) climate
clos enclosed
coin (m) corner
collègue (m/f) colleague
combien (de) how much/ many
comme as, like
commencer to begin
comment how, what like; pardon?
commission (f): faire les commissions to do the shopping
compagne (f) partner
compagnon (m) partner
complet/complète full
compliqué complicated

comprendre (pp compris) to understand
comprimé (m) tablet
comptable (m/f) accountant
concessionaire (m/f) agent, dealer
conducteur/trice (m/f) driver
conduire to drive
confortable comfortable
confortablement comfortably
congé (m) leave
connaître to know
conseil (m): salle (f) du conseil boardroom
conseiller to advise
contacter to contact
contemporain modern, contemporary
content pleased, satisfied
continuer to continue
contraire: au contraire on the contrary
contre against
convenable convenient
copain (m) boyfriend
cornichon (m) gherkin
Corse (f) Corsica
côte (f) coast
côté (m): à côté de next to
coude (m) elbow
couleur (f) colour
coup (m): coup de soleil sunburn
tout d'un coup suddenly
coupe (f) cup
couper to cut
couramment fluently
courant fluent
courir (pp couru) to run
course (f) à pied running
cousin(e) (m/f) cousin
couteau (m) knife
coûter to cost
créer to create
crème (f) cream
crêpe (f) pancake
crier to shout
crois from croire (I) think,

believe
cuillerée (f) spoonful
cuire (pp cuit) to cook
cuisine (f) cooking, food, kitchen

D

d'abord first of all
d'accord OK, agreed
dangereux/euse dangerous
dans in
danser to dance
de of, from
de la, de l' some, any
décembre (m) December
décider to decide
défaire to undo
défendeur (m) defender
degré (m) degree
déguster to taste
dehors: en dehors de outside
déjà already
déjeuner (m) lunch
délégué (m) delegate
délicieux/euse delicious
demain tomorrow
demander to ask
demi(e) half
demi-frère (m) stepbrother, half brother
demi-pension (f) half-board
demi-soeur (f) stepsister, half sister
départ (m) departure
dépasser to exceed
dépenser to spend (money)
depuis since, for
dernier last, latest
derrière behind
des some, any
désagréable unpleasant
descendre to go down
désirer to want: vous désirez? can I help you?
désolé sorry
dessert (m) dessert
dessin (m) drawing, design
dessinateur (m) designer
détail (m) detail
détester to hate

deux two
deuxième second
devant in front (of)
devoir to have to; to owe
d'habitude: comme d'habitude as usual
diarrhée (f) diarrhoea
difficile difficult
digestif (m) liqueur
dimanche (m) Sunday
dimensions (f pl) size
dîner (m) dinner
dîner to have dinner
dire (pp dit) to say
directeur/trice (m/f) director
se diriger to head (towards)
dis(-moi) from dire tell (me)
discours (m) speech
discuter to discuss
divorcé divorced
dodo (m) sleep (slang)
doigt (m) finger
domicile (m) place of residence
dommage: (c'est) dommage (it's a) pity
donc therefore, so
donner to give
dormir to sleep
dos (m) back
douceur (f) sweet
douleur (f) pain
doux/douce gentle
drap (m) sheet
droit: tout droit straight ahead
droite: à droite on/to the right
du some, any

E

eau (f) water
eau minérale (f) mineral water
échalote (f) shallot
école (f) school
écologique ecological
écouter to listen (to)
écrire (pp écrit) to write

s'écrire to be spelt
Edimbourg Edinburgh
effet (m): en effet indeed
église (f) church
embrasser to kiss
emploi (m) job
emporter to take away
en in, by; of them
enchanté pleased to meet
    you
encore yet; another, more
enfant (m/f) child
enlever to take off
ennuyeux/euse boring
ensemble together
ensuite then
entendre to hear
s'entraîner to train
entre between
entrer to enter, go in
environ about, approximately
environs (m pl) outskirts
envoyer to send
épicerie (f) grocer's
épinards (m pl) spinach
équipe (f) team
escargot (m) snail
Espagne (f) Spain
espagnol Spanish
espérer to hope
essayer to try
est from être is
et and
étage (m) floor
était from être was
États-Unis (m pl) United
    States
été (m) summer
éteint extinct
êtes from être (you) are
étranger (m) foreigner,
    stranger
étranger/ère foreign
à l'étranger abroad
être (pp été) to be
études (f pl) studies
étudiant(e) (m/f) student
étudier to study
examen (m) exam
européen(ne) European

F

façon (f) way
face (f): en face de opposite
facile easy
faim (f): avoir faim to be
    hungry
faire (pp fait) to do, make
fait: en fait in fact; tout à
    fait completely
famille (f) family
fatigué tired
faut: il faut you/we/I must,
    it is necessary
favori favourite
férié: jour férié (m) public
    holiday
femme (f) woman, wife
fenêtre (f) window
ferme (f) farm
fermé closed
fête (f) party, holiday
feu (m) fire, heat
feuilleton (m) soap opera
feux (m pl) traffic lights
février (m) February
fille (f) girl, daughter
film (m) film
fils (m) son
finalement finally
finir to finish
fixé fixed
fleur (f) flower
fois (f) time
fondamental basic
font from faire (they) do,
    make
football (m) football
forêt (f) forest, woods
formidable amazing
four (m) à micro-ondes
    microwave oven

frais/fraîche chilled
fraise (f) strawberry
français French
frapper to knock
frère (m) brother
frites (f pl) chips
froid cold
fromage (m) cheese
fromagerie (f) cheese shop
fruits (m pl) de mer seafood
fumé smoked
fumer to smoke
furieux/euse furious

G

gagner to win
garçon (m) boy
garder to keep
gare (f) station
gare routière (f) bus station
gâteau (m) cake
gauche left
    à gauche on/to the left
génial great, cool
genou (m) knee
gentil(le) kind, nice
gîte (m) holiday home
glace (f) ice cream
gorge (f) throat
goûter to taste
grand big, tall
grand magasin (m)
    department store
grand-mère (f) grandmother
grand-père (m) grandfather
gratter to scratch
gratuit free
grave serious
grève (f) strike
grippe (f) flu
gris grey
gros(se) fat
groupe (m) group
guide (m/f) guide

H

habillé dressed
s'habiller to get dressed
habiter to live
habitude (f): comme

d'habitude as usual
hacher to chop
haricot (m) bean
haut: en haut upstairs
herbe (f) herb
hésiter to hesitate
heure (f) hour, o'clock, time
heureusement fortunately
heureux/euse happy
hier yesterday
homard (m) lobster
homme (m) man
homme politique (m)
    politician
hôpital (m) hospital
horaire (m) timetable
horreur (f): film (m) d'horreur
    horror film
    quelle horreur! how
    horrible!
hors-d'oeuvres (m pl) starter
hôtel (m) hotel
hôtel (m) de ville town hall
hôtesse (f) de l'air air
    hostess
huile (f) oil
huître (f) oyster
humide humid

I

ici here
idéal ideal
idée (f) idea
il y a ago; there is/are
important important
imposant imposing
incroyable unbelievable
inculte uncultivated
indiquer to show
infirmier/ière (m/f) nurse
ingénieur (m/f) engineer
insectifuge (m) insect
    repellent
interdit prohibited
intéressant interesting
s'intéresser (à) to be
    interested (in)
intérieur (m) inside
    à l'intérieur on the inside
interprète (m/f) interpreter

inviter to invite
italien(ne) Italian

J

jamais: ne ... jamais never
jambe (f) leg
jambon (m) ham
janvier (m) January
jardin (m) garden
jardinage (m) gardening
jardinerie (f) garden centre
jean (m) pair of jeans
jeudi (m) Thursday
jeune young
jeune (m/f) young person
joli pretty
jouer to play
joueur (m) player
jour (m) day
journal (m) newspaper
journée (f) day
juillet (m) July
juin (m) June
jumelle (f) twin
jus (m) juice
jusqu'à until, up to
juste fair

L

la the; her, it
là-bas over there
laid ugly
laisser to let, leave
lait (m) milk
langue (f) language
lave-linge (m) washing
    machine
laver to wash
lave-vaisselle (m) dishwasher
le the; him, it
lecteur DVD (m) DVD player
légume (m) vegetable
lent slow
lentement slowly
les the; them
leur their
se lever to get up
librairie (f) bookshop
libre free
lieu (m) place

ligne (f): en ligne online
linge (m) washing
linge (m) de toilette
    bathroom linen
lire (pp lu) to read
lit (m) bed
livraison (f) delivery
livre (m) book
location (f) hire
loin far
long(ue) long
lotion solaire (f) suntan
    lotion
louer to hire
lui him
lundi (m) Monday
lune (f) moon

M

ma my
madame (f) Mrs, madam
mademoiselle (f) Miss
magasin (m) shop
magnifique wonderful
mai (m) May
main (f) hand
maintenant now
mairie (f) town hall
mais but
maison (f) house
    à la maison (at) home
mal: avoir mal (à) to hurt,
    ache; de mal en pis from
    bad to worse; pas mal
    not bad
malheureusement
    unfortunately
manger to eat
manteau (m) coat
marché (m) market
marché (m) aux puces flea
    market
marcher to walk
mardi (m) Tuesday
mari (m) husband
mariage (m) marriage
marié married
se marier to get married
Maroc (m) Morocco
marocain Moroccan

marque (f) brand, model
mars (m) March
matin (m) matinée (f)
    morning
mauvais bad
méchant naughty
médecin (m/f) doctor
médiéval medieval
méditerranéen(ne)
    Mediterranean
meilleur better
mélanger to mix
même some; even
ménage (m) housekeeping,
    housework
mentionner to mention
menu (m) à prix fixe fixed-
    price menu
mer (f) sea
merci thank you
mercredi (m) Wednesday
mère (f) mother
merveilleux/euse wonderful
mes my
métro (m) underground,
    metro
mettre (pp mis) to put
micro-ondes (f pl): four (m) à
    micro-ondes microwave
    oven
midi midday
milliers (m pl) thousands,
    lots
minute (f) minute
moi me
moins less; to (clock time)
    au moins at least
mois (m) month
mon my
monastère (m) monastery
monde (m) world
monsieur (m) Mr, sir
montagne (f) mountain
monter to climb, go up
mosquée (f) mosque
mot (m) word
moto (f) motorbike
mots croisés (m pl)
    crossword
mourir (pp mort) to die

moyen (m) de transport
    means of transport
Moyen-Orient (m) Middle
    East
muraille (f) wall
musée (m) museum
musique (f) music

N

nager to swim
naître (pp né) to be born
natation (f) swimming
neiger to snow
n'est-ce pas? isn't it? haven't
    you? don't you? etc
neveu (m) nephew
nièce (f) niece
noir black
noix (f) nut
nom (m) name, surname
non no
nord (m) north
Normandie (f) Normandy
note (f) bill
notre, nos our
nourriture (f) food
nous we
nouveau/nouvelle new
novembre (m) November
nuit (f) night
numéro (m) number

O

occupé busy
octobre (m) October
œil (m) eye
œuf (m) egg
œuf (m) au plat fried egg
office (m) du tourisme
    tourist office
offrir (pp offert) to offer, give
    as a present
oignon (m) onion
olive (f) olive
ombragé shaded
on we, you, one
oncle (m) uncle
ont *from avoir* (they) have
oreille (f) ear
organiser to organise

ou or
où where
oublier to forget
oui yes
ouvert open

P

pain (m) bread
palais (m) palace
panne (f): en panne broken
    down
pantalon (m) trousers
paquet (m) parcel
par by, via
parapluie (m) umbrella
parc (m) park
parce que because
pardon excuse me, sorry
parent (m) parent, relative
parfait perfect
parfum (m) flavour, perfume
parking (m) car park
parler to speak
parole (f) word
parti (m) (political) party
partir to leave
partout everywhere
pas de no, not any
pas du tout not at all
pas mal not bad
pas tellement not much
passager (m) passenger
passeport (m) passport
passer to spend (time)
se passer to happen
passe-temps (m) hobby
passionnant exciting
pastille (f) lozenge
pâte (f) pastry, batter
pâtisserie (f) cake shop
payer to pay
pays (m) country
paysage (m) scenery
peau (f) skin
peinture (f) painting
pelouse (f) lawn
penser to think
pension complète (f) full
    board
perdre to lose

père (m) father
périple (m) trip, trek
permis de conduire (m) driving licence
persil (m) parsley
personne (f) person
personne ne ... nobody
petit small
petit à petit bit by bit
petit déjeuner (m) breakfast
petit-enfant (m/f) grandchild
petite-fille (f) granddaughter
petit-fils (m) grandson
petit pois (m) pea
peu: un peu a little
à peu près approximately
peur (f): avoir peur to be afraid
peut-être perhaps, maybe
peut *from pouvoir* (he/she/it) can
peux *from pouvoir* (I) can
pharmacie (f) chemist's
pharmacien(ne) (m/f) chemist, pharmacist
photo (f) photo
photocopieuse (f) photocopier
pièce (f) room
pied (m) foot
à pied on foot
pierre (f) stone
piquant spicy
piqûre (f) bite, sting
piscine (f) swimming pool
pistache (f) pistachio
pittoresque picturesque
place (f) room (space), seat, square
placer to put
plage (f) beach
plan (m) map
plante (f) plant
plat (m) dish: œuf au plat fried egg
plat (m) du jour day's special
plat (m) principal main course
plateau (m) tray, platter

pleurer to cry
pleut *from pleuvoir*
il pleut it's raining
plombier (m/f) plumber
plongée sous-marine (f) deep-sea diving
pluie (f) rain
plus more
non plus either
ne ... plus no more, no longer
plusieurs several
pneu (m) tyre
poche (f) pocket
poids (m) weight
poésie (f) poetry
poire (f) pear
poireau (m) leek
poisson (m) fish
poissonerie (f) fishmonger's
poivre (m) pepper
police (f) police
pomme (f) apple
pomme de terre (f) potato
pont (m) bridge
populaire popular
portable (m) mobile phone
porte (f) door, gate
porter to wear
poste (f) post office
poste (m) de police police station
pot (m) drink
poulet (m) chicken
pour for
pourquoi why
pousser to push
pouvoir to be able to, can
pratique practical
préférer to prefer
premier/ière first
premier ministre (m) prime minister
prendre to take
prénom (m) first name
préparer to prepare
près (de) near
présenter to introduce
presque almost
presse (f) press

pressing (m) dry cleaner's
prie: je vous en prie it's a pleasure, don't mention it
principal main
printemps (m) spring
privatif/ive private
privé private
prix (m) price
problème (m) problem
prochain next
professeur (m/f) teacher
projet (m) plan
promenade (f) walk
se promener to go for a walk
promettre to promise
promouvoir (pp promu) to promote
proposer to suggest
propre clean
propriété (f) property
provenance: en provenance de coming from
puis then
pupitre (m) music stand

Q

quai (m) platform
qualité (f) quality
quand when
quartier (m) district
quatrième fourth
que than; who, that: ne ... que only
que ... que whether ...
qu'est-ce que? what?
quel(le) what, which
quelque chose something
question (f) question
qui who, which
quitter to leave
quoi what

R

radio (f) radio
rafraîchissements (m pl) refreshments
ragoût (m) stew
raisin (m) grape
raison (f): avoir raison to be right

ranger to tidy
rapide rapid
rater to miss
récemment recently
recette (f) recipe
recevoir (pp reçu) to receive
rechercher to look for
recyclage (m) recycling
refroidir to cool down
regarder to watch, look at
régime (m) diet
région (f) area
régional regional
régler to pay, settle
regretter to be sorry
se relaxer to relax
remarquer to notice
remettre to put on again,
    put back
remontant (m) pick-me-up
remplir to fill
remuer to move
(se) rencontrer to meet
rendez-vous (m) appointment
rendre to give back
rendre visite to visit
rénover to renovate
rentrer to return/go home
repas (m) meal
répéter to repeat
répondre to reply
se reposer to relax, rest
réserver to book, reserve
rester to stay
résultat (m) result
retard (m): en retard
    (running) late
retour (m) return
retourner to return
retraite (f) retirement
    en retraite retired
réunion (f) meeting
réussir to succeed
réveille-matin (m) alarm
    clock
revenir (pp revenu) to come
    back
revoir: au revoir goodbye
rez-de-chaussée (m) ground
    floor

rhum (m) rum
rhume (m) cold
riad (m) riad (traditional
    Moroccan
    accommodation)
rien: ne ... rien nothing
    de rien it's nothing, don't
    mention it
roman (m) novel
roman (adj) Roman
rond-point (m) roundabout
rose pink
rôti roast
rouge red
rouler to drive
rue (f) street
ruelle (f) alley

S

sa his, her
sais, sait from savoir (I)
    know, (he/she) knows
saison (f) season
salade (f) salad
sale dirty
salle (f) hall
salle à manger (f) dining
    room
salle de bains (f) bathroom
salle d'eau (f) shower room
salle de gym (f) gym
salon (m) living room
salut hi
samedi (m) Saturday
sans without
saucisse (f) sausage
saucisson (m) sausage
saumon (m) salmon
savoir (pp su) to know
sèche-linge (m) tumble dryer
séjour (m) living room
sel (m) salt
semaine (f) week
septembre (m) September
serveur (m) waiter
serveuse (f) waitress
serviette (f) briefcase
servir to serve
ses his, her
seulement only

si if; so
siècle (m) century
sifflet (m) whistle
s'il vous plaît please
sirop (m) syrup, mixture
société (f) company
sœur (f) sister
son his, her
soif (f): avoir soif to be
    thirsty
soir (m), soirée (f) evening
soldes (m pl) sales
soleil (m) sun
    il fait du soleil it's sunny
    coup de soleil (m)
    sunburn
sommes from être (we) are
sommet (m) top
sont from être (they) are
sortie (f) exit
sortir to go out, exit
souffrir to suffer
sous under
sous-marin underwater
sous-sol (m) basement
souvent often
spacieux/euse spacious
spectacle (m) show
sport (m) sport
sportif/ive sporty
stade (m) stadium
stage (m) course
station de taxis (f) taxi rank
stationner to park
succès (m) success
sucer to suck
sucre (m) sugar
sud (m) south
suggérer to suggest
suis from être (I) am
Suisse (f) Switzerland
suivre to follow
sur on
supermarché (m)
    supermarket
sûr: bien sûr of course
surprenant surprising
surprendre to surprise
surtout especially
sympathique nice

T

ta your
tabac (m) tobacconist's
tante (f) aunt
tard late
tarte (f) pie, tart
technicien(ne) (m/f)
    technician
télé (f) TV
télécharger to download
téléphoner to phone
télévision (f) television
tellement so; so much
temps (m) time; weather;
    tense
        de temps en temps
        from time to time
tenue (f) outfit
terrain (m) pitch, plot
terrasse (f) terrace
terminer to finish
terre (f) ground
tes your
tête (f) head
TGV (m) TGV (very fast train)
thé (m) tea
théâtre (m) theatre
thon (m) tuna
tiens! gosh!
tirer to pull
tomate (f) tomato
tomber to fall
tomber amoureux to fall
    in love
ton your
tort: avoir tort to be wrong
tôt early
toujours always
tour (m) tour
touriste (m/f) tourist
touristique touristy
tourner to turn
tous all, everyone
    tous les deux both
Toussaint (f) All Saints' Day
tout all, everything
        du tout at all
        tout à fait completely
        tout de suite
        immediately

tout le monde everyone
tout près very near
toux (f) cough
traditionnel(le) traditional
train (m) train
tranche (f) slice
se transformer to be
    transformed
travail (m) work
travailler to work
traverser to cross
très very
troisième third
trop too
trouver to find
se trouver to be situated
tu you
Tunisie (f) Tunisia
typique typical

U

un, une one
Union européenne (f)
    European Union
université (f) university
utiliser to use

V

vacances (f pl) holidays
va *from aller* (he/she, it)
    goes
vache (f) cow
vais *from aller* (I) go
vaisselle (f) dishes
valise (f) suitcase
vas *from aller* (you) go
vedette (f) film star
véhicule (m) vehicle
vélo (m) bike
vendre to sell
vendredi (m) Friday
venir (pp venu) to come
venir de (+ inf) to have just
vent: il fait du vent it's
    windy
ventre (m) stomach
vérifier to check
verre (m) glass
vers about, towards
vert green

veste (f) jacket
vétérinaire (m/f) vet
veut *from vouloir* (he/she,
    it) wants
veux *from vouloir* (I, you)
    want
vie (f) life
Vietnam (m) Vietnam
vietnamien(ne) Vietnamese
vieux/vieille old
vilain bad, ugly
village (m) village
ville (f) town, city
vin (m) wine
visite (f) visit
visiter to visit
visiteur (m) visitor
vite fast
vivre to live
voici here you are
voilà there you are
voir (pp vu) to see
voisin (m), voisine (f)
    neighbour
voiture (f) car
voix (f) voice
vol (m) flight
volcan (m) volcano
vont *from aller* (they) go
votre, vos your
voudrais *from vouloir* (I, you)
    would like
vouloir (pp voulu) to want
vous you
voyage (m) journey, trip
voyager to travel
vrai true
vraiment really
vue (f) view

W

week-end (m) weekend

Y

yeux (m pl) *from œil* eyes
y there

English–French glossary

A

a un, une
able: to be able pouvoir
    (pp pu)
about à peu près, environ,
    vers
abroad à l'étranger
accent accent (m)
to accept accepter
accountant comptable (m/f)
to ache avoir mal
active actif/ive
actor acteur (m), actrice (f)
to add ajouter
address adresse (f)
to admire admirer
to adore adorer
advance: in advance à
    l'avance
to advise conseiller
aeroplane avion (m)
afraid: to be afraid avoir peur
Africa Afrique (f)
after après
afternoon après-midi (m)
against contre
age âge (m)
ago il y a
air hostess hôtesse de l'air (f)
all tout
    at all du tout
allergic allergique
alley ruelle (f)
almost presque
Alps Alpes (f pl)
already déjà
also aussi
always toujours
amazing formidable
amusing amusant
ancient ancien(ne)
and et
animal animal (m)
ankle cheville (f)

apple pomme (f)
apply appliquer
appointment rendez-vous (m)
to appreciate apprécier
approximately à peu près,
    environ
April avril (m)
architect architecte (m/f)
are: see 'to be' être
area région (f)
arm bras (m)
to arrive arriver
as comme
    as usual comme
    d'habitude
to ask demander
at à
atmosphere ambiance (f)
August août (m)
aunt tante (f)
autumn automne (m)

B

baby bébé (m)
back dos (m)
bad mauvais
baker's boulangerie (f)
balcony balcon (m)
banana banane (f)
bank banque (f)
bank holiday jour férié (m)
bar bar (m)
basement sous-sol (m)
basketball basket (m)
to bathe se baigner
bathroom salle de bains (f)
bay baie (f)
to be être (pp été)
beach plage (f)
bean haricot (m)
beautiful beau, belle
because parce que
bed lit (m)
bedroom chambre (f)

beef bœuf (m)
beer bière (f)
before avant (de)
to begin commencer
behind derrière
Belgium Belgique (f)
better meilleur
between entre
bicycle vélo (m)
big grand
bike vélo (m)
bill note (f)
birthday anniversaire (m)
bit: a bit un peu
bite piqûre (f)
black noir
blue bleu
boat bateau (m)
bookshop librairie (f)
boring ennuyeux/euse
to be born naître (pp né)
boss chef (m)
both tous les deux
bottle bouteille (f)
boxing boxe (f)
boyfriend copain (m)
book livre (m)
to book réserver
boy garçon (m)
bread pain (m)
breakfast petit déjeuner (m)
bridge pont (m)
Brittany Bretagne (f)
brother frère (m)
Brussels Bruxelles
building bâtiment (m)
business affaires (f pl)
bus autobus (m)
bus station gare routière (f)
bus stop arrêt (m)
busy occupé
but mais
butcher's boucherie (f)
butter beurre (m)

to buy acheter
by par; en
bye! à bientôt!, salut!

C

café café (m)
cake gâteau (m)
to call appeler
called: to be called s'appeler
camping: to go camping faire du camping
campsite camping (m)
can boîte (f)
can, to be able pouvoir (pp pu)
cancelled annulé
canteen cantine (f)
car voiture (f)
car park parking (m)
case valise (f)
castle château (m)
cathedral cathédrale (f)
cellar cave (f)
centre centre (m)
century siècle (m)
certainly bien sûr
to change changer
to check vérifier
cheese fromage (m)
chemist pharmacien(ne) (m/f)
chemist's pharmacie (f)
cherry cerise (f)
chicken poulet (m)
child enfant (m/f)
Chinese chinois
chocolate chocolat (m)
choice choix (m)
to choose choisir
Christmas Noël (m)
church église (f)
cinema cinéma (m)
city ville (f)
clean propre
client client (m)
climate climat (m)
to climb monter
closed fermé
coach car (m)
coast côte (f)
coffee café (m)

cold froid
  to be cold avoir froid
  to have a cold avoir un rhume
colleague collègue (m/f)
colour couleur (f)
to come venir
to come back revenir (pp revenu)
to come in entrer
comfortable confortable
company société (f)
completely tout à fait
complicated compliqué
conference conférence (f)
to consult consulter
to contact contacter
content content
to continue continuer
convenient convenable
cooking cuisine (f)
corner coin (m)
correct correct
Corsica Corse (f)
to cost coûter
cough toux (f)
country pays (m); campagne (f)
countryside campagne (f)
course stage (m)
course: of course bien sûr
cousin cousin(e) (m/f)
crab crabe (m)
cream crème (f)
credit card carte (f) de crédit
to cross traverser
crossroads carrefour (m)
crossword mots croisés (m pl)
to cut couper

D

to dance danser
dangerous dangereux/euse
daughter fille (f)
daughter-in-law belle-fille (f)
day jour (m), journée (f)
dear cher/chère
December décembre (m)
to decide décider

degree degré (m)
delegate délégué (m)
delicious délicieux/euse
delivery livraison (f)
dentist dentiste (m/f)
department store grand magasin (m)
departure départ (m)
designer dessinateur (m)
dessert dessert (m)
destination destination (f)
detail détail (m)
diarrhoea diarrhée (f)
to die mourir (pp mort)
difficult difficile
dining room salle à manger (f)
dinner dîner (m)
to have dinner dîner
director directeur/trice (m/f)
dirty sale
dish plat (m)
dishwasher lave-vaisselle (m)
divorced divorcé
DIY bricolage (m)
to do faire
doctor médecin (m/f); docteur (title)
documentary documentaire (m)
dog chien (m)
to download télécharger
dressed habillé
  to get dressed s'habiller
drink boisson (f), pot (m)
to drink boire (pp bu)
to drive conduire, rouler
driver conducteur/trice (m/f)
driving licence permis de conduire (m)
dry cleaner's pressing (m)
DVD player lecteur DVD (m)

E

each chaque
ear oreille (f)
early tôt
easy facile
to eat manger

egg œuf (m)
elbow coude (m)
end bout (m)
energetic énergique
engineer ingénieur (m/f)
England Angleterre (f)
English anglais(e) (adj);
    (language) anglais (m)
to enjoy oneself s'amuser
enough assez
to enter entrer
especially surtout
Europe Europe (f)
European européen(ne)
evening soir (m), soirée (f)
every chaque
everyone tous, tout le
    monde
everything tout
everywhere partout
exactly exactement
exam examen (m)
to exceed dépasser
excellent excellent
exciting passionant
excursion excursion (f)
excuse me excusez-moi,
    pardon
exit sortie (f)
to exit sortir
expensive cher/chère
extraordinary extraordinaire
eye œil (m) (pl yeux)

F

to fall tomber
family famille (f)
far loin
farm ferme (f)
fast rapide, vite
fat gros(se)
father père (m)
favourite préféré, favori
February février (m)
film film (m)
to find trouver
fine bien; (weather) beau
finger doigt (m)
to finish finir
first premier/ière

first (of all) d'abord
first name prénom (m)
fish poisson (m)
fishmonger's poissonerie (f)
flat appartement (m)
flavour parfum (m)
flight vol (m)
floor étage (m)
flower fleur (f)
flu grippe (f)
fluently couramment
foggy: it's foggy il fait du
    brouillard
food nourriture (f), cuisine (f)
foot pied (m)
    on foot à pied
football football (m)
for pour; depuis
foreign étranger/ère
foreigner étranger (m)
    étrangère (f)
forest forêt (f)
to forget oublier
fortunately heureusement
fourth quatrième
France France (f)
free gratuit; libre
French français (adj);
    (language) français (m)
frequently souvent
fresh frais/fraîche
Friday vendredi (m)
friend ami (m), amie (f)
from de
front: in front (of) devant
full complet/complète
funny amusant
furious furieux/euse

G

garage garage (m)
garden jardin (m)
gardening jardinage (m)
garlic ail (m)
gate porte (f)
gentle doux/douce
German allemand (adj);
    (language) allemand (m)
to get dressed s'habiller
to get up se lever

girl fille (f)
to give donner
glass verre (m)
to go aller
to go down descendre
to go for a walk se promener
to go home rentrer
to go in entrer
to go out sortir
to go up monter
goat chèvre (f)
goat's cheese chèvre (m)
golf golf (m)
good bon(ne)
goodbye au revoir
good day bonjour
good evening bonsoir
good-looking beau/belle
good morning bonjour
grandchild petit-enfant (m/f)
granddaughter petite-fille (f)
grandfather grand-père (m)
grandmother grand-mère (f)
grandson petit-fils (m)
great génial
green vert
grey gris
ground floor rez-de-chaussée
    (m)
group groupe (m)
guide guide (m/f)
gym salle de gym (f)

H

hair cheveux (m pl)
half demi(e)
half-board en demi-pension
half past et demie
half sister demi-sœur (f)
ham jambon (m)
hand main (f)
to happen se passer
happy heureux/euse
hard difficile
hat chapeau (m)
to hate détester
to have avoir
to have to devoir, il faut
head tête (f)
to hear entendre

heating chauffage (m)
hello bonjour, allô (on phone)
to help aider
her la; son, sa, ses
here ici
here you are voici
hi salut
him le; lui
hire: for hire en location
to hire louer
his son, sa, ses
hobby passe-temps (m)
holiday fête (f)
holiday home gîte (m)
holidays vacances (f pl)
home: at home à la maison
to hope espérer
horror film film (m) d'horreur
horse cheval (m)
hospital hôpital (m)
hot chaud
    to be hot avoir chaud
hotel hôtel (m)
hour heure (f)
house maison (f)
    at the house of chez
housekeeping ménage (m)
housework ménage (m)
how comment
how are you comment allez-vous/vas-tu?; ça va?
how many/much combien (de)
humid humide
hungry: to be hungry avoir faim
to hurt avoir mal
husband mari (m)

I

ice cream glace (f)
idea idée (f)
if si
immediately tout de suite
important important
in à; en; dans
incredible incroyable
indeed en effet
inside intérieur (m)

on the inside à l'intérieur
interesting intéressant
international international
internet internet (m)
to introduce présenter
to invite inviter
is: see 'to be' être
Italian italien(ne) (adj); (language) italien (m)
itinerary itinéraire (m)

J

jacket veste (f)
January janvier (m)
jeans jean (m)
jogging jogging (m)
journey voyage (m)
juice jus (m)
July juillet (m)
June juin (m)

K

to keep garder
key clé (f)
kilometre kilomètre (m)
kiss bisou (m)
to kiss embrasser
kitchen cuisine (f)
knee genou (m)
knife couteau (m)
to knock frapper
to know (fact) savoir; (person, place) connaître

L

language langue (f)
large grand
last dernier/ière
late en retard, tard
laundry linge (m)
lawyer avocat (m), avocate (f)
to learn apprendre
least: at least au moins
to leave partir; laisser; quitter
left gauche
    on/to the left à gauche
leg jambe (f)
lemon citron (m)

less moins
to let laisser
life vie (f)
lift ascenseur (m)
like: like that comme ça
to like aimer
to listen (to) écouter
little petit
    a little un peu
to live habiter, vivre
living room salon (m), séjour (m)
to loathe détester
lobster homard (m)
long long(ue)
longer: no longer ne ... plus
to look at regarder
to look for chercher
lorry camion (m)
to lose perdre
lot: a lot (of) beaucoup (de)
lotion lotion (f)
lounge salon (m), séjour (m)
to love aimer beaucoup, adorer
low bas(se)
lozenge pastille (f)
luck chance (f)
lucky: to be lucky avoir de la chance
lunch déjeuner (m)
    to have lunch déjeuner

M

magnificent magnifique
main principal
to make faire
man homme (m)
many beaucoup (de)
map plan (m)
March mars (m)
market marché (m)
marriage mariage (m)
married marié
    to get married se marier
marvellous merveilleux/euse
match match (m)
May mai (m)
maybe peut-être
me me; moi

meal repas (m)
Mediterranean
    méditerranéan(ne)
to meet (se) rencontrer
meeting réunion (f)
to mention mentionner
menu carte (f)
microwave oven four à micro-
    ondes (m)
midday midi
milk lait (m)
mineral water eau minérale (f)
minute minute (f)
to mix mélanger
mobile phone portable (m)
modern moderne,
    contemporain
Monday lundi (m)
money argent (m)
month mois (m)
more plus
    no more ne ... plus
morning matin (m)
Moroccan marocain
Morocco Maroc (m)
mosque mosquée (f)
mother mère (f)
mother-in-law belle-mère (f)
motorbike moto (f)
motorway autoroute (f)
mountain montagne (f)
mountain-climbing alpinisme
    (m)
mouth bouche (f)
to move bouger
Mr monsieur (m)
Mrs madame (f)
museum musée (m)
music musique (f)
must il faut; to have to
    devoir
my mon, ma, mes

N

name nom (m)
    first name prénom (m)
naughty méchant
near près (de)
neighbour voisin (m), voisine
    (f)

nephew neveu (m)
never ne ... jamais
new nouveau/nouvelle
newspaper journal (m)
next prochain
next to à côté de
nice sympathique, gentil(le)
niece nièce (f)
night nuit (f)
no non
nobody personne ne ...
normally normalement
Normandy Normandie (f)
north nord (m)
not bad pas mal
nothing ne ... rien
novel roman (m)
November novembre (m)
now maintenant
number numéro (m)
nurse infirmier/ère (m/f)
nut noix (f)

O

o'clock heure(s) (f)
October octobre (m)
to offer offrir (pp offert)
office bureau (m)
often souvent
oil huile (f)
OK d'accord, très bien, OK
old vieux/vieille; ancien(ne)
olive olive (f)
onion oignon (m)
online en ligne
only seulement
open ouvert
opinion avis (m), opinion (f)
opposite en face de
or ou
orange orange (f)
orchestra orchestre (m)
to organise organiser
other autre
our notre, nos
outfit tenue (f)
outside extérieur (m):
    on the outside à
    l'extérieur
oven four (m)

over there là-bas
oyster huître (f)

P

painting peinture (f)
pancake crêpe (f)
parcel paquet (m)
parent parent (m)
park parc (m)
to park stationner
particularly surtout
partner compagnon (m),
    compagne (f)
party fête (f), soirée (f);
    (political) parti (m)
passenger passager (m)
passport passeport (m)
to pay payer, régler
pea petit pois (m)
peaceful calme
pear poire (f)
pepper poivre (m)
perfect parfait
perhaps peut-être
person personne (f)
pharmacist pharmacien (m),
    pharmacienne (f)
phone téléphone (m);
    (mobile) portable (m)
to phone téléphoner
picnic pique-nique (m)
picturesque pittoresque
pie tarte (f)
pink rose
pistachio pistache (f)
pitch terrain (m)
pity: (it's a) pity (c'est
    dommage
plan projet (m)
plane avion (m)
plant plante (f)
platform quai (m)
to play jouer
pleasant agréable
please s'il vous plaît
pleased to meet you
    enchanté
plot terrain (m)
plumber plombier (m/f)
pocket poche (f)

police police (f)
police station poste de
    police (m)
politics politique (f)
popular populaire
post office poste (f)
potato pomme de terre (f)
practical pratique
to prefer préférer
to prepare préparer
pretty joli
price prix (m)
private privatif/ive, privé
problem problème (m)
property propriété (f)
to put mettre

Q

quality qualité (f)
question question (f)
queue queue (f)
quick rapide, vite
quiet calme

R

radio radio (f)
rain pluie (f)
to rain pleuvoir: it's raining
    il pleut
rapid rapide
to read lire (pp lu)
really absolument, vraiment
to receive recevoir (pp reçu)
recently récemment
recipe recette (f)
to recommend recommander
red rouge
refreshments
    rafraîchissements (m pl)
region région (f)
regional régional
regular régulier/ière
relative parent (m)
to relax se reposer
to remain rester
to remove enlever
to repeat répéter
to reply répondre
to reserve réserver

to rest se reposer
restaurant restaurant (m)
result résultat (m)
retired en retraite
return retour (m)
return (ticket) aller retour (m)
to return rentrer, retourner
right droite
    on/to the right à droite
    to be right avoir raison
road rue (f)
room pièce (f); (in a hotel)
    chambre (f)
roundabout rond-point (m)
to run courir (pp couru)

S

salad salade (f)
sales soldes (m pl)
salmon saumon (m)
salt sel (m)
same même
sandwich sandwich (m)
satisfied content
Saturday samedi (m)
sauerkraut choucroute (f)
sausage saucisson (m),
    saucisse (f)
to say dire (pp dit)
scenery paysage (m)
school école (f)
to scratch gratter
sea mer (f)
seafood fruits de mer (m pl)
seaside bord (m) de la mer
seat place (f)
second deuxième
secretary secrétaire (m/f)
to see voir
see you soon à bientôt
to sell vendre
to send envoyer
September septembre (m)
serious grave
to serve servir
service service (m)
several plusieurs
shady ombragé
sheet drap (m)

shoe chaussure (f)
shop magasin (m)
shopping shopping (m)
shopping centre centre
    commercial (m)
should (you, we, I etc) il faut
to show indiquer
shower douche (f)
shower room salle d'eau (f)
shy timide
since depuis
to sing chanter
single célibataire
single (ticket) aller simple (m)
sister sœur (f)
sit down asseyez-vous
situated situé
to be situated se trouver
situation situation (f)
ski ski (m)
to ski faire du ski
sky ciel (m)
to sleep dormir
slice tranche (f)
slow lent
slowly lentement
small petit
to smoke fumer
snail escargot (m)
to snow neiger
so si; donc; alors
soap opera feuilleton (m)
sofa bed canapé
    convertible (m)
some du, de la, de l', des; en
something quelque chose
son fils (m)
son-in-law beau-fils (m)
song chanson (f)
sorry désolé; pardon
to be sorry regretter
soup soupe (f)
south sud (m)
spacious spacieux/ieuse
Spain Espagne (f)
Spanish espagnol (adj);
    (language) espagnol (m)
to speak parler
speciality spécialité (f)

spectacular spectaculaire
speech discours (m)
spell: to be spelt s'écrire
to spend (time) passer;
    (money) dépenser
spinach épinards (m pl)
sport sport (m)
sporty sportif/ive
spring printemps (m)
square place (f)
stadium stade (m)
starter hors d'œuvres (m pl)
station gare (f)
to stay rester
stepbrother demi-frère (m)
stepmother belle-mère (f)
stepsister demi-sœur (f)
stepson beau-fils (m)
still toujours
sting piqûre (f)
stomach ventre (m)
to stop s'arrêter
straight ahead tout droit
stranger étranger (m)
    étrangère (f)
strawberry fraise (f)
street rue (f)
student étudiant(e) (m/f)
to study étudier
to succeed réussir
success succès (m)
to suck sucer
to suffer souffrir
sugar sucre (m)
to suggest proposer
suitcase valise (f)
summer été (m)
sun soleil (m); it's sunny
    il fait du soleil
sunburn coup de soleil (m)
Sunday dimanche (m)
suntan lotion lotion solaire (f)
supermarket supermarché (m)
surname nom (m)
surprise surprise (f)
to surprise surprendre
surprising surprenant
to swim nager, se baigner
swimming pool piscine (f)

Switzerland Suisse (f)
symptom symptôme (m)

T

table table (f)
tablet comprimé (m),
    cachet (m)
to take prendre
takeaway repas (m)
    à emporter
tall grand
to taste déguster, goûter
tea thé (m)
teacher professeur (m/f)
team équipe (f)
tee shirt t-shirt (m)
television télévision (f)
tennis tennis (m)
tennis court court de
    tennis (m)
terrace terrasse (f)
than que
thank you merci
that ça, cela; ce
the le, la, les
theatre théâtre (m)
their leur
them les
then ensuite, puis
there y; là
    over there là-bas
there is, there are il y a
there you are voilà
therefore donc
these ces
they ils, elles
thing chose (f)
to think penser
third troisième
thirsty: to be thirsty avoir soif
this ce, cette
those ces
throat gorge (f)
Thursday jeudi (m)
ticket billet (m)
time fois (f); temps (m),
    heure (f)
    from time to time de
    temps en temps

timetable horaire (m)
tin boîte (f)
tired fatigué
today aujourd'hui
together ensemble
toilet toilette (f)
tomato tomate (f)
tomorrow demain
too aussi; trop
top sommet (m)
tourist touriste (m/f)
tourist office office du
    tourisme (m)
towards vers
town ville (f)
town hall hôtel de ville (m),
    mairie (f)
traditional traditionnel(le)
traffic lights feux (m pl)
train train (m)
to train s'entraîner
to travel voyager
travel agent's agence de
    voyage (f)
trip voyage (m)
trousers pantalon (m)
true vrai
to try essayer
Tuesday mardi (m)
tumble dryer sèche-linge (m)
tuna thon (m)
Tunisia Tunisie (f)
to turn tourner
two deux
typical typique
tyre pneu (m)

U

ugly laid
umbrella parapluie (m)
unbelievable incroyable
uncle oncle (m)
under sous
underground (train) métro (m)
to understand comprendre
    (pp compris)
unforgettable inoubliable
unfortunately
    malheureusement

United States États-Unis
(m pl)
university université (f)
unpleasant désagréable;
(weather) mauvais
until jusqu'à
up to jusqu'à
us nous
to use utiliser
usual: as usual comme
d'habitude
usually généralement,
d'habitude

V

vanilla vanille (f)
very très
via par
Vietnam Vietnam (m)
Vietnamese vietnamien(ne)
view vue (f)
village village (m)
visit visite (f)
to visit visiter
visitor visiteur (m)
volcano volcan (m)

W

to wait (for) attendre
waiter serveur (m)
waitress serveuse (f)
walk promenade (f)
to walk marcher
to go for a walk se promener
to want vouloir
warm chaud: to be warm
avoir chaud
to wash laver
washing linge (m)
washing machine
lave-linge (m)
to watch regarder
water eau (f)
to wear porter
weather temps (m)
Wednesday mercredi (m)
week semaine (f)
weekend week-end (m)
weight poids (m)
welcome bienvenue

well bien; alors
wet room salle d'eau (f)
what? qu'est-ce que?
quel(le)? quoi?
when quand
where où
which que; quel(le); qui
white blanc/blanche
white coffee café crème (m)
who que; qui
why pourquoi
wife femme (f)
window fenêtre (f)
windy: it's windy il fait du
vent
wine vin (m)
winter hiver (m)
with avec
without sans
woman femme (f)
wonderful magnifique,
merveilleux/euse
woods forêt (f)
word mot (m)
work travail (m)
to work travailler
world monde (m)
wrestling catch (m)
to write écrire
wrong: to be wrong avoir tort

Y

year an (m); année (f)
yes oui
yesterday hier
yet encore
you tu, vous
young jeune
your ton, ta, tes; votre, vos

Transcripts and answers

Chapter 1

Activity 3
The Restaurant Aragon's chef loves local products. He prefers to offer his clients seasonal ingredients. The restaurant is very popular and reservations are necessary.

Activity 4
A
- **Bonjour** madame, je m'appelle Louis Duval.
- **Bonjour** monsieur, je m'appelle Madeleine Dugard.
- **Au revoir** Madeleine. A bientôt!
- **Au revoir** Louis.

- **Bonjour** monsieur, je m'appelle Paul Bousquet. Je vous présente Jérôme Martin.
- Enchanté messieurs. Je m'appelle Charles Fournier.

- **Bonjour** messieurs, dames. Je m'appelle Henri Lacroix.
- Enchantée monsieur. Je m'appelle Sylvie Gauthier. Je vous présente Jean-Claude Arnaud, Victor Bellenger et Catherine Hugo.
- Enchanté messieurs, madame.

- **Au revoir** Henri. A bientôt!
- **Au revoir**, Sylvie.

Activity 5
1 Bonjour madame.
2 Bonsoir monsieur.
3 Au revoir monsieur.
4 Bonjour mesdames.
5 Au revoir messieurs, dames.

Activity 6
A
Enchanté(e); À bientôt; Je vous présente ...

B
1 Enchanté(e) madame.
2 À bientôt.
3 Enchanté messieurs.
4 Bonjour madame, enchanté(e).

Activity 7
I am called ... – Je m'appelle ...

- **Bonjour madame.**
- Bonjour. Vous vous appelez comment?
- **Je m'appelle ...**
- Bonsoir. Je vous présente Madeleine Dugard.
- **Enchanté(e) madame.**
- **Bonsoir monsieur. Vous vous appelez comment?**
- Je m'appelle Henri Lacroix.
- **Enchanté(e).**
- Au revoir.
- **Au revoir, à bientôt.**

Activity 8
A
- Bonjour madame. Comment allez-vous?
- Très bien, merci, et vous?
- Oui, très bien.

- Bonjour monsieur. Comment allez-vous?
- Bien, merci.

- Bonjour monsieur. Comment allez-vous?
- Pas mal, merci, et vous?
- Bien, bien.

- Bonjour madame. Comment allez-vous?
- Je vais très bien, merci. Et vous?
- Je vais bien, merci.

well – bien; very well – très bien; not bad – pas mal

B
- Bonjour. Comment allez-vous?
- **Bien, merci.**
- Bonjour. Comment allez-vous?

- **Pas mal, merci. Et vous?**
- Bien, merci.

- **Bonjour madame. Comment allez-vous?**
- Je vais bien, merci. Et vous?
- **Très bien, merci.**

Thank you. – Merci.

Activity 9

A
Hi: Sophie, Nicolas, Christine, Jean-Claude
Goodbye: Jérôme, Paul

B
Comment vas-tu? and Ça va?

- Salut Sophie. Comment vas-tu?
- Salut. Je vais bien, merci.

- Salut Jérôme. À bientôt.
- Salut.

- Salut Nicolas. Comment vas-tu?
- Salut. Très bien, merci.

- Salut Christine. Ça va?
- Salut. Ça va bien, merci.

- Salut Paul. À bientôt.
- Salut. À bientôt.

- Salut Jean-Claude. Ça va?
- Salut Marie-Thérèse. Ça va très bien merci.

Activity 10

- Bonjour, Monsieur. Comment allez-vous?
- **Bonjour, Monsieur. Ça va, merci. Comment allez-vous?**
- Bien, merci. Je vous présente Christine Dufour.
- **Enchanté. Je m'appelle Paul.**

- **Bonsoir, Madame Clément. Comment allez-vous?**
- Bonsoir, Madame Grieux. Je vais bien, merci. Et vous?
- **Je vais très bien, merci. Je vous présente Henriette Margaux.**

- Salut, Philippe. Ça va?
- **Salut. Ça va ... Salut, à bientôt!**

Activity 11

hôpital – hospital; île – isle, island; hâte – haste; hôte – host; honnête – honest; arrêt – arrest, stop; étudiant – student; école – school; écarlate – scarlet; épine – spine (thorn); éponge – sponge; étendard – standard (flag); étrange – strange; étrangler – strangle

Endgame
sheet

Chapter 2

Activity 1
un hôtel: un parking, une chambre pour deux personnes
un restaurant: un menu à prix fixe, des spécialités de la région
un café: des omelettes, des sandwichs
un office de tourisme: un plan de la ville, une liste des spectacles

Activity 2
une chambre pour deux personnes; une liste des spectacles; un plan de la ville

Activity 3

A
1 - Bonjour madame, vous désirez?
- Vous avez un plan de la ville?
2 - Oui, monsieur?
- Vous avez une liste des spectacles dans la région?
3 - Bonjour madame!
- Bonjour madame! Vous avez un menu à prix fixe?
4 - Vous désirez, monsieur?
- Vous avez une chambre?
5 - Oui, madame? Vous désirez?
- Vous avez un guide des hôtels?
6 - Bonsoir monsieur!
- Bonsoir madame! Vous avez des spécialités de la région?
7 - Vous désirez, monsieur?
- Vous avez un restaurant?

Dans un office de tourisme: 1, 2, 5
Dans un restaurant: 3, 6
Dans un hôtel: 4, 7

B
1 Vous avez des omelettes?
2 Vous avez des sandwichs?
3 Vous avez un parking?

4 Vous avez un café?

Pronunciation activity
Comment‿allez-vous?
Vous vous‿appelez comment?

Activity 4
- Mesdames, messieurs, bonjour. Vous désirez?
- Bonjour monsieur. Vous avez un guide de la région?
- Non, je regrette.
- Alors, un plan de la ville, s'il vous plaît.
- Voilà messieurs, dames
- Merci, au revoir, monsieur.

They ask for a guide to the region and a map of the town. They don't get the guide but do get the map.

- Bonsoir monsieur.
- Bonsoir madame. Vous désirez?
- Vous avez une table pour deux personnes?
- Oui madame. Par ici. Suivez-moi.
- Merci.

The woman asks for a table for two and they have one available.

- Bonjour madame. Vous désirez?
- Bonjour madame. Pour moi, un café crème, s'il vous plaît. Vous avez des pizzas?
- Non madame, je suis desolée.
- Alors, vous avez des sandwichs?
- Oui madame. Pâté? Camembert?
- Pâté, s'il vous plaît.

The woman asks for a milky coffee and a pizza. She doesn't get pizza so opts for a pâté sandwich.

Activity 5
- **Bonjour monsieur.**
- Bonjour monsieur. Vous désirez?
- **Vous avez un restaurant?**
- Oui monsieur. Juste là.

- **Bonjour madame.**
- Bonjour, madame. Vous désirez?
- **Vous avez une table?**
- Oui, bien sûr, suivez-moi.
- **Vous avez un menu à prix fixe?**

- Non madame, à la carte seulement.
- **Vous avez des spécialités de la région?**
- Oui madame, voici une liste.
- **Un coq au vin, s'il vous plaît.**

Activity 6
A
Lille, il y a un musée d'histoire naturelle, des monuments historiques, une cathédrale et des églises, des parcs, des jardins, un centre commercial, un marché, des boutiques, des restaurants, des bars, des hôtels. En fait, tout pour le touriste.

1 des
2 cathédrale (f), musée (m), marché (m) and centre (m)
3 churches
4 pour

Activity 7
A
un café – des cafés
un animal – des animaux
une région – des régions
un château – des châteaux
un accident – des accidents
un marché – des marchés
une ville – des villes
un cheval – des chevaux

B
animaux; chevaux

Activity 8
A
- Il y a un marché à Lille?
- Oui, il y a un marché.
- Il y a un camping ici?
- Non, je regrette, il y a des hôtels seulement. Voici une liste.
- Il y a un stade de football?
- Oui, et un stade de rugby.
- Il y a des musées?
- Oui, il y en a beaucoup. Voici un guide des musées.
- Il y a un casino à Lille?
- Oui, bien sûr.
- Il y a des cinémas à Lille?
  Oui, il y en a beaucoup

1 campsite

2 football
3 museums and cinemas
4 market
5 yes, there's a casino

B
1 Il y a un bar?
2 Il y a des campings?
3 Il y a un château?
4 Il y a une cathédrale?
5 Il y a des parcs?

Activity 9

A
1 In an office
- Bonjour Monsieur Duval. Comment allez-vous?
- Bien, merci. Je vous présente mon collègue Jérôme Bousier.
- Enchanté.
- Vous avez des documents pour moi?
- Oui monsieur, les voilà.
- Merci beaucoup. Il y a une photocopieuse ici?
- Oui, monsieur, juste ici.

2 In a café
- Bonjour. Vous désirez?
- Un thé, s'il vous plaît.
- Et pour moi, une bière.
- Vous avez des hamburgers?
- Non, je regrette.
- Alors, une pizza, peut-être?
- Des pizzas, oui, de toutes sortes.

B
- Salut, ça va?
- Salut, ça va.
- Voici le café de la Gare.
- Vous avez une table pour deux personnes?
- Oui, voilà une table là-bas.
- Bonjour madame, monsieur. Vous désirez?
- Un café crème, s'il vous plaît. Vous avez des omelettes?
- Ah non, je regrette, mais j'ai des sandwichs, un croque-monsieur...
- Un croque-monsieur, s'il vous plaît.

C
- Bonjour monsieur.
- Bonjour monsieur, vous avez un plan de la ville?
- Oui, voilà, monsieur.
- Merci, il y a des musées?
- Oui monsieur, il y en a beaucoup, le musée des vins, le musée des Beaux Arts.
- Très bien, il y a un marché?
- Oui, monsieur, sur la Place Charles de Gaulle.
- Vous avez une liste des hôtels, s'il vous plaît.
- Oui, bien sûr, voici.
- Merci beaucoup monsieur, au revoir.

Activity 10
l'université (f), la qualité, la philosophie, la sociologie, l'optimisme, le communisme

Chapter 3

Activity 1
Louis Pasteur: chemist; André Breton: writer, poet and surrealist theorist; Ferdinand Foch: a Marshal of France and Allied Supreme Commander in World War I; Battle of the Marne: First World War battle; Charles de Gaulle: first president of the fifth republic of France

Activity 2
Les magasins: le supermarché, le pressing, le tabac, la librairie

Les bâtiments municipaux: l'hôtel de ville, l'hôpital, la poste, le poste de police

Le voyage: la gare, la gare routière, la station de taxis, l'aéroport, l'arrêt de bus

Activity 3
un supermarché – le supermarché – les supermarchés
un café – le café – les cafés
un bureau – le bureau – les bureaux
un magasin – le magasin – les magasins
un canal – le canal – les canaux
une avenue – l'avenue – les avenues
un hôpital – l'hôpital – les hôpitaux

Activity 4
A
where is – où est; excuse me – pardon

B
- Pardon, madame. Où est le café du marché, s'il vous plaît?
- Il est dans l'allée André Breton

- Pardon, mademoiselle. Où est la poste, s'il vous plaît?
- Elle est place Charles de Gaulle.
- Merci.
- Je vous en prie.

- Pardon, monsieur. Où est la gare, s'il vous plaît?
- Elle est dans la rue Pasteur.

market café: allée André Breton
post office: place Charles de Gaulle
station: rue Pasteur

Activity 5
- **Pardon, où est la station de taxis, s'il vous plaît?**
- Voyons, il y en a une dans l'avenue Montaigne.

- **Pardon, où est le poste de police, s'il vous plaît?**
- Le poste de police, il est dans la rue Mouffetard, je crois. Oui, oui la rue Mouffetard.

- **Pardon, où est le pressing, s'il vous plaît?**
- Alors il y en a un boulevard Tisserand.

- **Pardon, où est la gare routière, s'il vous plaît?**
- Je regrette, je ne sais pas. Henri, tu sais où est la gare routière?
- Oui, elle est dans la rue Descartes.

- **Pardon, où est le marché aux puces, s'il vous plaît?**
- Il est place Paul Painlevé près de la gare.

taxi rank – D, police station – A; dry cleaner's – B; bus station – C; flea market – E

Activity 6
B
- **Pardon, monsieur, où est l'hôpital, s'il vous plaît?**
- Vous avez dit l'hôpital? Il est Boulevard de la Marne.
- **Désolé(e), je n'ai pas compris. Voulez-vous répéter, s'il vous plaît?**

- L' hôpital est Boulevard de la Marne.
- **Vous avez dit Boulevard de la Marne?**
- Oui, c'est bien ça.

Activity 7
A
lawyer – avocate (f)
secrétaire – secretary (m/f)
directrice marketing – marketing manager (f)
comptable – accountant (m/f)
directeur qualité – quality manager (m)
interprète – interpreter (m/f)
technicien – technician (m)

B
- Bonjour, je suis Eugénie Colomba. Je suis comptable. Je vous présente, Luc Vacherin. Il est technicien. Voici Marie-Chantal Dupuis, elle est avocate.

- Madame Dupuis, bonsoir, je vous présente Christophe Lebrun. Il est interprète.
- Bonsoir, monsieur.
- Enchanté, madame.

- Je vous présente Valérie Sochaux, elle est directrice qualité. Non, pas qualité, elle est directrice marketing.

- Madame Sochaux, bonsoir, je vous présente Béatrice Prévert et Henri Legrand, ils sont secrétaires ici.
- Bonsoir, madame, monsieur.

Henri Legrand – secretary; Valérie Sochaux – marketing manager; Eugénie Colomba – accountant; Christophe Lebrun – interpreter; Luc Vacherin – technician; Marie-Chantal Dupuis – lawyer; Béatrice Prévert – secretary

Activity 8
Je vous présente Guillaume Souchet – il est avocat.
Je vous présente Roselyne Flon – elle est directrice générale.
Je vous présente Marguerite Dormoi – elle est comptable.
Je vous présente Pascal David – il est directeur qualité.
Je vous présente Alfred Laroche – il est interprète.

Activity 9

A

un conducteur – une conductrice
un acteur – une actrice
un technicien – une technicienne
un pharmacien – une pharmacienne
un avocat – une avocate
un étudiant – une étudiante
un secrétaire – une secrétaire
un dentiste – une dentiste
un infirmier – une infirmière
un boulanger – une boulangère
un coiffeur – une coiffeuse
un serveur – une serveuse

B

1 Je suis Brigitte Laurent; je suis professeur.
2 Je suis Anne David; je suis conductrice de bus.
3 Je suis Paul Roux; je suis dentiste.
4 Je suis Angélique Bonnet; je suis pharmacienne.
5 Je suis Roland Petit; je suis ingénieur.

Être ou ne pas être
To be or not to be

Activity 10

A

1d; 2e; 3b; 4c; 5a

B

- Bonjour, je suis Marie-Claude Vacherin. Vous êtes Jean-Marie Le Coq?
- Ah, non, je ne suis pas Jean-Marie. Il n'est pas ici aujourd'hui; il est à Paris.
- Le bureau, il est Place Victor Hugo?
- Non, non, il n'est pas Place Victor Hugo, il est Place de la Liberté.
- Je suis architecte dans la société Dufour.
- Ah, vous n'êtes pas avec la société Concord, alors?

1 In Paris
2 Place de la Liberté
3 He's an architect.

Activity 11

Tu n'es pas professeur de mathématiques?
La poste n'est pas Place du Marché.
Je ne suis pas dans le train.

Nous ne sommes pas à Paris.
Les portables ne sont pas indispensables.

Activity 12

- Allô, oui?
- Salut Julie.
- Salut Joseph. Tu es où?
- Je suis dans le café de la Gare. Je suis désolé, je suis en retard.
- Tu as dit le café de la gare?
- Oui, oui. Tu es où?
- Je suis dans le supermarché, Boulevard André Breton, en route pour le café.
- Alors, à bientôt!
- Salut.

1 In the Café de la Gare; he's apologising because he's late.
2 the supermarket

Activity 13

A

Edimbourg – Edinburgh
choux de Bruxelles – Brussels sprouts

B

- Je m'appelle Thomas Espinasse et je suis de Grenoble.

- Vous vous appelez comment?
- Carole Rey.
- Bonjour Carole. Vous êtes d'ici?
- Non, je ne suis pas d'ici, je suis de Metz.

- Bonjour, voici Monique Delahaye.
- Bonjour Monique, vous êtes d'où?
- Je suis de Marseille.

- Vous êtes Habib?
- Oui, je m'appelle Habib Taieb et vous?
- Je suis Michel Gallet
- Et moi, je suis Thérèse.
- Enchanté! Vous êtes d'où ?
- Nous sommes de Québec et vous?
- Moi, je suis d'Andorre.

Monique Delahaye – Marseille
Thomas Espinasse – Grenoble
Michel et Thérèse Gallet – Québec
Carole Rey – Metz
Habib Taieb – Andorre

Activity 14

- **Bonjour madame. Je suis Mark**

Thompson.
- Enchantée, je suis Valérie de Lafayette.
Je vous présente Jean-Pierre Renard.
- **Enchanté monsieur. Vous êtes d'ici?**
- Non, je ne suis pas de Toulouse, je suis
de Cahors. Et vous?
- **Je suis de Manchester. Je suis interprète.**
- Ah bon, vous êtes ici pour la conférence,
alors?
- **Oui, vous êtes interprète?**
- Non, je suis technicien.
- **Où est la salle de conférence?**
- Elle est dans le hall d'exposition.
- **Merci et au revoir.**

- **Bonsoir monsieur, comment allez vous?**
- Tres bien merci, et vous?
- **Très bien. Voici Marthe Paoli, elle est
professeur.**
- Enchanté, vous êtes tous les deux
professeurs alors?
- **Non, je ne suis pas professeur, je suis
acteur.**
- Tiens! Il y a un théâtre ici?
- **Oui, il y un théâtre dans la rue Grenelle.**

Activity 15

visual artist and human rights activist; born
in Besançon and died in Paris

Endgame

Chapter 4

Activity 1

1b; 2e; 3c; 4g; 5h; 6a; 7d; 8f

Activity 2

A

- Bonjour madame. Vous désirez?
- Je voudrais une flûte, s'il vous plaît.
- Voilà et avec ça?
- Un pain de campagne, s'il vous plaît.
- Très bien. C'est tout?
- Oui, c'est tout, merci. C'est combien?
- Six euros, s'il vous plaît.
- Voilà.
- Merci. Au revoir, madame.

- Bonjour madame.
- Bonjour. Vous désirez?
- Je voudrais une crème antiseptique, s'il
vous plaît.
- Voilà, Monsieur. Avec ceci?
- Un insectifuge.
- Voilà. Ce sera tout?
- Oui, c'est tout, merci. C'est combien?
- Vingt-six euros, s'il vous plaît.
- Voilà.
- Merci. Au revoir, monsieur.

1 a bakery and a chemist's
2 a flûte, a country loaf, antiseptic cream
and insect repellent

B

1 Je voudrais un Bordeaux, s'il vous plaît.
2 Je voudrais six éclairs au chocolat, s'il
vous plaît.
3 Je voudrais un pain de campagne, s'il
vous plaît.
4 Je voudrais un vin rosé, s'il vous plaît.

Activity 3

- C'est combien, le Bordeaux?
- C'est neuf euros cinquante.

- Monsieur, s'il vous plait, c'est combien la
lotion solaire?
- C'est six euros vingt.

- Les croissants, c'est combien?
- C'est un euro la pièce.

- Le bœuf, c'est combien?
- C'est à huit euros quarante le kilo.

- C'est combien, le Camembert?
- Un camembert, cinq euros trente.

- Pardon, madame, c'est combien le
saumon?
- Alors, pour ceci, onze euros quatre-

vingts.

1 €9.50; 2 €6.20; 3 €1 each; 4 €8.40 a kilo; 5 €5.30; 6 €11.80

Activity 4

- Bonjour. Vous désirez?
- Je voudrais un crabe, s'il vous plaît.
- Voilà et avec ça?
- Un homard, c'est combien?
- Dix-huit euros vingt.
- Très bien, un homard s'il vous plaît.
- Avec ceci?
- Je voudrais douze langoustines et six huîtres, s'il vous plaît.
- Voilà, ce sera tout?
- Oui, c'est tout, merci. C'est combien?
- Quarante euros quatre-vingt-dix, s'il vous plaît.
- Voilà. Merci. Au revoir.

Activity 5

A

- Deux kilos, ça fait huit euros soixante.
- Deux cents grammes, c'est trois euros soixante.
- Alors deux, ça fait soixante-quatorze euros.
- Cinq cents grammes, c'est treize euros.
- Trois kilos, dix-huit euros soixante.
- Alors, huit euros dix pour les trois.

2 kilos onions, 200g ham, 2 bottles cognac, 500g Roquefort, 3kg potatoes, 3 tins tuna

C

un kilo d'oignons
cinq tranches de saucisson
une bouteille d'eau minérale
deux cent cinquante grammes de salami
deux boîtes de tomates

Activity 6

- Bonjour monsieur. Vous désirez?
- Je voudrais deux cent cinquante grammes de Roquefort, s'il vous plaît.
- Voilà monsieur, avec ceci?
- Quatre tranches de jambon.
- C'est tout?
- Non, je voudrais six bouteilles de vin rouge, s'il vous plaît.
- Du Bourgogne? Du Beaujolais?
- C'est combien le Bourgogne?

- Neuf euros la bouteille.
- Six bouteilles de Bourgogne. Vous avez une boîte d'olives?
- Oui, voilà. Ça sera tout?
- Oui, c'est tout, c'est combien?
- Soixante-douze euros cinquante, s'il vous plaît. Vous payez par carte de crédit?

'Are you paying by credit card?' was the final question.

Activity 7

B

Vous prenez deux tranches **de** pain. Mettez **du** beurre sur les deux tranches. Sur une tranche vous mettez **du** jambon et **du** Gruyère et avec l'autre tranche, vous formez un sandwich. Mettez le sandwich au gril. Mettez **des** œufs au plat sur le sandwich avant de servir.

A croque-madame has egg on top

C

- Je voudrais des œufs.
- Vous avez du pain?
- Je voudrais de l'eau.
- Vous avez de la crème?

Activity 8

A

What is ...? – Qu'est-ce que c'est ...
What do you have in the way of ...? –
Qu'est-ce que vous avez comme ...?

B

1 Qu'est-ce que c'est la bouillabaisse?
a C'est un ragoût de poissons.

2 Qu'est-ce que c'est la bisque?
d C'est une soupe aux fruits de mer.

3 Qu'est-ce que c'est la ratatouille?
c C'est un ragoût de légumes.

4 Qu'est-ce que c'est le gratin dauphinois?
b Ce sont des pommes de terre avec de la crème et du fromage.

Activity 9

A

Bonjour messieurs, dames. Aujourd'hui, en hors d'œuvres, des crêpes au saumon et une soupe aux champignons. Pour le plat principal, nous avons le steak au poivre ou le poulet à la crème et en dessert, notre chef pâtissier propose une mousse au chocolat ou une tarte aux pommes.

2 la soupe aux champignons; 3 le steak au poivre; 6 la tarte aux pommes; 1 les crêpes au saumon; 5 la mousse au chocolat; 4 le poulet à la crème

le bœuf au vin rouge isn't mentioned

starter – hors d'œuvres; main course – plat principal; dessert – dessert

B
Messieurs, dames, qu'est ce que vous prenez comme dessert?
- Alors pour moi une crème brûlée à la vanille, s'il vous plaît.
- Et pour nous, un fondant au chocolat noir et les fruits exotiques flambés au rhum.
- Je voudrais une tarte à la banane, ah, non, une tarte aux fruits de saison, non, même pas ça, un moelleux aux pommes!
- Et pour moi une glace à la fraise.

fondant au chocolat noir; crème brûlée à la vanille; fruits exotiques flambés au rhum; moelleux aux pommes; tarte à la banane; tarte aux fruits de saison; glace à la fraise

Activity 10
1 Je voudrais une tarte à l'oignon.
2 Je voudrais une soupe aux champignons.
3 Je voudrais de la glace à la vanille.
4 Je voudrais une crêpe au jambon.
5 Je voudrais un sandwich au fromage.

Activity 11
A
1 salade au saumon fumé
2 salade aux épinards/salade au fromage de chèvre
3 garlic
4 lemon

B
PAIN À L'AIL (garlic bread)
SALADE CÉSAR AU POULET (chicken caesar salad)
Tranches de poulet grillées servies sur

notre salade césar
SALADE AUX ÉPINARDS (spinach salad)
Épinards frais garnis de champignons, d'oignons rouges et mayonnaise piquante au citron
SALADE AU FROMAGE DE CHÈVRE (goat's cheese salad)
Fromage de chèvre chauffé, couvert de noisettes, tomates, concombres, salades vertes avec une vinaigrette aux herbes fines
SALADE AU POULET ET AUX POIRES RÔTIES (chicken and roasted pear salad)
Poulet, poires rôties, Gorgonzola et noix caramélisées, servis sur salade verte mixte
SALADE AU SAUMON FUMÉ (smoked salmon salad)
Saumon fumé de l'Atlantique servi sur salade verte, avec oignons rouges, olives noires, câpres, et une vinaigrette à l'huile citronnée

Activity 12
Alors le numéro de téléphone pour Le Pont de La Tour est le zéro un, seize, cinquante-quatre, douze, zéro neuf, et pour La Bonne Bouche zéro sept, soixante-seize, onze, quatre-vingt-douze, soixante-sept, Chez Mimi zéro cinq, quarante-deux, quatre-vingt-huit, dix-neuf, trente-six et Café Antigone zéro deux, trente-trois, vingt-neuf, cinquante-cinq, quatre-vingt-treize.

Le Pont de La Tour – 01 16 54 12 09; La Bonne Bouche – 07 76 11 92 67; Chez Mimi – 05 42 88 19 36; Café Antigone – 02 33 29 55 93.

Activity 13
- Vous avez choisi?
- **Oui, je voudrais le menu à vingt-cinq euros, s'il vous plaît.**
- Bon, qu'est-ce que vous prenez en hors d'œuvres?
- **Je voudrais la salade au fromage de chèvre et le poulet au vin rouge.**
- Très bien.
- **Qu'est-ce que vous avez comme desserts?**
- Nous avons la tarte à la fraise et le

clafoutis.
- Qu'est-ce que c'est, le clafoutis?
- C'est un gâteau aux cerises.
- Non, merci, vous avez des glaces?
- Vanille, chocolat, rhum raisin.
- Une glace au chocolat, s'il vous plaît.
- Et pour boire, vous désirez?
- Une bouteille de vin blanc et de l'eau, s'il vous plaît.

The tools of the trade

Activity 1

1 Canal becomes canaux in the plural and is a masculine noun.
2 Être is a verb.
3 National becomes nationaux in the masculine plural and is an adjective.

Activity 2

B
In my bedroom there are blind people (instead of 'blinds') on the window.

Shop till you drop!

I support West Ham.

Chapter 5

Activity 2

A
Appartement 1: Marianne Dugard; divorced; Antoine Lesieur is her half brother
Appartement 2: Philippe Rocard; partner of Julie Corot; Antoine Lesieur's cousin
Appartement 3: Annette Metzger; divorced; stepmother of Antoine Lesieur
Appartement 4: Julie Corot; partner of Philippe; Marianne Dugard's cousin
Appartement 5: Antoine Lesieur; married; Annette Metzger is his stepmother

B
1 Julie Corot est la compagne de Philippe Rocard./Philippe Rocard est le compagnon de Julie Corot.
2 Marianne Dugard est la demi-sœur d'Antoine Lesieur./Antoine Lesieur est le demi-frère de Marianne Dugard.
3 Antoine Lesieur est le cousin de Philippe Rocard./Philippe Rocard est le cousin d'Antoine Lesieur.

Activity 3

- Philippe, vous n'êtes pas marié mais vous avez une compagne ici?
- Oui, ma compagne s'appelle Julie. Sa tante, Annette, est l'ex-femme de mon oncle, Pierre.

- Antoine, qui est votre sœur?
- J'ai une demi-sœur qui s'appelle Marianne. Elle est la cousine de Julie.

- Annette vos enfants, en fait toute votre famille, habitent La Résidence?
- Oui, c'est vrai, j'ai mes enfants, Marianne et Antoine, mes petits-enfants, ma nièce et le neveu de mon ex, ils sont tous ici.

1 Who Philippe's partner is and who Antoine's sister is.
2 Children, grandchildren, niece, and nephew of her ex.

Activity 4

Je suis divorcée deux fois avec deux enfants. **Ma** fille s'appelle Marianne et **son** demi-frère est Antoine. **Mon** ex-mari, le père d'Antoine, est Pierre. **Son** neveu Philippe habite dans l'appartement numéro deux. La partenaire de Philippe, Julie, est **ma** nièce. Antoine, **sa** femme et **leurs** deux enfants habitent dans l'appartement numéro cinq. Nous sommes vraiment 'en famille' dans La Résidence!

Activity 5

- J'ai une Citroën, ma femme a une Peugeot.
- Il a son appartement à Paris et sa maison à Antibes.
- Où est ton verre?
- Ils ont leur bureau à côté de la poste, dans la Rue Foucauld.
- Oui, nous avons une piscine dans notre jardin.
- Lucille et Martine ont leurs photos de Marrakech.

7 a swimming pool; 6 an office; 8 a garden; 3 a flat in Paris; 4 a house in Antibes; 5 a glass; 1 a Citroën; 2 a Peugeot; 9 photos of Marrakech

Activity 6

A

Alors, je suis mariée avec Antoine.
Nous avons deux enfants, Xavier et
Sophie. Xavier a quatre ans et sa sœur a
seulement deux ans. Antoine, il a toute sa
famille à la Résidence, donc nous avons
toujours une baby-sitter! Nos enfants ont
leur grand-mère au numéro trois et leur
tante au numéro un.

1 Xavier
2 There's always a babysitter

B

j'ai; tu as; il/elle **a**; nous **avons**; vous
avez; ils/elles **ont**

C

Elle s'appelle Annette Rosalie Metzger.
Elle est divorcée.
Elle a cinquante-deux ans.
Elle est serveuse à temps partiel.
Elle a une fille, un beau-fils et deux petits-
enfants.

Activity 7

1g; **2**c; **3**a; **4**f; **5**b; **6**d; **7**h; **8**e

Activity 8

La famille a cinq appartements à La
Résidence. Nous n'avons pas de jardin
mais le parc est à côté et j'ai un balcon.
On n'a pas de restaurants dans les
environs, mais on a des magasins tout
près, une boulangerie, une pharmacie
et un supermarché et on est près de la
gare et de la gare routière. On est bien ici
mais je voudrais prendre ma retraite à la
campagne!

1 She's got a balcony and there's a park
nearby.
2 train and bus
3 the countryside

Activity 9

Je n'ai pas **de** sœurs.
On n'a pas **de** piscine dans notre villa.
Vous n'avez pas **de** cousins?
Il n'est pas **le** neveu de Marguerite.
Je ne voudrais pas **d'**appartement. Je
voudrais un hôtel.

Ce ne sont pas **des/les** photos de ta
famille?

Activity 10

A

- Didier, dis-moi, qui est Jean-Claude?
- C'est mon père.
- Il a quel âge ton père?
- Il a soixante-dix-huit ans.
- Tu as un frère, n'est-ce pas?
- Oui, on est deux enfants dans la famille,
moi et mon frère Gustave. Gustave a
quarante-neuf ans et je suis le bébé, j'ai
quarante-sept ans.
- Vous êtes mariés tous les deux?
- Moi, oui, Gustave est divorcé. Il a une
fille, Béatrice qui a vingt-cinq ans et un
fils Marc, qui a dix-huit ans.
- Qui sont Monique et Chantal?
- Ce sont mes filles. Elles ont vingt ans et
sont jumelles, tu vois!

Family tree: Didier's father is Jean-Claude
and his brother is Gustave. Didier has
twin daughters Monique and Chantal and
Gustave has a son, Marc, and a daughter,
Béatrice.

female twins – jumelles; male twins –
jumeaux

B

- Qui est Gustave?
- Mon frère.
- Qui est Béatrice?
- La fille de Gustave, ma nièce.
- Qui est Marc?
- Mon neveu.
- Qui sont Monique et Chantal?
- Mes filles.

C

Jean-Claude est son père.
Gustave est son frère.
Monique et Chantal sont ses filles.
Béatrice est sa nièce et Marc est son
neveu.

Ce sont leurs cousins.

Activity 11

Marie-France **est** mariée avec Franck. Les
Legrand **ont** trois enfants, un fils et deux
filles. Leur fils **est** technicien à Paris. Il **a**

une fille qui s'appelle Sophie qui a deux ans. Les filles des Legrand ne **sont** pas mariées. Sylvie **a** vingt-six ans et elle est infirmière. Sa sœur, Thérèse, **a** dix-huit ans et elle **est** étudiante à l'Université de Strasbourg.

Activity 12

A

- Vous vous appelez comment?
- Antoine Charles Lesieur.
- Vous êtes célibataire?
- Non, je suis marié.
- Vous avez quel âge?
- Trente et un ans.
- Quel est votre emploi?
- Je suis sans emploi.
- Votre famille?
- Ma femme qui a vingt-sept ans et deux enfants.

Nom	Lesieur
Prénom	Antoine Charles
Situation de famille	Marié
Âge	Trente et un
Emploi	Sans emploi
Famille	Femme et deux enfants

Activity 13

1 Anne d'Autriche
2 Henri IV and Marguerite d'Autriche-Styrie
3 Marie de Médicis – Italian; Henri IV – French; Marguerite d'Autriche-Styrie – Austrian; Philippe III – French
4 four and a half

Endgame

1e; 2h; 3g; 4d; 5b; 6f; 7a; 8i; 9c

Chapter 6

Activity 1

1 un avion – a plane
2 un vélo – a bicycle
3 un autobus – a bus
4 une voiture – a car
5 un car – a coach

Activity 2

A

1 Coach
2 Paris and Lille
3 It's environmentally friendly and there are no parking problems.
4 One of them is short of time.

B

je **prends**
tu **prends**
il/elle **prend**
nous prenons
vous prenez
ils/elles prennent

Word builder

Take it or leave it.

Activity 3

A

- Vous prenez des vacances, Stéphanie?
- Oui, en juillet avec mon mari. On va à Nice.
- Vous prenez l'avion?
- Non, on prend le train de Lille à Paris. À Paris on prend le métro de la Gare du Nord à la Gare de Lyon, ensuite le TGV pour Nice.
- Et votre hôtel?
- L'hôtel est dans le centre de Nice et on est en demi-pension; on prend le petit déjeuner et le dîner à l'hôtel. Pour le déjeuner on prend un snack au café.
- Attention, ne prenez pas de poids! Bonnes vacances!

1 her husband
2 train Lille to Paris; metro in Paris; TGV to Nice
3 half board
4 Don't put on weight.

B

Stéphanie **prend** ses vacances avec son mari à Nice. Ils **prennent** le train de Lille à Paris et le TGV pour Nice. Leur hôtel est dans le centre de Nice. Ils **sont** en demi-pension mais ils **ont** des plans pour le déjeuner - ils **prennent** un snack à midi. Régime Low Carb après les vacances!

Activity 4

huit heures quarante-cinq; onze heures cinquante-trois; neuf heures trois; dix-sept heures treize; dix-neuf heures quarante-six; dix-huit heures vingt et une; vingt heures quarante-huit

11h37 is not mentioned

Activity 5

1 Le car pour Rennes part à quelle heure?
2 Le ferry pour La Corse part à quelle heure?
3 L'avion de Montréal arrive à quelle heure?
4 Le train de Rome arrive à quelle heure?

Activity 6

- Allô
- Allô, ici Jean-Louis.
- Salut Jean-Louis.
- Dis, le train de Chartres arrive à quelle heure?
- À douze heures cinq.
- Et l'avion de Londres arrive à l'aéroport à douze heures trente-huit?
- Non, il part de Londres à dix heures quarante-deux et il arrive à onze heures cinquante-cinq.
- Et le car de Metz, il arrive à quelle heure?
- À treize heures dix-sept à la gare routière.

1 train, plane, coach
2 dix heures quarante-deux (10.42)
3 douze heures cinq (12.05); douze heures trente-huit (12.38); onze heures cinquante-cinq (11.55); treize heures dix-sept (13.17)

Activity 7

- Le train en provenance de Marseille a quinze minutes de retard. Il arrive à vingt heures quarante au quai numéro sept.

- Le TGV à destination de Lille a trois minutes de retard. Il arrive à neuf heures douze au quai numéro quatre.

- Le train à destination de Nice est annulé.

- Le train en provenance de Dijon a vingt minutes de retard. Il arrive à vingt heures quarante au quai numéro trois.

- Le train à destination de Besançon est annulé.

origin/ destination	arriving/ leaving	status
Nice	leaving	cancelled
Dijon	arriving	20 minutes late
Besançon	leaving	cancelled
Lille	leaving	3 minutes late
Marseilles	arriving	15 minutes late

Activity 8

A

un aller retour – return; un aller simple – single; une réservation – reservation; en seconde classe – second class; en première – first class; un tarif enfants – child's fare; une carte senior – senior travel card

C

- Bonjour. Vous désirez?
- **Je voudrais un aller retour pour Clermont Ferrand, s'il vous plaît.**
- En première ou en seconde?
- **En première, c'est combien?**
- C'est quatre-vingt-quatre euros soixante-cinq.
- **Très bien, j'ai une Carte Senior.**
- Bon, le tarif est soixante-seize euros soixante-cinq.
- **Merci, le train part à quelle heure?**
- A dix heures trente-cinq et il arrive à quatorze heures vingt. Voici votre billet.
- **Merci et au revoir.**
€76.65 and 14.20

Activity 9

Je vais à Paris **par** le train.
On va à Saint Tropez **à** vélo.
Elle ne va pas en autobus, elle préfère aller **en** taxi.
Ils vont **en** car entre Lille et Bruxelles.
Vous allez en Angleterre **par** le TGV ou **en** avion?

Activity 10

A
je **vais**
tu vas
il/elle **va**
nous allons
vous **allez**
ils/elles **vont**

B
- Vous allez où en vacances?
- On va au Canada.
- Vous avez un vol direct?
- Non, nous allons par Amsterdam.

- Vous allez où?
- Je vais en Guadeloupe pour une conférence.
- Vous ne prenez pas de vacances?
- Non, on va aux Seychelles en octobre. La Guadeloupe c'est pour le travail.

- Ils vont à Cayenne en Guyane. Ils ont de la famille là-bas.
- Ils vont souvent en Guyane alors?
- Oui, je crois.
- Ce sont vos cousins, n'est-ce pas?
- Oui, mais nous, nous n'allons pas en Guyane malheureusement.

- Nous, on va aux Antilles, en Martinique.
- Tiens, vous avez de la chance! Vous allez souvent en vacances?
- Non, c'est pour mon anniversaire, j'ai quarante ans.

- Elle va en Nouvelle Calédonie; son fils est là-bas.
- Il est professeur, n'est ce pas?
- Non, il est ingénieur.
- Elle va avec son mari?
- Il ne voyage pas en avion. Il a peur.

Guadeloupe 2; Canada 1; Guyane 4; Nouvelle Calédonie 6; Seychelles 3; Martinique 5

1 40th birthday
2 cousins, fils, mari
3 The husband of the woman who is going to New Caledonia; he is afraid of flying.
4 Canada
5 For a conference.

C
en France; en Belgique; au Luxembourg; en Suisse; en Andorre; au Vietnam

D
Je vais à Besançon, en France.
On va à Lausanne, en Suisse.
Luc et Sylvie vont à Papeete, en Polynésie française.
M. Cornouet va à Bruxelles, en Belgique.
Xavier va à Hanoï, au Vietnam.

Activity 11

B
Lundi je prends le train pour aller à Toulouse. Mardi matin, je vais à la société Concord. L'après-midi je suis au bureau. Mercredi matin je suis aussi au bureau. L'après-midi je vais à Clermont-Ferrand. Je ne vais pas au bureau jeudi matin, j'ai un rendez-vous chez le dentiste. Vendredi je prends congé. Je vais en vacances dans mon gîte en Normandie.

jour	matin	après-midi
lundi	Taking the train to Toulouse	
mardi	To Concord	In the office
mercredi	In the office	To Clermont-Ferrand
jeudi	Dentist's appointment	
vendredi	Holiday, gîte in Normandy	

Activity 12

Le gîte se trouve <u>dans</u> (in) le centre du village <u>près de</u> (near) la place principale. <u>À côté de</u> (next to) la maison, il y a un garage et <u>devant</u> (in front), un jardin. <u>Derrière</u> (behind), vous avez une terrasse et une piscine. <u>Sur</u> (on) la terrasse il y a un barbecue et des chaises longues. <u>Sous</u> (under) la maison il y a une cave où il y a des vélos à votre disposition. Si vous avez des problèmes, ma mère habite <u>en face</u> (opposite).

Activity 13

- Bon, le gîte c'est où exactement?
- C'est à côté de l'église. Vous avez un parc derrière.
- Parfait. Dis moi, il y a un arrêt de bus près du gîte?

- Il y en a un en face.
- Et il y a des courts de tennis?
- Oui, dans le parc derrière la propriété.
- Très bien et merci beaucoup.
- De rien, salut.

1 bus stop; **2** church; **3** tennis courts

Activity 14

Rooms: un séjour, une cuisine, une chambre, une salle de bains, un WC, un salon de jardin, un salon, une salle à manger, une salle d'eau

Outside space: une terrasse, un terrain privé, un jardin privatif, un parking clos

Facilities: un lecteur DVD, un lit, un lave-linge, un sèche-linge, un lave-vaisselle, le chauffage électrique, un barbecue, un canapé convertible, un four

Services: les draps en location, le ménage, le linge de toilette, les lits faits, connection Internet

Activity 15

A

Bonjour monsieur, bonjour madame, enchantée de faire votre connaissance. Je suis ici pour faire un tour de la maison. Entrons. Nous sommes ici dans le vestibule, devant il y a la cuisine où vous avez un lave-linge, un lave-vaisselle et un four à micro-ondes. Un sèche-linge? Non, je regrette, il n'y en a pas. Le séjour est ici en face de la salle à manger; vous avez une vue sur le jardin, et ça, c'est un canapé convertible à côté de la télévision. En haut, il y a deux chambres et une salle de bains. Le jardin est privatif et entoure toute la maison. Vous prenez le déjeuner sur la terrasse, peut-être? Sous la maison il y a un garage et tout pour la piscine. Si vous avez froid il y a le chauffage électrique. Allez! Bonnes vacances!

B
- Il y a une connection internet?
- Oui, oui c'est gratuit.
- **Où sont les magasins?**
- Alors vous avez une boulangerie en face et un supermarché dans la ville à côté.
- **Il y a des vélos?**

- Oui, ils sont dans le garage, sous la maison.
- **Il y a une gare près du gite?**
- Oui pas trop loin. À environ cinq kilomètres.

C

Downstairs there's a (kitchen, dining room) and lounge. The lounge has a (sofa bed) for extra guests and there's free (internet). In the kitchen there's a lot of kit but there isn't a (tumble dryer). There are (two) bedrooms and a bathroom. Outside there's a garden, a pool and (a terrace) where we can eat. The stuff for the pool is in (the garage under) the house; there are (bikes) in there too. We'll have to go to (the next town) for supermarket shopping but (the baker's) is opposite. The (station) is about five kilometres away.

Activity 16
- **Salut, Sabine. Ca va?**
- Salut, oui ça va bien merci. Tu vas où?
- **Je vais à la gare.**
- Ah bon, tu vas en vacances, n'est-ce pas?
- **Oui, je vais à Deauville.**
- Tu ne vas pas en voiture alors, tu prends le train?
- **Oui, je prends le train. Il part à dix heures quarante-cinq.**
- Tu restes dans un hôtel à Deauville?
- **Non, j'ai un gîte en face du casino.**
- Bonnes vacances!
- **Merci, au revoir.**

Activity 17

It's only two hours from Paris so there are lots of weekenders and holidaymakers.
pour cent means 'per cent'

Chapter 7

Activity 1
A
to prefer; to arrive; to admire; to fix; to explore; to turn; to hate (detest); to live (inhabit); to travel; to accept; to start

B
inviter; confirmer; comparer; changer;

voter; consulter; continuer; exister;
transformer; imaginer

C

rester – to stay; assister – to attend;
attendre – to wait for; embrasser – to kiss;
blesser – to wound; demander – to ask;
travailler – to work; quitter – to leave

Activity 2

A

1 the climate, lifestyle and the cuisine
2 spring and autumn
3 tennis and swimming
4 her partner, Christophe and their dog,
Roger

B

Je suis Madeleine Dugard – vétérinaire.
Mon compagnon, Christophe et moi nous
habitons un appartement à Nice. On
travaille ensemble à Cannes; Christophe
est vétérinaire aussi. Je suis du nord,
mes parents habitent à Strasbourg, mais
j'aime bien le sud: le climat, le style de vie
et la cuisine. Je voyage beaucoup mais je
reviens toujours ici.

Christophe adore Nice, sa famille habite
Lyon mais il préfère être au bord de la
mer.

Ici, il joue au tennis et il nage. On se
promène sur la plage tous les jours avec
notre chien, Roger. On s'amuse bien ici.

On aime l'été quand les touristes arrivent
et la région se transforme; mais nous
préférons le printemps et l'automne, c'est
plus calme.

C

travailler; habiter; voyager

Activity 3

Je travaille	Il travaille	Nous travaillons
J'aime	Il aime	Nous aimons
J'adore	Il adore	Nous adorons
J'habite	Il habite	Nous habitons
Je joue	Il joue	Nous jouons

Activity 4

A

- Je cherche le bureau de Monsieur Martin.

Il est où, s'il vous plaît?
- Il est là-bas mais, je regrette, Monsieur
Martin travaille à Paris à présent. Vous
désirez parler avec sa secrétaire?
- Oui, merci.

- Nous travaillons pour la Société Dupont.
Je suis Nicolas Bourdin, dessinateur et je
vous présente mon collègue, Julien Legros
qui est technicien.
- Enchantée. Je suis Corinne De Marchand.
Je travaille chez Peugeot. Vous habitez
Besançon?
- Non, nous habitons à Lyon.

- J'aime bien ce candidat. Il parle anglais
couramment.
- Oui mais je préfère Mlle Lefarge. Elle
parle anglais et allemand.

- Les délégués arrivent à Paris le trois mai.
Ils désirent un rendez-vous avec nous à
midi.
- D'accord. Ils voyagent par le train ou en
avion?
- Par le train et ils restent deux jours
seulement.

- Tu restes à Bordeaux ce week-end?
- Oui, et toi? Tu habites près de la poste,
n'est-ce pas?
- Oui, je préfère l'ambiance du centre. Tu
cherches un appartement dans le centre?

1 He's working in Paris.
2 Dupont
3 two, English and German
4 by train
5 the atmosphere

B

tu travailles, vous cherchez and ils/elles
habitent don't appear

Activity 5

	arriver	chercher
Je/j'	arrive	cherche
Tu	arrives	cherches
Il/elle/on	arrive	cherche
Nous	arrivons	cherchons
Vous	arrivez	cherchez
Ils/elles	arrivent	cherchent

	parler	rester
Je/j'	parle	reste
Tu	parles	restes
Il/elle/on	parle	reste
Nous	parlons	restons
Vous	parlez	restez
Ils/elles	parlent	restent

Activity 6

Je **joue** au tennis dans le parc. Belle matinée!

Ils **mangent** les céréales; moi, je **préfère** le pain

Journée importante, les parents **arrivent**. Attention!

Bizarre! Elle **parle** anglais avec Sophie. Pourquoi?

On **commence** le régime aujourd'hui. Pas de chocolat!

Mon compagnon **demande** une augmentation de salaire – bonne chance!

Nous **quittons** la ville pour la campagne. À bientôt!

Activity 7

A

He will visit the south of France and then go to Paris; a stage pratique is work experience

B

- Quand vous <u>finissez</u> vos études, vous <u>retournez</u> à la maison?
- Si je <u>réussis</u> à mes examens, non. J'<u>attends</u> les résultats et ensuite je <u>descends</u> dans le sud pour les vacances. En octobre je <u>commence</u> mon stage pratique chez Michaud à Paris.
- Vous <u>choisissez</u> une vie bien loin de Rennes alors?

Oui, mais mes parents <u>comprennent</u> l'importance de ce choix.

Activity 8

A

- Ma journée de travail finit à dix-huit heures.
- A six heures on se promène avec les chiens.
- Elle attend son collègue à la gare tous les jours.
- Nous arrivons toujours au bureau à huit heures.
- Les week-ends, je rends visite à mes parents.
- Je passe tous les soirs dans le jardin.
- On se baigne dans la mer le jour de Noël.

B

Elle arrive à son lieu de travail à six heures le matin. D'abord elle lave la vaisselle, elle range les bouteilles et elle prépare la machine à café. Les premiers clients arrivent à six heures trente; ils sont en route pour leur travail. Elle travaille, mais en même temps elle parle avec tout le monde, elle s'amuse. Sa période de travail finit à midi, elle attend l'arrivée de son collègue et elle rentre, fatiguée, mais contente.

Il habite dans un appartement près du stade. De lundi à vendredi il s'entraîne dans la salle de gym et avec son équipe sur le terrain. Samedi, il arrive au stade; il s'habille en t-shirt et en short. Lui et ses dix coéquipiers arrivent au stade à quatorze heures et le match commence; quand il marque un but ou s'ils gagnent le match, ils passent la soirée au bar!

Elle passe la journée dans le métro. Elle arrive à temps pour le premier train et elle s'installe près de l'escalator. Elle choisit la musique, elle fixe son pupitre et elle commence à jouer. Les passagers donnent de l'argent en passant. Elle finit sa journée dans le café du coin.

café worker; footballer; busker

C

Je passe la journée dans le métro. J'arrive à temps pour le premier train et je m'installe près de l'escalator. Je choisis la musique, je fixe mon pupitre et je commence à jouer. Les passagers donnent de l'argent en passant. Je finis ma journée dans le café du coin.

Activity 9

Il arrive ✓	Ils arrivent	arriver
Il descend	Ils descendent ✓	descendre
Ils parlent	Il parle	parler
Elles aiment ✓	Elle aime	aimer
Elle mange	Elles mangent	manger
Elle réagit ✓	Elles réagissent	réagir
Il se promène	Ils se promènent	se promener
Ils entendent	Il entend ✓	entendre
Elle vend	Elles vendent ✓	vendre
Elle s'habille	Elles s'habillent	s'habiller

Activity 10

A

Ça commence tôt. Petit à petit, des hommes, des femmes, des jeunes, des enfants même remplissent les rues. C'est une armée en uniforme bleu qui se dirige vers le stade. Ils s'arrêtent dans les cafés et les bars; ils mangent; ils prennent un verre; ils discutent le match. Une queue se forme; un par un ils entrent dans le stade; ils trouvent leur place. D'abord, un murmure de milliers de voix; ensuite ils chantent; ils applaudissent; ils crient les noms des joueurs. À trois heures on donne un coup de sifflet; le match débute. Qu'ils gagnent ou qu'ils perdent, on retourne chaque semaine pour encourager l'équipe.

B

1 Je m'arrête dans un bar.
2 Nous discutons le match.
3 J'entre dans le stade.
4 Nous chantons.
5 Nous applaudissons.
6 Je retourne chaque semaine.

Activity 11

A

- Tu aimes le football?
- Non, pas tellement, je préfère le rugby.

- Tu préfères le tennis ou le golf?
- J'adore le tennis mais j'aime beaucoup le golf aussi.

- Tu aimes la boxe?
- Non, pas du tout, mais j'apprécie le catch.

- Vous aimez le cyclisme?
- Non, je n'aime pas trop le cyclisme; je préfère la course automobile.

- Il aime le basket?
- Non, pas tellement, mais il admire les joueurs.

- Vous aimez la natation?
- Non, je déteste nager mais j'adore me promener sur la plage.

rugby tennis badminton, cycling basketball wrestling swimming hockey, motor racing football golf trekking, boxing

Activity 12

A

- Je déteste le shopping mais j'aime faire les achats en ligne
1 J'aime le vin, mais je préfère la bière.
2 J'aime aller au cinéma, mais je n'aime pas trop aller au théâtre.
3 Je n'aime pas tellement la musique pop; je préfère le jazz.
4 Je n'aime pas regarder la télé, mais je déteste écouter la radio.
5 Je n'aime pas les romans, mais j'apprécie la poésie.
6 Je déteste regarder les documentaires, mais j'aime beaucoup les feuilletons.

C

1 Vous aimez regarder la télé ou écouter la radio?
2 Vous préférez parler français ou allemand?
3 Vous aimez le jazz ou le rock?
4 Vous préférez habiter Paris ou Londres?

D

1 Il aime le sport?
2 Tu aimes/Vous aimez la cuisine française?
3 Vous aimez Monet?
4 Tu aimes/Vous aimez les films de science fiction?

Activity 13

A

Il est dix-neuf heures, mardi. Philippe et Julie sont dans l'appartement numéro deux; ils regardent la télé.

Natalie attend le retour d'Antoine dans son appartement (numéro cinq). Il se promène dans le parc avec les enfants et les chiens.

Annette travaille dans la cuisine de l'appartement numéro trois. Elle prépare un repas pour sa fille, Madeleine.

Madeleine n'est pas dans son appartement, elle rentre de son travail à vélo.

Dans l'appartement numéro quatre une personne entre par la fenêtre ...

Appartement 1	Appartement 2
	Philippe and Julie are watching television.

Appartement 3	Appartement 4
Annette is working in the kitchen. She's preparing a meal for her daughter, Madeleine.	Someone is entering the flat via the window.

Appartement 5
Natalie is awaiting Antoine's return. He's walking in the park with the children and the dogs.

B

Plus tard ...
Dans l'appartement numéro quatre Philippe **téléphone** à la police. Sa compagne Julie **pleure**.
Madeleine **mange** avec sa mère. Elles **entendent** les pleurs de Julie à côté mais elles **continuent** à manger.
Antoine, les enfants et les chiens **rentrent**. Ils remarquent la porte ouverte au numéro quatre mais ils n'entrent pas.
Natalie **se repose** dans le salon. Elle **choisit** un magazine sur la table.

Activity 14
- Qu'est-ce que tu fais?
- **Je me repose; je regarde la télé.**
- Qu'est-ce tu regardes?

- **Je regarde un documentaire.**
- Tu aimes les documentaires?
- **Je préfère les feuilletons, mais j'aime les documentaires aussi.**
- Tu travailles demain?
- **Non, je ne travaille pas; je reste à la maison, j'attends une livraison, mais je travaille mercredi.**
- Bon, à mercredi alors!

Chapter 8

Activity 1
A
1 statement; **2** question; **3** statement; **4** question; **5** question; **6** statement **7** question; **8** question

C
1 Vous avez des brioches?
Est-ce que vous avez des brioches?
Avez-vous des brioches?

2 Vous avez un jardin?
Est-ce que vous avez un jardin?
Avez-vous un jardin?

3 Vous avez l'heure?
Est-ce que vous avez l'heure?
Avez-vous l'heure?

D
1 Où est-ce qu'ils habitent?
Ils habitent où?

2 Quand est-ce que la conférence commence?
La conférence commence quand?

3 Comment est-ce qu'il arrive?
Il arrive comment?

4 À quelle heure est-ce que l'avion part?
l'avion part à quelle heure?

Activity 2
A
1 Est-ce que vous travaillez?/Travaillez-vous?
2 Est-ce que vous habitez Calais?/Vous habitez Calais?
3 Vous faites du sport?/Faites-vous du sport?
4 Est-ce que vous aimez le théâtre?/Aimez-vous le théâtre?

5 Est-ce que vous voyagez souvent à l'étranger?/Voyagez-vous souvent à l'étranger?

B
- Vous travaillez?
- Oui, je travaille pour Eurostar. (She works for Eurostar.)
- Vous habitez Calais?
- Non, j'habite à la campagne près de Boulogne. (No, she lives in the country near Boulogne.)
- Est-ce que vous faites du sport?
- Non, je déteste le sport et je n'ai pas le temps d'aller à la gym, je travaille trop. (No, she hates sport and doesn't have time to go to the gym, she works too much.)
- Aimez-vous le théâtre?
- Je n'aime pas du tout le théâtre, je préfère le cinéma surtout les films d'horreur. (She doesn't like the theatre, she prefers the cinema, especially horror films.)
- Vous voyagez souvent à l'étranger?
- Je voyage entre la France et l'Angleterre tous les jours, c'est mon travail. Je suis hôtesse. Pour les vacances je reste en France. (She travels between France and England every day for work. She's a hostess. She stays in France for her holidays.)

Activity 3

A
- Voulez-vous manger au Restaurant Leclerc, samedi soir?
- Oui, je veux bien, on se rencontre à quelle heure?

- Tu veux faire une promenade sur la plage demain?
- Désolée, je ne peux pas, je n'ai vraiment pas le temps.

- Voulez-vous prendre un pot après la réunion?
- Oui, je veux bien, on va au café de la Gare?

- Veux-tu venir chez moi pour un repas chinois mardi?
- Mardi, je regrette, je suis occupée. Mais mercredi je suis libre.

- Vendredi soir, vous voulez voir le nouveau film de Scorcese?

- Nous allons au cinéma vendredi avec nos voisins.

	Oui	Non
prendre un pot	x	
aller au cinéma		x
faire une promenade sur la plage		x
manger au restaurant	x	
venir chez moi	x	

B
1 Veux-tu aller au théâtre?
2 Voulez-vous visiter mon bureau?
3 Vous voulez venir chez moi?
4 Voulez-vous voyager par le train?
5 Tu veux manger à la Brasserie Flo?
6 Voulez-vous prendre un pot?
7 Tu veux rencontrer Marie-Claire?

je **veux**	nous voulons
tu **veux**	vous **voulez**
il/elle/on veut	ils/elles veulent

Activity 4

A
1 - Pardon, monsieur, je cherche un garage, pouvez-vous m'aider?
- Non, je regrette, je ne suis pas d'ici.

2 - Bonjour, Monsieur.
- Bonjour, Monsieur. Je reste deux jours seulement à Avignon. Est-ce que vous pouvez me proposer un itinéraire?
- Oui, vous voulez voir le Palais des Papes? Çela vous intéresse?

3 - Bonjour, mademoiselle, pouvez-vous me recommander une excursion?
- Mais oui, vous aimez les châteaux?

4 - Bonjour, madame.
- Bonjour, vous pouvez m'indiquer le Musée des Beaux Arts sur le plan, s'il vous plaît?
- Oui, voilà le musée, à côté de la cathédrale.

5 - Est-ce que vous pouvez m'appeler un taxi pour aller à l'aéroport, s'il vous plaît?
- Oui, vous voulez partir maintenant?
- Oui, tout de suite, s'il vous plaît. Je suis en retard.

	Help to do ...?	Help received?
1	Find a garage	no
2	An itinerary	yes
3	An excursion	yes
4	Find a museum	yes
5	Phone a cab for the airport	yes

B
1 Vous pouvez me recommander un restaurant?
2 Vous pouvez m'appeler un taxi?
3 Vous pouvez m'aider, je veux aller à la gare?

C
Je peux entrer dans le château?
Nous pouvons réserver les billets?
On peut déguster les huîtres?
On peut choisir les vins?
Je peux voir la chambre?

D
je **peux**   nous **pouvons**
tu **peux**   vous **pouvez**
il/elle/on **peut** ils/elles peuvent

Activity 5
Vous pouvez venir dimanche?
Vous savez télécharger la musique?
Vous savez changer un pneu?
Vous pouvez partir à seize heures?

Activity 6
A
- Qu'est-ce que vous faites le week-end?
- On fait du sport, du yoga et du snowboard.
- Qu'est-ce que vous faites quand vous ne travaillez pas?
- Moi je fais de la musique, je joue dans un orchestre.
- Qu'est-ce que tu fais le samedi matin?
- Je reste au lit, je poste des messages sur mon blog, je joue avec ma Xbox ...
- Qu'est-ce tu fais en vacances?
- Je vais au bord de la mer, je passe tous les jours sur la plage, je fais du surf.

- Qu'est-ce que vous faites quand vous ne travaillez pas?
- Alors, j'ai beaucoup de passe-temps, la généalogie, la politique, les mots croisés, le bridge. Je fais toujours quelque chose.
- Qu'est-ce que vous aimez faire?
- De la course à pied. Je fais du jogging tous les jours et je m'entraîne pour un marathon.

sports: yoga, snowboarding, surfing, jogging, marathon

leisure pursuits: playing in an orchestra, music, staying in bed, blogging, Xbox, genealogy, politics, crosswords, bridge

Activity 7
A
- Vous aimez le sport?
- **Pas tellement, mais je fais du jogging.**
- Vous faites d'autres sports?
- **Oui, je fais du ski.**
- Votre compagnon fait du sport?
- **Oui, il fait de la natation et du vélo.**
- Vous avez d'autres passe-temps, tous les deux?
- **Nous faisons du jardinage et mon compagnon aime faire du bricolage.**
- Et c'est vous qui faites la cuisine à la maison?
- **Non, mon compagnon fait la cuisine et la vaisselle aussi!**

B
1 Mon compagnon ne fait rien dans le jardin.
2 Mes enfants ne font rien à la maison.
3 Nous ne faisons rien le week-end.

C
1 On ne fait jamais de bricolage.
2 Elle ne fait plus de musique.
3 On ne fait jamais de conversation.
4 Nous ne faisons plus de golf.

Activity 8
1 Quel film? (Which film?);
2 Quelle sorte de cuisine? (What sort of cuisine?)
3 the match: Quels sports? (Which sports?)

Activity 9
- **Vous préférez quels vins?**
- J'aime bien le blanc mais je préfère le rouge.

- **Vous aimez quels parfums?**
- J'aime la vanille et le chocolat, je n'aime pas la pistache.

- **Vous aimez quelle maison?**
- On aime bien la maison avec deux chambres.

- **Tu préfères quelles régions?**
- J'adore le Jura et le pays Basque.

1 false; 2 true; 3 false; 4 false

Activity 10
Salut Didier, c'est Louis. **Qu'est-ce que** tu fais mardi? Tu peux m'aider? Je veux changer ma voiture mais je ne sais pas quoi faire? **Quelle** marque préfères-tu? **Quels** concessionnaires? **Qu'est-ce que** tu suggères? Je peux venir à ton appartement à douze heures si tu es libre. Sinon, tu peux proposer **quelle** autre journée? **Quel** est ton numéro de portable?

Activity 11
- **Bonsoir, comment vous appelez-vous?**
- Je m'appelle Olivier David.
- **Vous avez quel âge?**
- J'ai vingt-six ans.
- **(Est-ce que) vous travaillez?**
- Oui je suis plombier.
- **Vous habitez où?**
- J'habite chez mes parents à Toulouse.
- **Qu'est-ce que vous faites quand vous ne travaillez pas?**
- Alors, je ne sais pas, pas grand chose.
- **Vous ne faites rien? (Est-ce que) vous aimez le sport?**
- Oui, oui.
- **Vous aimez quels sports?**
- Le rugby, le football.
- **Vous savez jouer au rugby?**
- Non, je regarde les matchs à la télé!
- **Vous voyagez beaucoup?**
- Un peu, en vacances.
- **Vous voulez visiter quels pays?**
- Je voudrais bien aller au Vietnam et en Chine.
- **Merci et bonne chance.**

Activity 12
1 That they don't like work and often go on holiday.
2 There's a 35-hour working week, with five weeks' paid holiday a year, 11 public holidays, 16 weeks' maternity leave for women and two weeks' paternity leave for men.
3 If a public holiday falls on a Thursday they can also take the Friday off, and if one falls on a Tuesday they can take the Monday off.
4 1700 hours.
5 Retirement from the age of 60.

Chapter 9

Activity 2
A
- Bonjour madame. Comment allez-vous?
- Très bien, merci, et vous?
- Bien aussi. **Il fait beau**, n'est-ce pas?
- Oui, très beau.

- Salut Ernestine. Ça va?
- Salut. Oui ça va bien. **Il fait du brouillard,** n'est-ce pas?
- Oui, je ne vois presque rien!

- Allô, oui
- C'est toi, Pierre?
- Oui, c'est moi.
- Comment vas-tu? Il fait beau?
- Ça va. **Il fait du soleil** ici. Il fait chaud; au moins 28 degrés. On va à la plage.
- Oh là! Alors ici **il fait du vent** et il pleut. Tu as de la chance! Moi, je reste à la maison.

1 28 degrees
2 one person is going to the beach, the other is staying at home.

B
1 Il fait du soleil, n'est-ce pas?
2 Il fait du vent, n'est-ce pas?
3 Il fait mauvais, n'est-ce pas?

Activity 4

un homme important – une femme importante
un musée contemporain – une peinture contemporaine
un ami amusant – une amie amusante
un obstacle évident – une question évidente
un paysage charmant – une vue charmante

Activity 5

A

Ils habitent **une belle maison** sur la côte méditerranéenne. Ils ont **un grand salon charmant, une cuisine moderne et spacieuse** et trois chambres. Du jardin on a **une vue spectaculaire** sur la baie. Il y a **une petite piscine** avec **une terrasse ombragée.**

B

belle, grand and petite

Activity 6

A

Euh, ça fait au moins cinq ans qu'Annie est avec Yves, personne ne sait pourquoi. Elle est petite et jolie. Elle est toujours bien habillée, très chic. Elle est de bonne humeur, charmante et sympathique. Elle est sportive. Yves au contraire est grand, pas beau, un peu gros et pas très gentil. Il n'est pas du tout sportif. Il porte toujours un vieux t-shirt et un jean pas propre. Mais, alléluia, ils se marient en septembre.
Annie's sister doesn't approve of Yves.

B

petit – Annie (petite); sympathique – Annie; gros – Yves; pas gentil – Yves; vieux – t-shirt

C

1 propre; 2 sympathique or gentil; 3 bonne; 4 joli

Activity 7

A

charmant and grande

B

Je suis au sommet d'un **grand** volcan **éteint** dans la **belle** région de l'Auvergne. La vue est **fabuleuse**; là-bas un **petit** village avec son église **ancienne**, les champs, les fôrets, une **vieille** habitation **fermière**. En effet une image **idéale** de la France rurale.

Activity 8

A

- Allô, Agence Belle Maison.
- Bonjour, je voudrais des détails sur la maison dans la Rue de la Fontaine.
- Qu'est-ce que vous désirez savoir précisément?
- Il y a combien de chambres?
- Il y a trois grandes chambres.
- Est-ce que la maison est moderne?
- C'est une maison traditionnelle et typique de la région. Ancienne à l'extérieur mais avec un intérieur contemporain.
- Il y a une grande cuisine?
- Oui, c'est une nouvelle cuisine et il y a une salle de séjour magnifique à côté.
- Est-ce que je peux visiter la maison?
- Oui, bien sûr. C'est une maison charmante dans un village très populaire.
Living room: magnificent, next to the kitchen
Bedrooms: three, large
kitchen: one, large, new

B

Située dans un village **populaire** cette maison **traditionnelle** est **typique** de la région. Avec une salle de séjour **magnifique**, trois **grandes** chambres et une grande cuisine, la maison **est** charmante. Son intérieur **contemporain** est surprenant mais d'un style **sympathique**. N'hésitez pas à visiter cette excellente propriété.

Activity 9

A

- La chambre est très confortable.
- Le plateau de fruits de mer est incroyable.

- Les vues sur la baie sont merveilleuses.
- L'ambiance est parfaite.
- Les vins rouges sont formidables.

1 views over the bay; 2 room;
3 atmosphere; 4 red wines;
5 seafood platter

B
1 La vue est belle.
2 Le repas est merveilleux.
3 Les vins blancs sont excellents.
4 Votre maison est charmante.

Activity 10
A
- Je regrette, mais la chambre est trop chaude.
- Je regrette, mais le vin est trop cher.
- Je regrette, mais les t-shirts sont trop grands.
- Je regrette, mais les dimensions sont trop petites.

1 It's too hot; 2 It's too expensive;
3 They're too big; 4 They're too small.

B
- Bonjour. Je peux vous aider?
- Oui. Je regrette mais la chambre est trop petite.
- Désolé, mais c'est une de nos chambres les plus populaires.
- Je comprends, mais je voudrais voir une autre chambre.
- Très bien.
- Et je veux une chambre avec une salle de bains spacieuse.
- Voici les clés de la chambre numéro cinq.
- Voici les clés. Le lit est vieux et inconfortable et il n'y a pas de télévision dans la chambre.
- Alors, nous avons seulement la chambre numéro huit. C'est une suite. Voici les clés.
- La chambre est parfaite. C'est combien?
- Cent euros par nuit.
- C'est trop cher. Au revoir.

Activity 11
A
- J'aime le tennis. C'est si énergique.
- Les voyages en train, ils sont tellement.

agréables
- Pour les vacances je préfère la Côte d'Azur qui est très belle.
- J'aime travailler à Paris. C'est une ville tout à fait passionnante.
- J'adore le steak frites. C'est mon plat favori.
- J'aime les romans policiers, surtout s'ils sont compliqués.

1d; 2a; 3b; 4f; 5e; 6c

B
1 énergique; 2 agréables; 3 belle;
4 passionnante; 5 favori; 6 compliqués

C
- Vous aimez les films de François Truffaut?
- Oui, je les trouve admirables.

- Vous vous intéressez à la politique?
- Je la déteste. C'est tellement ennuyeux.

- Quelle est votre opinion sur l'Union Européenne?
- Je suis pour mais c'est trop compliqué.

- Vous aimez les romans de Victor Hugo?
- Je ne les aime pas tellement, mais j'adore la comédie musicale, Les Misérables

- Le recyclage, c'est important?
- Je le trouve indispensable pour l'avenir de la planète.

- Que pensez-vous de la presse anglaise?
- Je la trouve de temps en temps trop intrusive.

admirables; compliqué; musicale;
important; indispensable; intrusive

D
Oui, je les trouve admirables.
Je la déteste.
Je ne les aime pas tellement.
Je le trouve indispensable pour l'avenir de la planète.
Je la trouve de temps en temps trop intrusive.

Activity 12
1 Il la déteste.
2 Vous les regardez?
3 Je les trouve magnifiques.

4 Il ne la donne jamais.

Activity 13

A

- Qu'est-ce que vous pensez du football?
- Je le déteste.

- Qu'est-ce que vous pensez de la décision?
- Je ne l'aime pas, elle est trop impulsive.

- Qu'est-ce qu'elle pense des plans?
- Elle ne les aime pas du tout.

- Qu'est-ce qu'ils pensent de la nourriture?
- Ils la trouvent acceptable.

- Qu'est-ce que vous pensez des magasins?
- Je les aime beaucoup.

- Qu'est-ce que tu penses du dessin?
- Je ne l'aime pas, c'est trop abstrait.

- Qu'est-ce que Christophe pense de la suggestion?
- Il la trouve intéressante.

- Qu'est-ce que vous pensez du vase bleu?
- Je l'aime bien, je le prends!

1b; 2g; 3f; 4d; 5a; 6c; 7e

B

1 Qu'est que vous pensez du sport?
2 Qu'est-ce que vous pensez de la vue?
3 Qu'est que vous pensez de l'euro?
4 Qu'est que vous pensez des feuilletons?

Activity 14

- Bonjour madame.
- **Bonjour, il fait froid, n'est-ce pas?**
- Oui, il fait très froid. Vous restez dans le gîte de Monsieur Colbert?
- **Oui, je l'aime beaucoup.**
- Qu'est-ce que vous pensez de la région?
- **Je l'adore. J'aime les petits villages et les belles montagnes.**
- Vous faites du ski?
- **Non, je ne fais pas de ski, je préfère visiter en octobre quand il fait beau.**
- Qu'est-ce que vous faites aujourd'hui?
- **Je vais à St. Germain, une très jolie ville. Je veux prendre des photos et déjeuner dans un restaurant traditionnel.**
- Alors, bonne journée madame.

Activity 15

épicé(es) – spicy; un regard – a look; boisé(es) – woody
1 fragrances 2 ciel 3 couleurs
Les nouveaux parfums ensoleillés arrivent

Chapter 10

Activity 1

push/pull; drive on the right; turn on your headlights; fasten your seatbelts; press the green button; stamp your ticket

Activity 2

B
Tournez à droite. **3**
Allez à gauche. **4**
Continuez tout droit. **7**
Prenez la première rue à droite. **2**
Passez la deuxième rue à gauche. **6**
Au rond-point, prenez la deuxième sortie. **1**
Au carrefour, tournez à gauche. **5**

C
Au bout de la rue, tournez à gauche. Dans deux cents mètres, traversez le rond-point, deuxième sortie. Dans cinq cents mètres gardez la droite. Prenez l'autoroute. Dans deux cents mètres, prenez la sortie. Au rond-point, troisième sortie. Vous êtes arrivé à votre destination.
2, 5 and 6 are incorrect

Activity 3

A
- Excusez-moi, où est le bureau du directeur financier, s'il vous plaît?
- Montez au premier étage, tournez à droite et c'est sur la gauche.

- Pardon, madame, je cherche la cantine. Elle est au premier étage?
- Non, non elle se trouve au sous-sol.

- Madame, j'ai rendez-vous avec le président directeur général. Où est son bureau, s'il vous plaît?
- Prenez l'ascenseur au cinquième étage, son bureau est en face de vous.

- Salut, Marcel. Tu vas à la salle de gym? Elle est où exactement?
- Au rez-de-chaussée, près de la réception.

- Je crois qu'il y a un restaurant panoramique. C'est vrai?
- Oui, au sixième.

- Je voudrais parler avec Henri Ducaste du service du personnel. Les bureaux du service sont où?
- Allez au troisième étage, passez par le service comptable et c'est sur la droite.

- Je suis en retard, pouvez-vous m'aider? Où sont les salles de réunion?
- Au quatrième étage, en sortant de l'ascenseur tournez à gauche.

sixième étage – le restaurant panoramique
cinquième étage – le bureau du président directeur général
quatrième étage – les salles de réunion
troisième étage – le service du personnel
deuxième étage – not mentioned
premier étage – le bureau du directeur financier
rez de chaussée – la salle de gym
sous-sol – la cantine

B
En sortant de la gare prenez la rue Rabelais à droite. Dans la rue Rabelais cherchez une petite rue à gauche, la ruelle de la Fontaine. Descendez la ruelle et vous arrivez sur la place du Marché. Traversez la place et vous voyez un grand bâtiment blanc. Entrez et montez au quatrième étage. Mon bureau est en face de l'ascenseur, c'est la salle numéro huit.

Activity 4
Assemblies are organised in semi-circle format. As the president faces the semi-circle, socialist parties sit to the left and conservative and liberal to the right.

Activity 5
A
You suck them three times a day and go to the doctor if the symptoms persist.

B
1 diarrhoea; 2 sunburn; 3 insect bites

C
un gratte-ciel is a skyscraper

- Qu'est-ce que vous avez contre une toux?
- Prenez le sirop quatre fois par jour. Consultez un médecin si les symptômes persistent. (Take the cough mixture four times a day. Go to the doctor if symptoms persist.)

- Qu'est-ce que vous avez contre la diarrhée?
- Prenez un cachet trois fois par jour. Buvez de l'eau. (Take a tablet three times a day. Drink water.)

- Qu'est-ce que vous avez contre un coup de soleil?
- Appliquez la lotion. Ne sortez pas au soleil. (Put lotion on and don't go out in the sun.)

- Qu'est-ce que vous avez contre des piqûres d'insecte?
- Appliquez la crème antihistaminique; ne les grattez pas. (Put antihistamine cream on and don't scratch them.)

Activity 6
B
- Qu'est ce que tu as, Annie? Tu es malade?
- J'ai mal à **la gorge**. Tu peux m'acheter quelque chose à la pharmacie?

- Allô, bonjour, Centre de Physiothérapie
- Bonjour, mon mari ne va pas bien. Il a mal **au dos** et il ne peut pas bouger. Je cherche un osteopate.

- Bonjour, École St Joseph.
- Je suis la mère de Pierre Martin. Il a mal **au ventre** et il ne peut pas aller à l'école aujourd'hui.
- Merci de nous prévenir.

- Qu'est ce qui ne va pas?
- J'ai vraiment mal à **la tête**.
- Tu veux des comprimés?

- Qu'est-ce qu'elle a, Dominique?
- Elle a mal **aux oreilles**. Alors elle ne peut pas faire de la natation lundi.

C
- Bonjour, qu'est ce qui ne va pas?
- J'ai mal à la tête.
- J'ai mal aux oreilles.
- J'ai mal au ventre.

- J'ai mal à la gorge.

D

- Bonjour, asseyez-vous, s'il vous plaît.
- **Bonjour, merci.**
- Comment est-ce que je peux vous aider?
- **J'ai mal à l'oreille et à la gorge.**
- Vous souffrez?
- **Oui, je ne peux pas manger et je ne peux pas dormir.**
- Bon, voici un antibiotique. Vous devez prendre deux comprimés trois fois par jour. Finissez la bouteille.

Activity 7

A

Planting a shrub. You must first of all dig a hole big enough to insert the plant comfortably in a mixture of soil and compost. For heavy soil, you should put a layer of gravel at the bottom of the hole to improve drainage. For potted plants, you should loosen the soil with a fork. Fill with the mixture of soil and compost, and water.

Activity 8

A

Je **dois** téléphoner pour un taxi pour nos visiteurs. Ils arrivent à la gare à neuf heures trente et ils **doivent** être dans la salle du conseil à dix heures quinze pour la présentation qui commence ponctuellement à dix heures trente. Madeleine **doit** organiser les rafraîchissements et le technicien **doit** vérifier la connexion Internet. Toi, tu **dois** préparer un discours. Nous **devons** être totalement préparés pour cette visite; vous **devez** remuer ciel et terre pour assurer un succès.

'move heaven and earth' – remuer ciel et terre

B

Je dois
Tu dois
Il/elle/on doit
Nous devons
Vous devez
Ils/elles doivent

Word builder activity

A

normal – normalement
fondamental – fondamentalement
rapide – rapidement
régulier – régulièrement
heureux – heureusement

B

constant – constamment
récent – récemment
fréquent – fréquemment
courant – couramment

Activity 9

A

1d; 2e; 3b; 4a; 5c

B

- Qu'est-ce qu'il faut faire pour louer des skis?
- Allez au magasin de sports en ville.

- Pour réserver des billets pour le match, qu'est-ce qu'il faut faire?
- Appeler ce numéro.

- On doit quitter l'hôtel très tôt, qu'est-ce qu'il faut faire pour régler notre note?
- Vous pouvez payer quand vous voulez, la réception est ouverte vingt-quatre heures sur vingt-quatre.

- Qu'est-ce qu'il faut faire pour contacter Monsieur Legrand?
- Il faut demander à Mme Fourgat.

- Je dois envoyer un paquet, qu'est-ce qu'il faut faire?
- Allez à la poste qui est dans la rue principale.

- Qu'est-ce qu'il faut faire pour visiter les caves?
- Il y a des tours qui partent de l'hôtel tous les jours.

Pay the bill 3; Send a parcel 5; Visit the wine cellars 6; Hire skis 1; Contact Monsieur Legrand 4; Reserve tickets for the match 2

To say 'in order to ...' use pour + the infinitive

C

1 Qu'est-ce qu'il faut faire pour louer une

voiture?

2 Qu'est-ce qu'il faut faire pour avoir un permis de conduire international?

3 Qu'est-ce qu'il faut faire pour organiser un rendez-vous chez le médecin?

4 Qu'est-ce qu'il faut faire pour aller à l'aéroport?

D

1 dinner party 2 dinner party 3 business 4 dinner party 5 business 6 business 7 dinner party 8 business

Activity 10

A

- Le restaurant est au quatrième étage?
- Non, c'est au cinquième. Vous pouvez prendre l'ascenseur ou l'escalator. En sortant, tournez à gauche.
- Il faut réserver une table au restaurant?
- Normalement vous devez téléphoner à l'avance, mais aujourd'hui il y a des tables de libre.

B

- Qu'est-ce qu'il faut faire pour louer une voiture?
- Vous devez aller à notre bureau à l'aéroport.
- Il faut avoir un permis de conduire international?
- Non, vous devez avoir seulement votre permis de conduire anglais.
- Je dois ramener la voiture à l'aéroport?
- Non, vous pouvez la ramener à notre agence en ville, si vous voulez.

C

- Bonjour, je peux vous aider?
- J'ai mal au bras. Vous avez quelque chose contre les piqûres d'insecte?
- Vous êtes allergique aux antihistaminiques?
- Non, mais je préfère avoir une crème.
- Bien, voici, vous devez appliquer la crème trois fois par jour et si ça persiste, allez voir le médecin.
- Merci, je dois appliquer la crème trois fois par jour?
- Oui, c'est ça.

Activity 11

A

servez (servir – to serve); assaisonnez (assaisonner – to season); coupez (couper – to cut); enlevez (enlever – to remove); mélangez (mélanger – to mix)

B

1 no entry
2 don't walk on the grass
3 no parking
4 no bathing
5 no smoking
6 no picnicking

Chapter 11

Activity 1

1 masculine
2 bonsoir
3 adjective

Activity 2

Le président <u>rentre</u> demain des Etats-Unis
Taylor Swift <u>va passer</u> treize heures avec ses fans
Une nouvelle famille <u>va arriver</u> dans "La Résidence"
Obama <u>part</u> demain pour le Moyen-Orient
Les ministres <u>vont discuter</u> l'euro
Une vedette de la télé <u>va aller</u> en prison
Les Bleus <u>vont aller</u> en finale en juin
La France <u>va gagner</u> la coupe du Monde!

Activity 3

A

- Ce matin, je dois faire les commissions mais cet après-midi je vais jouer au tennis avec Claudine.

- Demain soir, je vais au cinéma et avant je vais rencontrer mon ami Charles. On va dîner ensemble au restaurant.

- Aujourd'hui, elle est au bureau toute la journée mais cet après-midi elle va assister à une réunion. Il faut téléphoner ce matin avant onze heures trente.

- Je vais aller voir Maxime cette semaine. Il va partir pour les États-Unis à la fin du mois.

- Pourquoi est-ce qu'il va à Menton la semaine prochaine? Parce qu'il a des clients là-bas. Il va prendre le TGV mardi et il va rentrer vendredi.

- L'année prochaine nous allons partir en vacances en juin parce que le mariage de notre fille est en septembre.
going to the theatre and going to watch a match

B
1 je vais jouer
2 je vais; je vais rencontrer; on va dîner
3 elle est; elle va assister
4 je vais aller voir; il va partir
5 il va; il va prendre; il va rentrer
6 nous allons partir; le mariage de notre fille est
this afternoon – cet après-midi; tomorrow evening – demain soir; next week – la semaine prochaine; next year – l'année prochaine; in June – en juin; in September –- en septembre

Activity 4
A
- Qu'est-ce tu fais cet après-midi?
- Je vais faire du shopping.
- Je ne suis pas libre ce matin, mais cet après-midi ça va, je peux venir?
- Mais oui, bien sûr. Je cherche une tenue pour le mariage de ma fille. Qu'est-ce que tu penses de cette tenue? Regarde la photo.
- Euh, cette photo n'est pas tellement facile à voir. De quelle couleur est la tenue?
- On peut l'avoir en plusieurs couleurs. Voici. J'aime bien la rose mais qu'est-ce que tu penses de cette verte?
- Je préfère la rose. Ces créations sont vraiment chic. Je vais voir s'il y a un pantalon. Tu vois ce pantalon noir, parfait pour le bureau!
- On va dépenser de l'argent, nous! On y va?
a wedding outfit and a pair of trousers

B
cet après-midi; ce matin; cet après-midi;

cette tenue; cette photo; cette verte; ces créations; ce pantalon

C
1 Cet après-midi il va à Paris.
2 Je ne travaille pas cette semaine.
3 Cet octobre nous allons visiter Marrakech.
4 Elle n'aime pas ces photos.
5 Vous allez prendre ce train?
6 Ils vont être au restaurant ce soir.

D
1 Je ne vais pas prendre ce train.
2 Ils ne vont pas être au restaurant ce soir.
3 On ne va rien faire cet après-midi.

Activity 5
A
Alors, vous allez rencontrer Cécile Martin, lundi le premier avril; l'après-midi vous avez la réunion du service personnel. Le rendez-vous est fixé pour onze heures. N'oubliez pas que vous allez à la salle de gym le soir. Mardi vous allez passer toute la journée à Clermont Ferrand. Mercredi soir, le trois avril, Robert Simone va dîner avec vous au Restaurant du Duc. Le matin vous allez à Concourès, l'après-midi vous êtes au bureau. Jeudi, l'après-midi, vous allez faire une présentation aux clients. Ils vont arriver à quinze heures et finalement vendredi, le cinq avril vous allez prendre le train de treize heures quatorze pour Toulouse; voici les billets et la réservation.

	lundi 1 avril	mardi 2 avril
Le matin	Rendez-vous avec Cécile Martin 11h00	Clermont-Ferrand toute la journée
L'après-midi	Réunion du service personnel	
Le soir	Salle de gym	

	mercredi 3 avril	jeudi 4 avril
Le matin	Visite à Concourès	Au bureau
L'après-midi	Au bureau	Présentation aux clients à 15h00
Le soir	Dîner avec Robert Simone Restaurant du Duc	Cinéma 21h00

	vendredi 5 avril
Le matin	
L'après-midi	Le train de 13h14 pour Toulouse
Le soir	

Activity 6

L'Armistice c'est le onze novembre.
La fête du travail c'est le premier mai.
La fête nationale c'est le quatorze juillet.
La Toussaint c'est le premier novembre.
Le jour de l'an c'est le premier janvier.
Noël c'est le vingt-cinq décembre.
la fête nationale – 14th July; la fête du travail – 1st May; le jour de l'an – 1st January; l'Armistice – 11th November; la Toussaint – 1st November; Noël – 25th December

Activity 8

- Quand est-ce que vous allez au Maroc?
- J'y vais en octobre; à ce moment-là il va faire beau et pas trop chaud.
- Et qu'est-ce que vous allez faire au Maroc?
- Je vais visiter la médina à Fez; faire un périple dans l'Atlas; passer trois jours à Marrakech.
- À Marrakech vous allez vous relaxer?
- Mais non, je vais me promener un peu partout. Je voudrais visiter la Place Jemaa el Fna et le jardin botanique. Je vais essayer la cuisine marocaine, aller à Guéliz, le quartier européen. J'ai l'intention d'étudier la culture, donc je vais visiter tous les musées et les mosquées.

passer deux jours à Casablanca; se relaxer (vous allez vous relaxer?)

Activity 9

A
2 Je vais visiter les ruines romaines à Carthage.
3 Je vais choisir des hôtels traditionnels.
4 Je vais manger dans des restaurants pas touristiques.
5 Je vais prendre le train et le car.

B
- Vous allez où en vacances?
- Je vais aller en Tunisie au mois de mai quand il fait toujours moins chaud.
- Ah bon, pourquoi la Tunisie?
- Parce que je veux voir Tunis et je vais visiter les ruines romaines à Carthage.
- Un voyage culturel alors?
- Oui, j'espère, je vais choisir des hôtels traditionnels, manger dans des restaurants pas touristiques.
- Et vous prenez le bateau pour arriver en Tunisie, pourquoi?
- Parce que je déteste les avions. Je vais prendre le train et le car, je n'aime pas conduire non plus.
- C'est une agence de voyages qui organise tout ça?
- Non, non je vais réserver par internet. C'est plus rapide et moins cher.
1 He hates planes; 2 online

Activity 10

1d; 2e; 3a; 4b; 5c

Activity 11

A
- Pourquoi est-ce que vous choisissez de voyager en bateau?
- Parce qu'un voyage en bateau est plus écologique qu'un voyage en avion.

- Vous prenez toujours vos vacances en mai?
- Non, mais pour les pays chauds il est plus pratique de visiter quand la température est plus agréable.

- Tu aimes la plongée sous-marine, je crois. Ce n'est pas dangereux?
- Dis, toi, tu fais de l'alpinisme. L'alpinisme est plus dangereux que la plongée sous-marine.

- Vous voyagez un peu partout, n'est-ce pas? Vous préférez la Bretagne ou cette région?
- Cette région est plus belle mais moins intéressante que la Bretagne.

- Quel est le meilleur moyen de transport pour aller en France, le train ou la voiture?
- Je pense que le train est le meilleur.

1 It's more environmentally friendly than travelling by plane.
2 The temperature is more pleasant, so it's more practical.
3 It's more dangerous than deep-sea diving.
4 It's not as pretty but is more interesting than this region.
5 It's a better way to travel than by car.

B
1 Cet hôtel est moins convenable que l'Hôtel Mercure.
2 Cette place est plus grande que la Place de la Concorde.
3 Il fait plus froid ici qu'en Belgique.
4 Les vacances en France sont plus populaires.
5 Je vais visiter le souk parce que c'est plus intéressant.
6 Ce train est plus rapide?

Activity 12

A
- Parlez-moi un peu de vos projets de vacances.
- **Je vais passer deux semaines à Madagascar.**
- Quand est-ce que vous allez visiter Madagascar?
- **Je vais y aller le 14 juin.**
- Pourquoi en juin?
- **Parce qu'il fait moins chaud et il ne pleut pas.**
- Qu'est-ce que vous allez faire?
- **Je vais voir les plantes et les animaux dans les parcs nationaux.**
- Vous vous intéressez à l'écotourisme

alors?
- **Oui, et je préfère des vacances plus actives. Ce voyage est parfait.**

B
- **Qu'est-ce que tu vas faire ce week-end?**
- Je vais passer le weekend en Normandie.
- **Pourquoi tu vas en Normandie?**
- Parce que je vais assister au mariage de mon cousin.
- **Tu vas partir à quelle heure?**
- Je vais quitter Paris ce soir à environ dix-neuf heures. Je dois être à la mairie à dix heures demain matin. Et toi, qu'est ce que tu fais ce weekend?
- **Je vais le passer chez moi avec un bon livre!**
- Alors, tu vas bien t'amuser! Bon week-end.
- **Bon week-end!**

Activity 13

1 the minaret of the Koutoubia Mosque
2 storytellers, people selling things and snake charmers
3 medieval times
4 clothes, jewellery and antiques
5 take the time to look and listen

Chapter 12

Activity 1

A
We tasted pho for the first time in a restaurant in Hanoi. Our friends visited Hanoi last January and they talked about its delicious cuisine. We mentioned the restaurant to our hotel receptionist. He suggested a taxi to get there. In the restaurant we asked for a traditional pho. We ate very well!

On a goûté le pho pour la première fois dans un restaurant à Hanoï. Nos amis ont visité le Vietnam en janvier dernier et ils ont parlé de sa cuisine délicieuse. Nous avons mentionné le restaurant au réceptionniste dans notre hôtel. Il a proposé un taxi pour y aller. Au restaurant on a demandé un pho traditionnel. On a très bien mangé!

B

on a goûté – goûter
nos amis ont visité – visiter
ils ont parlé – parler
nous avons mentionné – mentionner
il a proposé – proposer
on a demandé – demander
on a (très bien) mangé – manger

Activity 2

Tu **as** regardé le match à la télé?
Mes parents **ont** voyagé aux États-Unis en vacances.
Marie-Claire **n'a** pas aimé le film
Samedi, nous **avons** joué avec la Xbox toute la journée.
Qu'est-ce que vous **avez** pensé de ce camping?
J'ai trouvé une tenue, mais je **n'ai** pas trouvé les chaussures.

Activity 3

A

aimé; perdu; réagi; vendu; changé; rendu; saisi; entendu

B

Mercredi, j'ai **travaillé** au bureau le matin. J'ai **réussi** à contacter notre nouveau client. J'ai fini mon travail à midi et j'ai **déjeuné** au restaurant avec Christine. Elle m'a **attendu** dans le bar. On a **discuté** du match et on a **décidé** d'acheter des billets pour le prochain. L'après-midi j'ai **rencontré** Monsieur Dufour à seize heures. Le soir, j'ai **passé** un appel Skype à ma compagne avant d'aller au lit. Je n'ai pas bien **dormi**.

Activity 4

Je n'ai jamais envoyé de carte et je n'ai rien donné à Marcel pour son anniversaire. Je n'ai pas répondu à son invitation. Je n'ai pas téléphoné, je ne l'ai jamais visité, et lui ... Il ne va plus m'inviter à sa fête d'anniversaire!
She hasn't sent a card or given Marcel a birthday present, she hasn't replied to his invitation, she hasn't phoned and has never visited, so he's no longer going to invite her to his birthday party.

recevoir pp reçu; savoir pp su

Activity 5

- Vous avez visité Paris, je crois?
- Oui, j'y ai passé un week-end en avril. J'ai pris l'avion de Londres.
- Qu'est-ce que vous avez fait à Paris?
- Toutes sortes de choses touristiques! J'ai regardé les peintures dans le musée du Louvre; j'ai visité les monuments, la Tour Eiffel, la Grande Arche. J'ai pris le métro pour aller à Montmartre.
- Vous avez visité le Musée d'Orsay?
- Non, qu'est-ce c'est?
- C'est un musée d'art du dix-neuvième et du vingtième siècles.
- La prochaine fois peut-être.

Eiffel Tower, Musée d'Orsay, Grande Arche, Montmartre

1 April
2 plane and underground
3 vous avez and j'ai

Activity 6

A

Je n'ai pas entendu le réveille-matin donc j'ai raté le bus. J'ai voulu téléphoner pour un taxi mais je n'ai pas trouvé mon portable. J'ai cherché le portable dans mon sac, dans mes poches, partout sans succès. J'ai dû quitter la maison à pied, il a commencé à pleuvoir, j'ai laissé mon parapluie chez mes parents. J'ai couru et finalement quand j'ai voulu entrer dans le bureau! Fermé! J'ai compris – un jour de congé!
3 wanted to phone for a cab; 4 searched for my mobile; 2 missed the bus; 5 left my umbrella at my parents'; 6 ran; 1 didn't hear the alarm
It was a day off.

B

- Tu as passé une bonne journée?
- Pas tellement.
- Pourquoi elle n'a pas été bonne?
- D'abord j'ai dû faire une présentation ensuite j'ai passé la journée avec des clients très difficiles. Je n'ai pas eu le temps de manger à midi. J'ai entendu que

ma collègue a été promue et moi, je n'ai pas eu de promotion. Finalement, pas de trains ce soir et j'ai pris un taxi pour rentrer. Et toi?
- Moi, ça va. J'ai vendu une peinture. J'ai pris l'autobus pour aller en ville et j'ai fait les soldes. J'ai acheté des chaussures.
- Alors, pour certains la vie est belle. On dîne à quelle heure? J'ai vraiment faim?

1 He had to do a presentation, spent the whole day with difficult clients, didn't have time for lunch, didn't get a promotion and there were no trains in the evening so he had to come home by taxi.
2 It's alright for some.

Activity 7

A

drinking a coffee and smoking a cigarette

B

1 J'ai mis le café
Dans la tasse
J'ai mis le lait
Dans la tasse de café
J'ai mis le sucre
Dans le café au lait
Avec la petite cuiller
J'ai tourné
J'ai bu le café au lait
Et j'ai reposé la tasse
Sans lui parler

J'ai allumé
Une cigarette
J'ai fait des ronds
Avec la fumée
J'ai mis les cendres
Dans le cendrier
Sans lui parler
Sans la regarder

2 Il n'a pas mis le café
Dans la tasse
Il n'a pas mis le lait
Dans la tasse de café
Il n'a pas mis le sucre
Dans le café au lait
Avec la petite cuiller
Il n'a pas tourné
Il n'a pas bu le café au lait
Et il n'a pas reposé la tasse

Sans me parler
Il n'a pas allumé
Une cigarette
Il n'a pas fait des ronds
Avec la fumée
Il n'a pas mis les cendres
Dans le cendrier
Sans me parler
Sans me regarder

3 mettre (mis); tourner (tourné); boire (bu); reposer (reposé); allumer (allumé); faire (fait)

Activity 9

A

- Salut, Marianne, ça va aujourd'hui?
- Oui, ça va bien mais tu **as** entendu la dernière d'Antoine?
- Non, dis-moi, qu'est-ce qui s'**est** passé?
- Il **a** quitté Nathalie! Il **est** tombé amoureux d'une fille de dix-huit ans. Il **est** allé à la fête d'anniversaire de Philippe. La fille y **est** venue avec un autre.
- Non, ce n'est pas vrai. Il n'est plus à la maison alors?
- Non, il **est** parti lundi dernier. Il **est** allé chercher du pain le soir et il n'**est** pas rentré.
- Et Nathalie, comment va-t-elle?
- Je ne sais pas, elle n'**est** pas sortie de l'appartement. Sa mère **est** arrivée hier mais nous, on n'**a** rien appris ...

1 He's left Nathalie for an 18 year old.
2 last Monday evening
3 She hasn't left the flat and her mother arrived yesterday.

tomber, aller, venir, partir, rentrer, sortir, arriver

Activity 10

- Vous avez passé une bonne journée?
- Oui, merci, j'ai visité la ville.
- Qu'est-ce que vous avez vu?
- Je suis d'abord allé au musée, ensuite je me suis promené dans le parc. J'ai rencontré ma femme à midi. Elle a travaillé le matin et elle est venue me chercher au restaurant. Nous avons pris le déjeuner et ensuite nous sommes allés

au château mais nous n'avons pas eu le temps d'entrer.
- Maintenant vous avez besoin d'un remontant, qu'est-ce que vous prenez?
- Deux verres de vin rouge, s'il vous plaît.
1 He went to the museum and walked in the park.
2 They went to the castle but didn't go in.
3 red wine

Activity 11

A

La semaine dernière Corinne est allée à Clermont Ferrand. Elle a eu un rendez-vous d'affaires dans la ville, mais elle a des amies là-bas aussi. Après le rendez-vous elle a rencontré ses amies et elles sont allées déjeuner ensemble. Claudine et Nathalie ont proposé une visite de la ville. Elles sont parties du restaurant à quatorze heures et la visite a fini à dix-sept heures. Elles ont décidé de prendre des cocktails à dix-neuf heures dans un bar avant d'aller manger le soir. Elles sont sorties du restaurant et ont fini la soirée avec un digestif. Corinne a quitté Clermont Ferrand très contente de son voyage d'affaires!

B

Je suis sortie du bureau de Gérard Delémont vers onze heures trente. Tout d'un coup j'ai entendu un fracas. J'ai vu une voiture rouge, une Renault, je crois, et un camion. La voiture a tourné à droite devant le camion. Le chauffeur du camion n'a pas eu le temps de s'arrêter et les deux véhicules sont entrés en collision. L'automobiliste est sorti de sa voiture et il a commencé à crier et à gesticuler. Il a accusé l'autre de rouler trop vite mais ce n'est pas vrai.
1 false; 2 false; 3 true; 4 false; 5 true

Activity 12

next – ensuite/puis; first – d'abord; then – ensuite/puis; so – donc

Activity 13

A

Je suis arrivé(e) en avion jeudi le quinze.

Je suis resté(e) dans un hôtel au centre de Paris. Vendredi j'ai visité la Tour Eiffel et ensuite j'ai fait un tour en bateau mouche sur la Seine et puis le soir j'ai dîné dans un restaurant vietnamien. Samedi, d'abord j'ai regardé les peintures au Musée d'Orsay et ensuite j'ai pris le métro à la Grande Arche. Dimanche je suis parti(e) à neuf heures pour le Château de Versailles; je suis rentré(e) à dix-huit heures et puis j'ai dîné au restaurant de l'hôtel. Lundi l'avion est parti à quatorze heures cinq.

B

1 Quand est-ce que vous avez visité Paris?
2 Vous êtes allés à Paris par le train?
3 Vous avez fait un tour en bateau mouche?
4 Votre avion est parti à quelle heure?
5 Vous vous êtes promenés sur les Champs Elysées?
6 Vous vous êtes amusés?

Activity 14

last month – le mois dernier; last year – l'année dernière; yesterday afternoon – hier après-midi; yesterday evening – hier soir

Activity 15

- Vous apprenez le français depuis combien de temps?
- Je l'apprends depuis mars.
- Vous parlez très bien! Vous avez appris d'autres langues?
- J'ai appris l'espagnol il y a dix ans.
- Vous parlez espagnol encore?
- Non, l'année dernière je suis allé(e) en Espagne mais je n'ai pas parlé la langue. J'ai oublié beaucoup des mots essentiels.
- Dommage! Vous avez déjà visité la France?
- Non, je ne suis jamais allé(e) en France mais j'ai passé un week-end à Bruxelles en mai dernier.

Activity 16

A

En juillet dernier on est allé en Bretagne. La Bretagne, c'était formidable! Nous sommes partis de Metz à cinq heures du matin et nous sommes arrivés à Saint-Malo vers 18h00. On a trouvé le camping sans difficulté. La première soirée, on est allé tout de suite au lit après un si long voyage! On a fait le tour des musées, on a visité les sites touristiques, on a bien mangé et bien bu. Un jour Luc a voulu aller au Mont Saint Michel. Nous avons dû quitter le camping très tôt, mais ensuite on a passé une journée vraiment agréable et le monastère était magnifique. Nous sommes revenus dimanche dernier et puis lundi je suis retournée au travail. Quelle horreur!

1 They thought it was great.
2 18.00
3 at a campsite
4 They went to bed.
5 Mont St. Michel
6 Monday

B

1 A man and a woman; look at the ending of nous sommes reven<u>us</u> and je suis retourn<u>ée</u>. The masculine plural ending on revenu means they must be all men or a man and a woman; the feminine ending on retournée tells you that at least one person was female.
2 Because revenir is formed by adding a prefix to venir, which uses être as its auxiliary.

Activity 17

1 J'ai visité le Palais des papes à Avignon. C'était extraordinaire.
2 J'ai dégusté du vin dans le Beaujolais. C'était une expérience inoubliable.
3 J'ai fait du ski dans les Alpes. C'était merveilleux.
4 Je suis allée à la Martinique. C'était très, très bien.

Il pleuvait. – It was raining.

Activity 18

- Salut, comment vas-tu?
- **Salut je vais bien merci.**
- Qu'est-ce tu fais ici?
- **Je suis venu visiter Nathalie.**

- Tiens, moi aussi. As-tu vu Nathalie avant son départ en vacances?
- **Non, elle est allée où?**
- Elle et ses enfants sont partis passer le mois de juillet en Provence.
- **Pourquoi est-ce que Nathalie est allée en Provence?**
- Tiens, tu n'as pas entendu? Son mari a quitté la maison en mai. Il est parti vivre avec une fille de dix-huit ans! C'était tragique!
- **Non, il habite toujours avec la fille?**
- Non, elle a décidé d'aller travailler à l'étranger, en Afrique je crois.
- **Antoine est retourné dans son appartement?**
- Non, pas encore, il attend le retour de Nathalie, mais il ne va pas être content. Elle a trouvé un nouveau copain.
- **Oui, mais il doit accepter la situation. Il est parti et Nathalie a changé.**
- Oh, je dois partir maintenant. Je suis contente de t'avoir vu. A bientôt.
- **Oui, moi aussi, à bientôt.**

Activity 19

1 pancakes
2 her friend Aude's recipe
3 while her daughters were asleep
4 she ate one
5 Jacques, her neighbour
6 He thought they were delicious.

The four skills

Activity 1

1c; 2e; 3h; 4g; 5f; 6i; 7b; 8a; 9d

Activity 2

MSF is an international NGO which provides urgent medical assistance in circumstances such as armed conflict, natural disasters, epidemics and famine. Its headquarters are in Geneva, Switzerland, and it received the Nobel Peace Prize in 1999.

Activity 3

1 Christmas card ('Happy Christmas')
2 Birthday card ('My wishes for a happy birthday')

3 New Year ('Happy New Year')
4 Sympathy ('With our sincere condolences')
5 Wedding ('Congratulations on your wedding')
6 Valentine ('Happy Valentine's Day')
7 New baby ('All my best wishes on the birth of your baby')